Praise for
Rembrandt Is in the Wind

What I love about Russ Ramsey's latest project is that he understands down deep that Truth is exclusive to no party or sect; that Goodness arrives in the form of the lonely, the ill, and the outcast; and that Beauty, amid the church's moral twilight, might be the last apologetic that holds.

> **LEIF ENGER,** bestselling author of *Virgil Wander*
> and *Peace Like a River*

Sometimes when standing at a museum, I think to myself, *I wish somebody who knows something would explain this to me.* And I look around and see, on one side of me, someone expertly pointing out every intricacy in the painting and, on the other, someone bored and looking at a phone in hand. Somehow this book is able to captivate people in all those categories. Russ Ramsey walks us through a museum of artists and art works, showing how each of them illuminates something about God, humanity, and the meaning of life, and he does it in a way that won't bore the expert or intimidate the novice. Those who love art will find here new paths to the gospel. And those who love the gospel will find that they can love art. That's a lot to ask from a book, and this one delivers.

> **RUSSELL MOORE,** director of *Christianity Today*'s
> Public Theology Project

In these days fractured by those who aim to seize power, darkened by those who play dirty politics, and clouded by those who use platforms to polarize, perhaps the artists can lead us home. The artists featured in these pages—artists who devoted their lives and work to what is good, true, and beautiful—remind us that we can, and should, do the same.

> **KAREN SWALLOW PRIOR,** research professor of
> English and Christianity and Culture at Southeastern
> Baptist Theological Seminary and author of
> *On Reading Well*

Russ Ramsey helps us see some of the wonders seen and painted by great artists of the past. This book is full of surprises. What he offers is never a matter of beauty for its own sake, although we are drawn into a glorious journey of beauty through the ages; nor is it one of artistic skills and accomplishments, although every artist he focuses on could claim to have mastered their art; nor can this book be distilled into a mere fascinating overview of five centuries of human creativity, even though the stories told provide a superb entry point to the novice. The greatest joy of this book is that the accumulative effect of these nine artists helped me glimpse something of the world and of humanity as God our creator sees us. What a gift that is!

MARK MEYNELL, director (Europe & Caribbean) for Langham Preaching, cultural critic, and author of *A Wilderness of Mirrors* and *When Darkness Seems My Closest Friend*

Russ Ramsey was kind enough to give me an early chapter of this book a few years ago when I was preparing to go on a silent retreat and had asked him for a work of art I might meditate on. Thanks to Russ's recommendation, I spent hours contemplating Rembrandt's *The Storm on the Sea of Galilee*. I was shaken by the depiction of this scene and the disciples' question to Jesus, "Don't you care that we are perishing?" Russ's gentle shepherding of my understanding of the painting and the biblical story behind it was a balm in my life just when I needed it. I know this book will be the same for you.

SHAWN SMUCKER, author of *The Day the Angels Fell* and *The Weight of Memory*

Encountering paintings, drawings, and sculptures as a little boy set me up for my life arc; encountering Christ set me up for a lifelong love affair with my Creator. Russ Ramsey has gone to great lengths to examine art and faith in a way that helps us define our path forward. Artmaking is a sometimes lonely experience that requires us to rely on our own imagination and talent. This book illustrates the tightrope we must balance on to find the peace and beauty in expression. It's often difficult to maintain balance in the face of all that life offers. *Rembrandt Is in the Wind* helps us find a way forward by the examples and stories of artmakers who have gone before us.

JIMMY ABEGG, visual artist and musician with Rich Mullins and the Ragamuffin Band, Charlie Peacock, and Steve Taylor & the Perfect Foil (jimmyabegg.com)

It's easy to believe that enjoying and understanding art is only for those who have a PhD in art history. Russ Ramsey reminds us how simple and holy it is to be stirred by the mystery of images.

> **JOHN HENDRIX,** author/illustrator of *The Faithful Spy: Dietrich Bonhoeffer and the Plot to Kill Hitler* (johnhendrix.com)

Russ Ramsey is a deep lover of art and a student of art history. In this book, he takes the reader on an amazing guided tour through an art museum that doesn't exist. In this carefully curated collection of art from around the world, he offers us an experience that only someone who really loves art can. This book inspires the reader to engage art in an eye-opening way and understand how these famous works of art bring glory to God.

> **NED BUSTARD,** illustrator of the Every Moment Holy series, creative director of Square Halo Books, and artist and author of *History of Art* (worldsendimages.com; @nedbustard on Instagram and Twitter)

Russ Ramsey leads us well into one of the best possible uses of our time—engaging with art and beauty.

> **MARK MAGGIORI,** award-winning painter of the American West (markmaggiori.com; @markmaggiori on Instagram)

Russ Ramsey has gone deep into the histories of nine artists and their masterworks to reveal how each struggled in both their giftedness and fallenness to create beauty. I am reminded anew of how beauty leads us to God, the author of beauty. I can't wait to share this book!

> **DEBBIE TAYLOR,** visual artist (mayipaintyourdog.com)

Art and the act of creating are essential. Without them, we would not be here. To notice beauty is to be fully alive, and without the act of intimately engaging life, we are numb to ourselves and to the world around us. Russ Ramsey points us toward God through the raw, sensual power of the art, disrupting our unconscious lives that often want to grasp for whatever makes us unfeel.

> **WAYNE BREZINKA,** award-winning artist and illustrator (waynebrezinka.com)

REMBRANDT
IS IN
THE WIND

Rembrandt van Rijn, *The Storm on the Sea of Galilee*,
1633, oil on canvas, 160 × 128 cm, stolen from the
Isabella Stewart Gardner Museum in March 1990

REMBRANDT

IS IN

THE WIND

LEARNING TO LOVE ART THROUGH
THE EYES OF FAITH

RUSS RAMSEY

ZONDERVAN
REFLECTIVE

ZONDERVAN REFLECTIVE

Rembrandt Is in the Wind
Copyright © 2022 by Russ Ramsey

Requests for information should be addressed to:
Zondervan, *3900 Sparks Dr. SE, Grand Rapids, Michigan 49546*

Zondervan titles may be purchased in bulk for educational, business, fundraising, or sales promotional use. For information, please email SpecialMarkets@Zondervan.com.

ISBN 978-0-310-12974-5 (audio)

Library of Congress Cataloging-in-Publication Data

Names: Ramsey, Russ, 1973- author.
Title: Rembrandt is in the wind : learning to love art through the eyes of faith / Russ Ramsey.
Description: Grand Rapids : Zondervan, 2022. | Includes bibliographical references.
Identifiers: LCCN 2021042123 (print) | LCCN 2021042124 (ebook) | ISBN 9780310129721 (hardcover) | ISBN 9780310129738 (ebook)
Subjects: LCSH: Christianity and art. | Christianity and the arts. | Aesthetics—Religious aspects—Christianity.
Classification: LCC BR115.A8 R364 2022 (print) | LCC BR115.A8 (ebook) | DDC 261.5/7—dc23/eng/20211130
LC record available at https://lccn.loc.gov/2021042123
LC ebook record available at https://lccn.loc.gov/2021042124

Published in association with the literary agency of Wolgemuth & Associates, Inc.

Cover design: Studio Gearbox
Cover image: Public Domain
Interior design: Kait Lamphere

Printed in the United States of America

23 24 25 26 27 LBC 8 7 6 5 4

For Cathy Ferguson
and
Steve and Nancy Bayer,
my art teachers

CONTENTS

FOREWORD

Makoto Fujimura

During my first year as a college student, my literature teacher at Bucknell University, Professor Taylor, had us keep a diary. Each week, we were asked to write a brief essay in response to a short story. As a bicultural student, I struggled with writing in English—or any language. Every Thursday, I ended up in this professor's office to see if I had crafted just enough content to hand in on Friday. But my professor saw through my deficiencies and, to my astonishment, encouraged me to write more. In my junior year, I ended up taking several creative writing classes with him.

In my later entries of the diary homework, I pondered, "Why art?" In answer to my cry, my professor wrote back in typical eloquence, "Mako, that is one of the most important questions to ask. And I would like to push you to ask a deeper question through your art and writing: 'Why live?'"

Since then, I have tried to address this profound question— "Why live?"—in all of my art, my writings, and my lectures.

Art and our lives are indeed deeply connected. For Christians, we may extend that question a step further: "Why faith?" That is the ultimate question to ask ourselves as we probe deeply into our psyches, writing in our own diaries called life. The question "Why faith?" lies at the heart of the questions "Why live?" and "Why art?"

A book about art, written by a pastor, may seem superfluous

fluff in our stricken times, even if his illuminations on these known and unknown masterpieces are as keen as any of the commentaries of good art historians. Many Christians may see a discussion about art as secondary to the primary work of proclaiming the gospel to a dying world. We want to "use the arts" for the gospel's sake. In our churches, arts are at best peripheral to our existence—extra value added to the core realities of faith.

But what if our hearts are supposed to be full of the fruit of the Spirit, but instead they are stricken with fear, envy, and the cancerous fruits of the flesh? To such a predicament, this book reveals its worth. It's written as a result of seeking beauty, the report of a pastor's outward journey beyond the boundaries of the church walls to help him see into the unknown. By learning to truly see, we discover, one painting at a time, that the darkness within us is no longer hidden but is revealed in the light of painted countenance, guided by a shepherd meandering into museums.

Pastor Ramsey writes about art in a way that brings healing by *standing under* (the true meaning of *understanding*) each painting and loving each artist. Here's his description in appendix 1 of discovering Rembrandt:

> I discovered that Rembrandt's peers regarded him as The Master even while he lived. And I learned he was a man who loved the gospel. That opened up a new wing of the museum for me: Dutch Renaissance. Now I was looking for van Gogh and Rembrandt. Before long, Rembrandt introduced me to Caravaggio and Vermeer, and van Gogh introduced me to Gauguin, Seurat, and Cezanne.

Such a discovery could not happen without someone first having taught him to see. He writes, "In high school, I had the good fortune of having an art teacher who loved art. She wanted us to love it too, so she introduced us not only to great works of art but, more importantly, to the people who created them."

Pastor Ramsey's enthusiasm and candor make accessible these high art forms to connect deeply with our ordinary lives. Art, then, is finally connected to life, and life can become part of our art. Life, after all, is the great art of divine design.

"This is where beauty is so essential," Ramsey notes as he guides readers through van Gogh to Rembrandt. He also gives ample attention to little-known names such as Tanner and Trotter. To be a Christ follower is to behold the fragments before us, to pay attention and "consider the lilies,"[1] especially through the eyes of someone like Lilias Trotter, whose missionary gaze into the beautiful—not just her art but the art of her life— revealed astounding insight from the simple sight of a bee: "He was hovering above some blackberry sprays just touching flowers here and there, yet all unconsciously life, life, life was left behind at every touch."

We all wrestle to write, paint, and dance. Even our small struggles can lead to a larger revelation as we pay attention to that which captivates us. We also wrestle to preach, to live out our callings as Christ followers. Like the bee, we are in the business of leaving behind life "at every touch." This book is a gift to the next generation and beyond.

"There's nothing more genuinely artistic than to love people," said Vincent van Gogh.[2] Pastor Ramsey has loved well, and I am glad to read this account of his journey with these masterpieces that feed our souls. This book reminds us of the humble yet life-changing presence of everyday teachers, parents, pastors, and countless invisible influences that make our lives God's masterpiece.[3]

So "why live"? Through art, such deeper questions are etched in our minds and in eternity. This book clarifies that art makes possible our experience of the new creation on this side of eternity. In order to truly live, we must learn to see through the "eyes of our hearts,"[4] through the veils of our darkening reality into the illuminations of what artists have painted.

> *Makoto Fujimura,* artist and author of
> Culture Care, Silence and Beauty, and
> Art+Faith: A Theology of Making

BEAUTIFYING EDEN

Why Pursuing Goodness, Truth, and Beauty Matters

Vincent van Gogh, *Self-Portrait with Bandaged Ear*, 1889,
oil on canvas, 60 × 49 cm, Courtauld Gallery, London

There's so much beauty around us for just two
eyes to see. But everywhere I go, I'm looking.

Rich Mullins

Henri Nouwen wrote in *The Return of the Prodigal Son,* "Our brokenness has no other beauty but the beauty that comes from the compassion that surrounds it."[1] Our wounds are not beautiful in themselves; the story behind their healing is. But how can we tell the story of our healing if we hide the wounds that need it? This book is about beauty. To get at it, this book is filled with stories of brokenness.

If you've ever tried to make a realistic self-portrait, you've probably made this discovery: only the truth will work. In my high school art class, I was given the assignment to draw a self-portrait. As my eyes went back and forth from the mirror to the paper, I tried to draw what I saw—with a few improvements. I gave myself brighter eyes, a more chiseled nose, greater definition in my cheekbones, and a little less of a baby face. My vanity resulted in a portrait of someone who didn't look like me, and a B minus.

Vincent van Gogh (1853–1890) painted more than forty self-portraits. Some are not realistic at all. For example, when he was fascinated by Japanese art, he rendered himself with the distinct shaved head and Asian eyes of a Buddhist monk. But one of his self-portraits stands out as being brutally honest: *Self-Portrait with Bandaged Ear.* He painted it in January 1889, the year he produced *The Starry Night* and the year before he died of a gunshot wound to the abdomen.[2]

If you know anything about van Gogh outside of his art,

perhaps you know he was a tortured soul. Vincent suffered from depression, paranoia, and public outbursts so disconcerting that in March 1889 (two months after the completion of *Self Portrait with Bandaged Ear*), thirty of his neighbors in his little village of Arles, France, petitioned the police to deal with the *fou roux* (the redheaded madman). The officers responded by removing him from his rented flat—the Yellow House made famous in his painting *The Bedroom*.[3]

Shortly after his eviction notice, Vincent admitted himself into an asylum for the mentally ill—the Saint-Paul asylum in Saint-Rémy-de-Provence. Back in those days, most psychological maladies were simply called "madness." Debilitating depression, bipolar disorder, paranoia, and even acute epilepsy all fell under the umbrella diagnosis of madness. The "redheaded madman" checked himself in and remained in Saint-Rémy for a year, from May 1889 to May 1890.

What did Vincent do with his humiliation as a patient at Saint-Rémy? He painted. In fact, some of Vincent's most celebrated works—*Irises, The Starry Night,* and *Wheat Field with Cypresses*—were created on the grounds of that asylum. During his stay, he painted the asylum's gardens, grounds, and corridors. He painted the fields he could see beyond the asylum walls and the olive groves he would walk when he occasionally left the grounds. He painted portraits of his caregivers and fellow patients. He made his own versions of other artists' work that he loved. And he painted self-portraits. So much beauty came from that season of his life, but so much humiliation and public rejection facilitated it.

Beauty from Brokenness

What drove Vincent to check himself in to the asylum? What made his neighbors think he was mad and petition for his removal from their community? Though there were many contributing factors, the most ubiquitous episode came several weeks before his eviction from the Yellow House. He and his flatmate, the impressionist painter Paul Gauguin, had a falling out and Gauguin left. Soon after, Vincent took a blade to his ear, cut off the lobe, wrapped it in paper, and took it to a local prostitute named Rachel, who seems to have been a friend in his community of folks on the fringes. When he handed her the blood-soaked parcel, he said, "Take it, it will be useful."[4]

Word of this outburst spread quickly throughout the village, and the next morning, police found Vincent asleep in his bed, covered in blood. They took him to the hospital, and during his stay, Vincent began to count the cost of his outburst. His roommate, friend, and fellow artist had left, Vincent felt responsible. His body was permanently maimed, and his neighbors all knew why.

To add insult to injury, at the time Vincent cut off his ear, his star was just beginning to rise in the art world. After years of obscurity, he was on the verge of breaking through. So his public spectacle, which led to his eviction and detention in the asylum, piled on top of everything else a mountain of professional shame.

During his asylum year, Vincent painted more than 140 paintings—an average of one canvas every three days. Of those works, at least two were self-portraits with his bandaged ear showing. Rather than run or hide from this humiliating series of events, he captured the moment of his greatest shame.

It is hard to render an honest self-portrait if we want to conceal what is unattractive and hide what's broken. We want to appear beautiful. But when we do this, we hide what needs redemption—what we trust Christ to redeem. And everything redeemed by Christ becomes beautiful.

Van Gogh's *Self-Portrait with Bandaged Ear* indicts us. How willing are we to acknowledge the fact that we have a lot of things in us that aren't right? A print of *Self-Portrait with Bandaged Ear* hangs in my office to remind me that if I'm drawing the self-portrait dishonestly—pretending I'm okay when I actually need help—I'm concealing from others the fact that I am broken. But my wounds need binding. I need asylum. And if I can't show that honestly, how will anyone ever see Christ in me? Or worse, what sort of Christ will they see?

In Vincent's case, the story ends with a sweet bit of irony. *Self Portrait with Bandaged Ear*, in which van Gogh captured the moment of his spiritual and relational poverty, is now worth millions. That canvas faithfully captures a defining moment of shame and need for rescue by showing the bandaged side, and it has become a priceless treasure. This is how God sees his people. We are fully exposed in our shortcomings, yet we are of unimaginable value to him. This is how we should see others and how we should be willing to be seen by others: broken and of incalculable worth.

In this book, we'll explore the lives of nine primary artists, and many others by way of their connection to the nine. Each of them gave the world beautiful works of priceless art, but their stories are filled with a surprising measure of brokenness—and, in some cases, violence and corruption. Madeleine L'Engle reminds us that God often works through the most seemingly unqualified people to reveal his glory.[5] So does Scripture. There is beauty in the brokenness. That's what this book seeks to uncover, because beauty matters.

Goodness, Truth, Beauty, Work, and Community

From Socrates and Plato on down through Augustine, Thomas Aquinas, Meister Eckhart, and Immanuel Kant, philosophers and theologians have long wrestled with the question, What makes humanity so distinct from all other forms of life? Three properties of being that transcend the capacities of all other creatures, known as *transcendentals*, have risen to the surface: the human desire for goodness, for truth, and for beauty.

Scripture regards these three transcendentals as basic human desires that are essential for knowing God.[6] Why? Because these are three properties that define God's nature. Good and evil point to the reality of undefiled holiness. Honesty and falsehood point to the existence of absolute truth. Beauty and the grotesque whisper to our souls that there is such a thing as glory. Goodness, truth, and beauty were established for us by the God who is defined by all three.

Philosopher Peter Kreeft said, "These are the only three things that we never get bored with, and never will, for all eternity, because they are three attributes of God, and therefore [attributes] of all God's creation: three transcendental or absolutely universal properties of all reality."[7] Everything in creation participates in each property in some way. And because goodness, truth, and beauty are desires shared in some form by all people, they are, by nature, communal. None of them were intended to exist or be fully realized in isolation. The pursuit of goodness, the pursuit of truth, and the pursuit of beauty are, in fact, foundational to the health of any community.

This isn't just a philosophical position; it's a biblical one. We see it in the opening chapters of Genesis. What are the first things we learn about humanity from Scripture? Here are five quick observations from Genesis 1–2.

Goodness. First, in Genesis 1, we learn that when God created us, he pronounced his creation very good.[8] Goodness was a foundational part of our intended design from the beginning. To live according to the goodness inherent in our creation is a matter of both character and function; we're called to be good and to do good.

Truth. Second, just as we were created with inherent and functional goodness, we were made to obey God. In other words, we were created to live according to God's truth—which is absolute truth with a clear divide between what is evil and what is good.[9]

Consider the importance of truth. What precipitated the fall of humanity? Deception. Scripture says the serpent deceived the woman and the man, and they, in turn, lied to God and to themselves.[10] That rejection of the truth has brought immeasurable sorrow upon our species, and we have been longing to reclaim some sense of what is true and good ever since. In the confines of our created world, this is a uniquely human phenomenon. We are the only creatures who are consciously concerned with goodness and truth.

Beauty. Beauty, by definition, elevates and gives pleasure to the mind and senses. It engages us on multiple levels. We participate in beauty. Genesis 1 and 2 tell us that we are made in God's image, meaning we were created to be creative.[11] We see this responsibility to create in the act of naming the birds and beasts—a task God assigned to Adam.[12] While that might not seem like creation in a conventional sense, according to writer Maria Popova, "To name a thing is to acknowledge its existence as separate from everything else that has a name; to confer upon it the dignity of autonomy while at the same time affirming its belonging with the rest of the namable world; to transform its strangeness into familiarity, which is the root of empathy."[13] Creativity is a path to beauty. The creative work of naming is the work of ascribing dignity and speaking truth.

Work. Fourth, we see in Genesis that creativity is bound up in the act of work itself. Adam's creative work was a beautifying work. He was engaged in the true "oldest profession": landscaping, or gardening. Adam didn't just live in Eden; he worked there.[14] Our call to create stems from our first parents' call to care for *and beautify* Eden. Every one of us has an ember of that fire still smoldering in our hearts. When we set out to make something beautiful, we're drawing from that ancient instinct—however corrupted it may be from the fall—to care for and beautify Eden.

Community. Fifth, we learn that it is not good for people to be alone.[15] When God created Eve, he didn't just give Adam a wife; he gave him community. And together, Adam and Eve "created" others, in the sense that they were acting as what J. R. R. Tolkien described as "sub-creators."[16] We were created to create, and to do that in the context of community for the benefit of community.

Why Does Beauty Matter?

Genesis describes our origin as a union of goodness, truth, and beauty intended to aid in the work of building community. But we struggle to give goodness, truth, and beauty equal weight. C. S. Lewis described the struggle like this:

> The two hemispheres of my mind were in the sharpest contrast. On the one side a many-islanded sea of poetry and myth [beauty]; on the other a glib and shallow "rationalism" [goodness and truth]. Nearly all that I loved I believed to be imaginary; nearly all that I believed to be real I thought grim and meaningless.[17]

Do you feel that same struggle? Truth and goodness can be relegated to the empirical and measurable (and the "grim and meaningless"), while the "many-islanded sea" of beauty can seem to live in another realm altogether. It's as though goodness and truth are meant to be taken seriously, but beauty is merely a plaything, a hobby, even an obstacle to efficient, important work. Beauty cares very little whether the trains run on time.

In my experience, many Christians in the West tend to pursue truth and goodness with the strongest intentionality, while beauty remains a distant third. Yet when we neglect beauty, we neglect one of the primary qualities of God. Why do we do that?

One reason is that we can pursue forms of goodness and truth largely in isolation if we want to. We can reduce these two concepts to manageable, though deficient definitions. Goodness and truth can live largely in the realm of personal conduct and intellectual assent. We can establish certain codes to live by and focus our minds and interests on more cerebral matters, and in that way occupy ourselves with goodness we have reduced to conduct and truth we have relegated to the possession of knowledge. Of course, we have to become legalists in the process and minimize goodness and truth quite a bit to pull this off, but we can pursue some semblance of them both in isolation. People do this all the time.

This is where beauty is so essential. The pursuit of beauty requires the application of goodness and truth for the benefit of others. Beauty is what we make of goodness and truth. Beauty takes the pursuit of goodness past mere personal ethical conduct to the work of intentionally doing good to and for others. Beauty takes the pursuit of truth past the accumulation of knowledge to the proclamation and application of truth in the name of caring for others. Beauty draws us deeper into community. We ache to share the experience of beauty with other people, to look at someone near us and say, "Do you hear that? Do you see that? How beautiful!"

Beauty is a power wielded by the hand of God. Consider Abraham. When God promised Abraham he would become the father of a great nation—a great community—what did the Lord do? He took Abraham outside under the desert sky and told him to number the stars. So would his offspring be innumerable. God wanted Abraham to connect the covenant promise of descendants with a sense of glory.[18]

Have you ever seen a desert sky at night? It is beautiful. The heavens unfurl from horizon to horizon. Glory, mystery, and echoes of the divine spread out before our eyes. We may look, but *only* look—not touch. Since the dawn of time, such a sight has put into the souls of men and women around the world an ache for more. That beauty, and the ache that comes with it, is a powerful, necessary, shaping force for any who would desire to know God.

We have a theological responsibility to deliberately and regularly engage with beauty for three reasons. First, God is inherently beautiful. The book of Exodus tells us that Moses' desire to see God was a hunger to look upon beauty.[19] King David expressed the same longing in Psalm 27:

> One thing have I asked of the LORD,
> that will I seek after:
> that I may dwell in the house of the LORD
> all the days of my life,
> to gaze upon the beauty of the LORD
> and to inquire in his temple.[20]

Moses and David didn't just want to see beauty. They wanted to see God. They knew there was no greater beauty to see.

Second, God's creation is inherently beautiful. There is beauty all around us, and it points to the glory of God.[21] When God rested from creating, he said the world he made was "very good."[22] This goodness is not according to the world's standards, but to God's. And in God's kindness, the fall did not erase the beauty of creation. It's there to behold, if we'll only look. And when we see it, it will teach us about the Author of beauty.

Third, God's people shall be adorned in beauty for all eternity. Those who are in Christ will one day be "prepared as a bride adorned for her husband."[23] Psalm 149 describes this beauty as the glory of being "adorned with salvation."[24] These verses are meant to draw from us a response of praise. We should engage with beauty deliberately and regularly because these are the clothes we will walk around in for all eternity.

What Does Beauty Do?

We've discussed some of the foundational, theological reasons for why we should engage with beauty deliberately and regularly. But what does beauty actually do? What does it do for our communities? Though we miss the point if our goal is to distill beauty down to a list of functionalities, there are real benefits to be gained from deliberately and regularly engaging with beauty.

First, beauty attracts. I remember the first time I saw my wife. I was struck by her beauty. I had to do a double take just to make sure my eyes were not deceiving me. Her beauty drew me to pursue her. That attraction led me to discover the woman behind the beauty, which led to more than twenty-eight years together, twenty-six of them as husband and wife. We have made a life together. We have brought four children into the world and adopted another. We will send these children out into the world to, Lord willing, contribute goodness, truth, and beauty into the places and communities they join. All of this started because I was attracted to my wife's beauty.

Not only are we drawn to beauty, we are the only creatures who engage in certain behaviors purely for the sake of encountering beauty. We use vacation days to drive to places where we can see the sun come up over the ocean. We visit art museums, theatres, and symphonies. We look at the moon and the stars. We climb to high mountain lakes to put our feet in the frigid water to feel the rush and see the reflection of the summit in the ripples we have made. No other creature stops to behold something beautiful for no other reason than that it has stirred something in their souls. When we do these things, are we not like Moses and David, hungering to see the glory of God?

Furthermore, we can use beauty to attract others to what is good and true. For the Christian, this is an important part of what it means to carry out Christ's great commission, to bear witness to the story and the meaning of the death and resurrection of Jesus.[25] Truth without beauty is not enough. The same goes for good works. They need beauty to accompany them. Without beauty, truth and goodness lie flat, and they were not meant to. They were meant to be adorned. They were meant to be attractive.

Second, beauty shows us where we're wrong. In her book *On Beauty and Being Just*, Elaine Scarry explores the concept that beauty often appears to us unexpectedly, and when it does, that moment can transform something we might have regarded as ordinary or mundane our entire lives. She writes, "Something you did not hold to be beautiful suddenly turns up in your arms arrayed in full beauty."[26] The Pixar movie *Ratatouille* gives us a great picture of this when the unpleasable food critic Anton Ego begrudgingly takes a bite of protagonist Remy's food and is struck by a kind of simple beauty that teleports him back to when he was a child and happy. The beauty of this dish reveals that the dour, serious life he chose as an adult was a mistake pursued for the preservation of self at the expense of joy.

Beauty exposes error when we form impressions of people, places, and things based on biases. Without firsthand experience, we may decide we don't like a certain group of people or a foreign country and create impressions of those people or places in our minds to support our disdain. But then we may find ourselves sharing a meal with someone we've viewed mostly through prejudices or traveling to a country we've sized up and dismissed without ever having visited, and something in the experience—some encounter with beauty—changes our minds and reveals that the impressions we once held were wrong.

How is beauty able to have this effect? It brings specificity to prejudice. Scarry said, "Beauty always takes place in the particular, and if there are no particulars, the chances of seeing it go down."[27] Beauty corrects wrong general impressions by contrasting them with specific truths. The more we engage with beauty, the more we train our hearts to anticipate finding beauty, until eventually, everywhere we go, we're looking for it.

Third, beauty inspires creativity. Engaging with beauty sharpens our eye for what is pleasing, and it broadens our imaginations of what could be. Artists draw inspiration from other artists because beauty doesn't just fill us with wonder; it drives us to go create beautiful things ourselves. Scarry wrote, "Beauty brings copies of itself into being. It makes us draw it, take photographs of it, or describe it to other people."[28] Songwriters do not go home defeated when they see Paul Simon in concert; they go home hungry to write songs. Poets don't give up their craft when they hear Billy Collins read his work; they start scribbling down ideas on the back of the program before they leave the venue.

But we're not talking about mere inspiration here, the thunderbolt. Beauty inspires creativity by teaching us some fundamental principles. When we engage with art, we learn about the principles of composition, design, color, and perspective. We hone our creative instinct. We get better. When we create, we reflect the image of the Creator. There is a cycle of creation here: Beauty inspires creativity, and creativity is a path to more beauty.

Fourth, beauty arouses belief in God. Faith is a gift from God, but God is a God of means. He uses what is beautiful to quicken still hearts. Blaise Pascal wrote, "Every man is almost always led to believe not through proof, but through that which is attractive."[29] This is what happens when people stand on the North Rim of the Grand Canyon and are moved to worship, even if they don't know why. God uses beauty to woo and warm hearts.

Creation testifies to a Maker who delights in beauty for beauty's sake.[30] Consider the life of Jesus. The gospel of Matthew tells the story of a woman who came to Jesus just a few days before his crucifixion to anoint him with a very expensive perfume. The disciples reacted as people often do, concerned about the value of her perfume. As the scent filled the room, it seemed a waste. They winced. They thought about how much that perfume was worth and how they might have capitalized on its value if it were theirs. To voice such analysis may have seemed vulgar, but something needed to be said about her extravagance, so they dressed their indignation in the noble auspices of concern for those in need: "Why this waste? For this could have been sold for a large sum and given to the poor."[31]

This is the perspective of a world focused on function and economics. Perfume is seen as a commodity. But what is perfume for? It is meant to fill a room with its beautiful and startling aroma. In this sense, it is meant to be "wasted."

To Jesus, this was no waste. As the scent electrified the senses of everyone present, as it soaked into Jesus' clothing and hair, he said, "She has done a beautiful thing to me."[32] The woman was getting the greatest value out of her precious commodity. To Jesus, this "waste" was beautiful.

So many things in our world are beautiful but didn't need to be. God chose to make them that way so he might arrest his people by their senses to awaken us from the slumbering economy of pragmatism. That awakening is a vital function of beauty. This is the gift of beauty from an artist to their community—to awaken our senses to the world as God made it and to awaken our senses to God himself.

Nine Artists

The chapters that follow walk through the stories of nine different artists, spanning nearly four hundred years of art history in the West. Story is a trojan horse for truth. It can sneak truth past the gates of our defenses and prepare our hearts to hear things we might have resisted if they had come as mere declaration. Jesus relied on storytelling as his primary method of teaching for just this reason—to persuade Jews to empathize with Samaritans, wealthy people to care for the poor, and religious people to have compassion on society's fringe.

The following chapters are part art history, part biblical study, part philosophy, and part analysis of the human experience. But they are all story. I've arranged the chapters chronologically to provide a small sample of the arc of art history in the West from the Italian Renaissance to today. There is so much more I would have liked to include if the parameters of this book permitted. Some artists included here are well known, others not as much. Some lived lives of rich faith in God, others seem to have fought against God having any claim on their lives at all. But they all illustrate part of the struggle of living in this world and point to the beauty of the redemption available to us in Christ.

Michelangelo highlights our hunger for glory. Caravaggio raises the conundrum of an utterly corrupt person creating transcendently beautiful displays of gospel truth. Rembrandt takes us on a journey involving the greatest art heist in American history, asking whether we feel the brokenness of the world and what can be done about it. Vermeer reminds us that no one creates in a vacuum, but rather we rely on the technological innovations of others. Bazille takes it a step further, adding that we don't just rely on the innovations of others but on the others themselves for community and showing how generosity can yield exponential benefits for many. Van Gogh breaks our hearts as an example of someone striving for glory as he empties himself chasing a beauty that eludes him. Henry O. Tanner unpacks issues of race, the role of an artist in the late 1800s who wanted to promote the dignity of the marginalized, and the complicated choices that accompanied that journey. Edward Hopper delves into human loneliness and isolation, reminding us that talent and fame cannot give the heart what it hungers for most. And Lilias Trotter shows us what it means to set aside a passion for something good in order to follow after a greater calling and reveals the joys and sorrow that often accompany sacrificial obedience.

Each story is different. Some conclude with resounding triumph, while others land with the thud of despair. But all of them raise important questions about humanity's hunger and capacity for glory, and all of them teach us to see and love beauty. I hope this is your experience as you read this book.

In *Confessions*, Augustine wrote, "I have learnt to love you late, Beauty at once so ancient and so new! I have learnt to love you late! You were within me, and I was in the world outside myself."[33] There is no statute of limitations for training our eyes to see beauty. Look around the space where you are right now, and no doubt you will find some. If you have not yet learned to love beauty, learn to love it late. Cultivate the habit of pursuing beauty, because, as Annie Dillard wrote, "Beauty and grace are performed whether or not we will or sense them. The least we can do is try to be there."[34]

Beauty is a relic of Eden—a remnant of what is good. It comes from a deeper realm. It trickles into our lives as water from a crack in a dam, and what lies on the other side of that dam fills us with wonder and fear. Glory lies on the other side. And we were made for glory.

CHAPTER 2

PURSUING PERFECTION

Michelangelo's *David* and
Our Hunger for Glory

Michelangelo, *David*, 1501–1504, marble, 17 x 6-1/2 feet,
Gallery of the Academy of Florence, Florence
TravelFlow / Getty Images

> Without any doubt, this figure has put in the shade
> every other statue, ancient or modern, Greek
> or Roman . . . To be sure, anyone who has seen
> Michelangelo's *David* has no need to see anything
> else by any other sculptor, living or dead.
>
> **Giorgio Vasari, 1568**

The raw stone lay on its side in the back courtyard of the Florence Cathedral for decades. The church custodians and locals nicknamed the monolith "The Giant." It was hewn from the Fantiscritti quarries in the Apuan Alps just above Carrara. The Apuan Alps are home to around 650 quarry sites, about half of which are still producing. The Carrara quarries produce more marble than any other place on earth, and this marble has been incorporated into buildings and monuments all over the world, including the Pantheon in Rome, the Marble Arch in London, the Oslo Opera House in Norway, and the sea of crosses and stars of David at the American cemetery at Normandy. Ancient Rome first popularized Carrara marble, fashioning columns, statuary, and streets in the ivory and bone hues of this particular stone. It was also the medium of choice for the sculptors of the Italian Renaissance, who sought to evoke the work of the ancients.

Marble is a metamorphic rock that forms when limestone and other minerals like quartz, iron oxide, and graphite are exposed to extreme pressure and high temperatures over long periods of time. The calcite in the limestone crystalizes, forming a denser rock made up of clusters of these hard crystals. The color variants in marble are due to different minerals present with the limestone prior to recrystallization. White marble is prized for its purity.

The structural integrity of building material is measured in terms of tensile strength, compressive strength, and shear strength. An object's tensile strength is determined by the amount of force it takes to pull it apart. Imagine two teams in a game of tug-of-war; the rope needs high tensile strength so it won't snap in two. Compressive strength is the opposite. Materials with compressive strength can withstand inward force; it is measured by how much pressure is required to crush it. Moving boxes need high compressive strength when they're being stacked in a moving truck, or else they—and everything inside—will be compacted. Shear strength is a little more complex. It's an object's ability to resist shearing forces—two unaligned forces pushing in opposite directions. Think of a piece of paper being ripped in half; one hand pulls half of the page up, the other hand pulls the other half down, and the paper breaks because it has a lower shear strength than, say, a piece of wood. That's why scissors are sometimes called "shears," the two blades applying force in opposite directions to adjacent parts of an object, dividing it in two.

FORMS OF MATERIAL STRENGTH

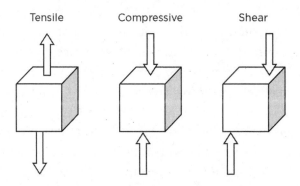

Tensile   Compressive   Shear

Marble has high compressive strength but low tensile and shear strength. The crystalline structure of marble makes it strong enough to support the force of a mountain pressing down, but brittle enough to burst apart when struck with a hammer and chisel.

That particular slab of marble that lay on its side in the back courtyard of the Florence Cathedral was massive, weighing in at twelve tons. How it got there was a marvel in itself.

The Stone

In 1463, an Italian sculptor named Agostino di Duccio was commissioned by the Florence Cathedral, also known as the Duomo, to carve one of a series of twelve Old Testament figures to adorn the buttresses of the Duomo's exterior. The Italian Renaissance master Donatello had begun the series fifty-two years earlier, in 1410, with a terra-cotta sculpture of Joshua. David would be next, and Agostino had won the contract.

Though he had no experience selecting raw stone, Agostino traveled to the Fantiscritti quarries and hired the quarrymen to hew for him a stone 18 feet long, weighing more than 24,000 pounds. The immense block deviated from the artist's contract, which permitted him to use four separate stones that could later be fitted together.[1] Instead, Agostino chose to attempt the project with a single massive slab. With the block cut, he chipped away some of the stone he knew would be shed in the sculpting process to lighten the monolith, bored a hole between where the legs would be, and commissioned a small army of movers to haul the thing over land and sea to Florence.

The Giant was transported from the Carrera region first along the western coast of the Ligurian Sea to Pisa, and then up the Arno River to Florence. The journey from the mountain to the city took close to two years.[2] In 1466, when the horses and men finally carted the slab into the cathedral courtyard, people flocked to see it. No one had ever seen a single block of marble this large. It was an unfathomable fascination how this stone had come down from the mountains to rest in their midst—human ingenuity and tenacity at their finest. It had been one thousand years since anyone had harvested a slab of this size. The people marveled at Agostino's achievement.

THE GIANT'S JOURNEY FROM THE FANTISCRITTI QUARRY TO FLORENCE

Designed by Brad Davis

They marveled until craftsmen who knew something about marble began to take a closer look at Agostino's slab. Sam Anderson, in a *New York Times Magazine* article about the stone, wrote:

> City leaders went to inspect the block, and they were dismayed. It had not only been badly chosen; it had also been badly carved. Agostino, as was traditional, had "roughed out" the block at the quarry—a quick whittling down to leave only what was necessary for the eventual statue. In doing so, however, he had compounded his previous mistake. The block had been strangely narrow to begin with, and Agostino had made it even narrower. He created an awkward hole in its middle. It was hard to see how this stone was ever going to become a plausible human form. Some believed that it was ruined, the city's investment was already lost.
>
> Agostino was fired. The block was abandoned. It sat there, on its side, getting rained on, hailed on, and fouled by birds.[3]

The stone became a fixture for the residents of Florence—a symbol of both incredible accomplishment and unmet potential. It lay dormant for ten years until 1476, when another sculptor, Antonio Rossellino, was commissioned to take over. He worked the stone for a short time but didn't get far until he too was dismissed from the project. The Giant lay undisturbed for the next twenty-six years, exposed to the elements, hardening in the sun, becoming increasingly brittle.

Still, the unparalleled size of the slab and the investment the city had made in procuring it caused it to remain a kind of asset in the minds of the people of Florence. In 1500, the stewards of the cathedral decided they would raise the fallen colossus to its feet and search once more for a suitable craftsman to take on the project of carving David from the Giant. In 1501, a twenty-six-year-old sculptor who had begun to make a name for himself a few years earlier when, at the age of twenty-four, he presented to Rome his *Pietà*, convinced the city officials that he should be hired to finish the sculpture that Agostino started eleven years before he had been born.

On August 16, 1501, the contract was awarded to Michelangelo di Lodovico Buonarroti Simoni.

The Sculptor

Michelangelo was born on March 6, 1475, in the little town of Caprese, just east of Florence. His father worked in banking and government. While Michelangelo was still very young, his mother took ill, and his father sent him to live with a nanny whose husband was a stonecutter at their family's quarry in Arezzo. The boy grew up around marble.

Michelangelo cherished his childhood, saying, "If there is some good in me, it is because I was born in the subtle atmosphere of . . . Arezzo. Along with the milk of my nurse I received the knack of handling chisel and hammer."[4]

As with many artists whom history remembers as elite, Michelangelo had little interest in his studies. Mostly he just wanted to create. He copied paintings he saw in churches (which he could reproduce from memory based on only a single viewing) and sought the company of other artists. Noticing his son's passion for creation, Michelangelo's father agreed to let him apprentice at the age of thirteen with the Florentine painter Ghirlandaio. There Michelangelo learned the fresco technique he would later use on the ceiling and wall of the Sistine Chapel.

In 1489, at the age of fourteen, Michelangelo began to study classical sculpture in the gardens of the governor of Florence, Lorenzo de' Medici. His talent and position brought him into contact with Florence's social elite, which gave him access to both opportunity and mentoring from some of the finest sculptors alive. He happily took advantage of these gifts.

Michelangelo regarded sculpture as the pinnacle of art. He hated painting—oil painting especially, which he described as "suitable for women . . . or for idlers."[5] For Michelangelo, painting held little virtue. Landscape painting was nothing but "a vague and deceitful sketch, a game for children and uneducated men,"[6] and portraiture was little more than "flattery of idle curiosity and of the imperfect illusions of the senses."[7] In a letter to a friend, Michelangelo wrote, "The more painting resembles sculpture, the more I like it . . . Sculpture is the torch by which painting is illuminated, and the difference between them is the difference between sun and moon."[8]

Did the man responsible for the ceiling of the Sistine Chapel, with its thousand square meters of space and over three hundred individual figures really despise painting this much? It seems so. Concerning that particular project, he wrote, "This is not my profession. I am wasting my time, and all for nothing. May God help me!"[9]

We know about his disdain for painting because he was willing to express it and even insult other painters in the process, as he did with a thinly veiled jab at his elder contemporary, Leonardo da Vinci, who held that painting was the nobler art. Michelangelo said, "If he who wrote that painting was more noble than sculpture shows the same understanding in other things as in that remark, my servant girl could do better."[10]

Michelangelo seemed to take pleasure in provocation. When he was seventeen, he made a derogatory comment about a fellow student's work. That student responded by punching Michelangelo in the nose, disfiguring him for life.[11] It would be naive to imagine that Michelangelo didn't hit back. He had strong opinions and a hot temper—a combination that not only got him into many fights but honed his artistic focus. Biographer Gilles Néret wrote, "Michelangelo never made any mystery of the fact that his entire life, from youth to old age, was consumed by passion."[12] Specifically, his was a passion for beauty. He was captured by it. And as it is with a great many passions, his hunger for beauty would become for him a source of torment—an appetite he could never fully satisfy, though his attempts to do so would have a corrupting effect on his soul.

Michelangelo wrote, "If in my youth I had realized that the sustaining splendor of beauty with which I was in love would one day flood back into my heart, there to ignite a flame that would torture me without end, how gladly I would have put out the light of my own eyes!"[13] This statement may ring a bit dramatic, but beneath those words lies the complexity of his particular struggle. Historians have little doubt that Michelangelo was homosexual.[14] His sexuality is present in his writing, in his art, and in the accounts of his personal life. At the same time, there is also little doubt about his personal sense of obligation to God. His lifestyle afforded him the opportunity to indulge any appetite he wanted—which he did—and his orthodoxy fought to bind his conscience to the love and law of the Savior he believed held his soul fast. As a young man, Michelangelo could not seem to shake either his faith or his carnal pursuits. This was his torment, which bore itself out in his work.

As an artist, Michelangelo possessed unmatched ability. He was a prodigy. His raw talent combined with his cultivated skill gave him the ability to render almost anything he wanted to make. What he delivered over the course of his life was a body of work that was at the same time divine and pagan, feminine and masculine, beautiful and violent. Somewhere between the poles of the pagan and the divine were human beings—yearning for glory while, at the same time, consuming corruption with an insatiable hunger.

The focal piece of his creative expression was the human form. He was captivated by the human body—the male body in particular. In his depictions of people, we see his struggle to portray a beauty that is both sensual and divine, powerful and vulnerable, masculine and feminine. Most of his subjects are male, many of them nude, and almost all are specimens of physical perfection. Even his women bear the musculature of the male form. Néret wrote, "The human body as it emerged from the hands of the Creator was Michelangelo's true medium of expression, on the ceiling above the papal altar as elsewhere. Human beauty as represented in his work is a reflection of divine beauty, and its contemplation leads the soul inexorably towards God."[15]

Michelangelo's artistic preferences were matters of conviction. Greater than landscape, portraiture, and all other subject matter was the human form. Above painting, etching, drawing, and every other technique was sculpture. And above clay, bronze, or any other material that could be added to in the event of a mistake was the single, unforgiving, solid block of marble. And there in the courtyard of the Duomo, resting on its side for forty years, lay the Giant. It called to Michelangelo for the convergence of his three great loves—a sculpture of the human form from a single slab.

Across the metaphorical "valley of completion" stood the master craftsman, full of swagger and grit, tormented by an insatiable longing to behold and create beauty, stretched between the poles of the carnal and the pure, the pagan and the divine, and able to render from stone pretty much anything he wanted. Michelangelo was a walking contradiction—spiritually complex, with an unusual natural talent and the untiring tenacity to practice, practice, practice. These were the qualities that prepared the young sculptor to deliver David from the Giant.

The Shepherd

David is perhaps the most famous character in the Old Testament. Everyone knows at least part of his story. So it's not unusual that David would be one of the early statues commissioned for the Duomo's set of twelve. It is also not hard to imagine that Michelangelo would be drawn to the shepherd-king. David's story and the complexity of his character as both an adulterer and a man after God's own heart aligned, at least in some ways, with Michelangelo's struggle between sensuality and devotion to the Lord.

One curious detail embedded in David's narrative in Scripture is the frequent mention of his beautiful appearance. When we first meet him, we're given three details: He was Jesse's youngest son, he was a shepherd, and "he was ruddy and had beautiful eyes and was handsome."[16] Then a few verses later, after David is conscripted into Saul's service, the king asks if there is anyone who can calm his tormented soul. One of Saul's servants says, "I have seen a son of Jesse of Bethlehem who knows how to play the lyre. He is a brave man and a warrior. He speaks well and is a fine-looking man. And the LORD is with him."[17] And finally, when David faces off against Goliath, "the Philistine looked and saw David, he disdained him, for he was but a youth, ruddy and handsome in appearance."[18] Three times David's beauty is mentioned. Scripture calls attention to the beauty of other men and women in the biblical text—Sarah, Rachel, Joseph, Saul, and Esther, to name a few[19]—but the recognition of David's beautiful appearance is unmatched in both frequency and detail.

David's physical beauty was not his only attractive quality. Consider what else we know of him. He worked the fields, fighting and killing lions and bears that tried to steal from his flock. He had mercy on his enemies (sometimes). He wrote psalms. He modeled confession and repentance. He oversaw building projects. His kingly reign was, in the minds and hearts of the generations to follow, Israel's Camelot era. People figured they would recognize the Messiah because he would be more like David than David was. Women desired him, and men wanted to be him—a poet, a theologian, a musician, a lyricist, a warrior, a lover, an architect, and a tactician. And along with all this innate ability and physical beauty, Scripture says David was also a man after God's own heart.[20] It's hard not to envy the guy.

Even when he was young and unknown, all the pieces for greatness were there. Consider the biblical story of his battle against Goliath.[21] Before David had risen to any level of fame, his brothers went off to war. Israel's king, Saul, and his army were dug in at the Valley of Elah in the hill country of Judah. Across the valley were the Philistines—clanking their spears and shields in the hopes that they might bait Saul's army into the killing fields.

Every day, their strongest, biggest warrior would call out across the valley for someone, anyone, to step forward to fight him in one-on-one combat. His name was Goliath of Gath. He stood 9 feet 9 inches tall. He was covered from head to toe in bronze armor, his coat of mail glistening like the scales of a serpent in the sun. He carried a javelin on his back, a spear in one hand, and a sword in another. The giant was a monolith of a figure, armed with iron and impenetrable as stone.

Every day, Goliath would call out, "Why have you come out for battle if you won't fight? Let's settle this man to man. Send over the best you've got; let him come down to me. Winner takes all."[22] Saul and his leaders were sick to their stomachs over Goliath's defiance and also over their inability to produce one single warrior who stood a chance against the giant. He was the perfect warrior. They had no answer.

One day, David came to the valley to bring supplies to his brothers. His father sent him with a care package from home. As he arrived, his brothers and the other soldiers were marching out for their daily standoff. David followed and saw the giant step into the sun, shimmering bronze. Goliath resumed his taunt. "Who will you send to fight me? Anyone? No one? Cowards!"

David watched as his countrymen shrunk back in fear. He could tell they had no fight in them at all, and this offended him. They were not just any army. They were the heirs of the exodus, the tribes that defeated Canaan, Edom, and Moab. Egypt was swallowed in the sea behind them, and Jericho fell before them. They were not just any clan. They were God's chosen people. How could they shrink in fear over the taunts of one man?

David said to the soldiers nearby, "Who does this guy think he is, anyway, to stand there and defy the armies of the living God?"[23] David's older brother Eliab heard what David said and chastised his little brother: "Why are you even here? And who's taking care of the flock at home? You snuck over here because you wanted to watch the battle, didn't you?" Others joined in the rebuke, but rather than wilt, David made his way directly to the king. He said to Saul, "Listen, you don't need to keep doing this. I'll go fight that giant."

Saul was incredulous. "You can't fight him. You're a boy, and he's the most terrifying warrior we've ever seen." David said, "I know how to handle this. When I was keeping watch over my father's herd, a lion came to snatch one away. I went after him, struck him, and delivered the lamb from his mouth. When he turned on me, I grabbed him by his beard, struck him again, and killed him with my knife. This giant across the valley will end up just like that lion. He defied the armies of the living God, and the Lord will deliver him to me."[24]

Saul recognized that the boy meant every word, and without a better plan, he said, "Well, go then. And may the Lord be with you." Saul dug out his best armor and weaponry and began to dress David in his coat of mail. Then the king handed David his sword. David stood under the weight of the armor, gripped the sword, and said, "I don't know this battle gear. This is not how I intend to fight." So he put it all down, picked up his staff and sling, placed five smooth stones from the brook of Elah in his pouch, and walked out to face the giant.

Goliath regarded the boy for a moment, laughed, and said, "Really? Do you think you can chase me away with a stick and some rocks like I'm a dog? Come to me if you must. But know this, I will feed your flesh to the birds and jackals if you do."[25]

David answered, "You come at me with your javelin, spear, and sword, but I come in the name of the Lord you have defied. And before this day is over, that same God will deliver you over to me and I will strike you down and cut off your head. You and your entire army will perish and every one of you will meet the fate of the birds and jackals. Then all the earth will know there is a God over Israel who doesn't need a giant's sword or spear. This battle belongs to him."[26] David watched as Goliath stood to his feet and began to make his way toward the young shepherd.

And . . . freeze that frame.

The Sculpture

That was the moment Michelangelo captured: David staring down his approaching foe. The story is all there; it's in his posture, in his hands, in his sling, in his vulnerability, in his eyes. The sling and stone signal to us that David is looking at Goliath, who is about to die. The look in David's eye tells us he has no doubt.

Traditionally, artistic depictions of David portray him after his victory, standing triumphant over the slain Goliath. Other Italian artists before Michelangelo—like Verrocchio, Bellano, and Donatello—showed David standing over Goliath's severed head. The deed was done. Victory was in hand. Lesson learned.

Not Michelangelo. For the first time ever, he chose to give us David before the fight. Gilles Néret wrote that Michelangelo "abandoned the traditional image of David as victor, inventing in its place a symbol that united *fortezza* (strength) and *ira* (anger)."[27]

The marble looks soft and smooth, like flesh. The shepherd is at the same time vulnerable in his nakedness and imposing in his size, standing more than 13 feet tall. David is tense, angry, ready to move. Michelangelo catches him at the peak of his focus. The warrior is alert but calm, equipped but patient, daring but confident. He stands in a way that conveys motion, as though he has just shifted his weight or taken a step—a classical pose known as *contrapposto*, where the figure stands with one leg holding his full weight and the other leg forward, causing the figure's hips and shoulders to rest at opposing angles, giving a slight S-curve to the figure's torso. The posture conveys a sense of life.

Artists often use the technique of exaggeration to convey scope. They amplify what is seen to imply what is unseen. The French painter of the American West, Mark Maggiori, uses this technique by painting skies with dramatic, exaggerated cloud formations. They supply within the frame of his canvas a sense of the epic expanse of sky viewers might see beyond it if they were standing there in person. He wants us to get a sense of the awe the people in his paintings must have felt as they took it all in.

In a similar form of exaggeration, David stands naked and defenseless—a detail not in Scripture but included to heighten the viewer's grasp of just how vulnerable he was against his unseen foe. The boy is naked, but he is anything but weak. The determination on his face and the weapon in his hands convey not only strength but confidence that the victory will be his. This was not a battle against flesh and blood.

His right hand holds the grip of the sling, and his left holds the pocket. The sling is draped across his back, hidden from Goliath, emphasizing that David's victory was one of cleverness, not brute strength. His approach was sophisticated and elegant. In his book *David and Goliath*, Malcolm Gladwell suggests that we usually read the story wrong, in the same way the forces of Israel misread the scene.[28] We look at the great size of Goliath and the small stature of David and assume David doesn't have a prayer. What we should be looking at, Gladwell says, are the weapons they've chosen for the fight. If we focus there, we see that the fight was over before it ever started and Goliath never stood a chance. Goliath's sword, javelin, muscles, and spear all depend on close to midrange combat. David's sling is a long-range weapon. A skilled slinger could take down an opponent armed with swords, spears, and javelins without ever coming within reach of his enemy's weapons. What's more, David believed God himself would guide the stone.

Of course David was confident. He knew Goliath would never even touch him. He knew the Lord would deliver the taunting scoffer into his hand. David would show up for the battle and sling the stone, and the Lord would drive it to its mark. And that is exactly what happened. The story is perfect—a perfect enemy, a perfect youth, a perfect cast of a lethal stone, a perfect ending. Michelangelo fit it all into a perfect statue of a perfect hero.

Michelangelo wanted to work on the stone in private, but because of its size, it could not be moved into a studio. So after standing it up, builders constructed a roofless shed around the giant block, where Michelangelo would disappear for days, hidden away in his work. It was a process of studying the stone, learning its intricacies, character, flaws, grain, and strengths. He made a wax model to work from and for two years chipped away at the Giant until David emerged.

Once the statue was finished, except for some minor touches Michelangelo would add later, the city devised a plan to move *David* a half mile from the workshop to the Piazza della Signoria. Historians wrote about the event, describing it as a stressful and difficult undertaking.[29] The crew leading the effort to move the

Giant had to dismantle the archway of the Duomo's courtyard to get it out because of its size. The entire city monitored the progress. Giorgio Vasari described a "strong wooden frame"[30] and a system of ropes suspending the statue. The scaffold was rolled slowly on greased logs. It took four days and forty men to move the statue the half mile to its destination. At night, vandals pelted it with rocks, trying to damage it, so a guard had to keep watch. Luca Landucci, an herbalist living nearby, wrote down the exceptional event of the transport in his chronicles: "It was midnight, May 14th, and the Giant was taken out of the workshop. They even had to tear down the archway, so huge he was. Forty men were pushing the large wooden cart where David stood protected by ropes, sliding it through town on trunks."[31]

After reaching its destination, it became apparent that there was no way to lift the statue all the way up to the Duomo's buttress. Besides, the wonder and perfection of the piece would be lost on people if it stood at such a distance. So they decided to put *David* on a pedestal in Florence's public square outside the Palazzo della Signoria, the seat of the city's civic government, where the young shepherd's battle-ready stare was turned toward the Goliath of Rome. It took almost a month to hoist him up onto his base.

Michelangelo kept working on finishing touches. That summer, the sling and tree stump were leafed in gold, and a gilded victory garland was placed around *David*'s neck. Weather and time have since destroyed the wreath and worn the gilding away.

Towering over 17 feet high on its pedestal, Michelangelo's *David* became a symbol of liberty and freedom for the people, displaying Florence's readiness to defend herself. David remained there in front of the Palazzo della Signoria until 1873, when it was moved into the Gallery of the Academy of Florence to protect it from the elements and further damage. He stands there still today—almost perfect.

We Work with What We're Given

No one is perfect—not in this life. We live in a world of limits. We all run up against them, and we all have them. If you're like me, you wish this weren't the case and find the whole business hard to accept. But limits are a fact of life—and part of God's design. Even our first parent, Adam, looked around when it was just him and said, "I need help. I need another."

Eve did not solve the problem of Adam's limitations. God didn't put the man to sleep and graft into him the rest of what he lacked. Instead, God took something out of the man and made a partner to come alongside, helpful but distinct. The gift of Eve confirmed that this was how things were going to be—how they were *meant* to be moving forward. We would not merely help ourselves. We would be given help. And we would be given *to* help.

Sometimes the help we're given requires us to adapt to a new course; the person who comes before us or alongside us has a personality that changes the rhythm of how we might move and work on our own. Perhaps they're faster than we are or more contemplative. They think in concrete terms, while we favor the abstract. They bring nuance into our otherwise rigid plans, structure to our hazy vision, or economic realities to our dream. Sometimes we inherit the work of others, and it falls to us to carry it across the finish line. Sometimes others inherit our work and build on what we started.

One of the beauties I see in this part of God's design is that our limits and our need for others end up producing results—beautiful, helpful, unexpected results—that none of us on our own would know how to create, or even *think* to create. The story behind Michelangelo's *David* helps us see this.

Michelangelo's statue began with limits. It was limited to what the stone could accommodate. When he began, Michelangelo had to adapt to the work of two prior sculptors whose creative choices and technical mistakes would determine, to a degree, how *David* would have to stand. That stance would affect everything about the end result—not only the composition of the piece, but also its structural integrity. Michelangelo was given a block of marble that others had a hand in shaping.

We work with what we're given. None of us build on an untouched foundation. Many people and their many decisions—for better or worse—have played a role in determining where our feet are planted. And the chances are good that we are each shaping some aspect of a foundation on which someone else will one day stand.

Lord, have mercy.

How different would Michelangelo's *David* have been if he had begun with a virgin stone? What artistic choices would he have made otherwise? Would that sculpture be as beloved as the one we've received? Michelangelo chipped away at the stone set before him. He had to accommodate the vision of the other sculptors. He had to accommodate the dimensions handed down by the stonemasons who first hewed the marble from the Tuscan Alps. He also had to accommodate the written word of Scripture; the story of David was not his to invent. These constraints played a role in drawing from that stone the shepherd he had read about and imagined. Some of those choices had already been made for him. Without them, we would have something—but it would not be Michelangelo's *David*.

I cannot think of a single thing in my life that doesn't bear the touch of others. I'm guessing you can't either. Of course we wish some of those chisel marks never happened—the ones that draw from us a plea for mercy, the ones that kindle a hunger for the renewal of all things. But other marks have been necessary to give us eyes to behold goodness, truth, and beauty we would not have known otherwise.

Living with limits is one of the ways we enter into beauty we would not have otherwise seen, good work we would not have chosen, and relationships we would not have treasured. For the Christian, accepting our limits is one of the ways we are shaped to fit together as living stones into the body of Christ. As much as our strengths are a gift to the church, so are our limitations.

Seeking Perfection in a World
That Is Wasting Away

There are cracks in David's ankles.

For more than five hundred years, nearly 6,000 pounds of marble have been pushing down on David's legs. Yet he stands. Through centuries of sun, rain, the tremors of thunder, and more than a few attacks by vandals—one as recently as 1991, when a forty-seven-year-old man named Piero Cannata took a hammer to David's left foot, chipping his toe before being wrestled to the ground, not by police, but by the other museumgoers[32]—David stands. The compressive strength of his stone legs has held.

But David stands on a bit of a tilt, adding torque to the pressure his weight puts on those tiny fissures. Torque requires tensile strength, of which marble has very little. In almost immeasurable ways, those fractures are growing, working their way up his legs. This deterioration cannot be reversed.

Florence sits near active fault lines that send tremors through the city. As the city develops, construction equipment shakes the earth. And as the daily queues of tourists form outside the Academy, the footsteps of a million pilgrims per year from all over the world create almost immeasurable but near constant seismic activity around the statue's base.

One day David will fall. In all likelihood, he will, ironically, be taken down by a stone—not by the force of a stone flung at him, but by the limitations of the very stone from which he is carved. He will collapse under his own weight because of his own flaws.

One of the many fractures will cause a catastrophic failure in the compressive integrity of the marble; the weight of his upper body will begin to shift; and pressure, torque, and momentum will finish the job.

In his article "David's Ankles: How Imperfections Could Bring Down the World's Most Perfect Statue," Sam Anderson imagined the scene:

> The first thing to hit the floor is his bent left elbow, the arm that holds the heroic sling, and it bursts along the lines of its previous breaks, old scars left over from an incident in the 16th century involving an unruly mob and a bench. Then the rest of the marble will meet the floor, and the physics from there will be fast and simple: force, resistance, the brittleness of calcite crystals, the shearing of microscopic grains along the axes on which they align. Michelangelo's David will explode.[33]

Museum and government officials in Florence insist that the fractures are not growing and that the statue is positioned to minimize the pressure of the downward force of his weight. They do not believe the statue is in any grave danger. The biggest concern at the moment is earthquakes, with the consensus being that if a major earthquake were to hit Florence, *David* would not be the only priceless piece of art to suffer.

A small comfort—this reminder that the world itself, which is wasting away, is utterly indifferent to preserving the finest art its inhabitants can produce. Just as pressure and time compress and crystalize limestone into marble without ever wondering what we might make from it, tectonic plates beneath the earth's surface give neither *David* nor any of the rest of us a moment's consideration. Time and pressure are happening now.

The same time and pressure that gave us the stone from

which *David* was cut could reclaim him at any moment. The stone was filled with all kinds of imperfections when the quarrymen hewed it from the mountain, before the first tap of the first sculptor's hammer and chisel. Though the marble was capable of accommodating the physical toll of the thousands of taps from the sculptor's tools, and even though it has managed to stand for more than five hundred years supporting its own weight in all kinds of conditions, *David* is made of a perishing material. Still, we flock to see him, standing there in all his glory.

To enter the room where David stands, you must pass through the Hall of Slaves—a passage lined with unfinished works Michelangelo had begun. These half-finished Hercules struggle, curled up and frozen in their prisons of stone, pleading for the recognition of the masses who cannot help but look away because there, at the end of the hall, stands the most perfect work of art ever achieved by any one of us.

We are drawn to beauty, and we instinctively know that somewhere, somehow, such a thing as perfection exists. We seek both beauty and perfection, at great expense of money and time. Beauty we can find. It's all around us, in a million different forms. Perfection, on the other hand, eludes us. It is as though, to borrow an expression attributed to Meister Eckhart, perfection inhabits our true home, but we are walking in a distant country. We are like revenants. On the other side of the veil is the tangible glory of unfailing perfection, but it is just out of our reach. So we have given ourselves to the pursuit of making copies from the dust of the earth, compressed by time, crafted by pressure, but conceived by something more than mere imagination. Our best attempts at achieving perfection this side of glory come from an innate awareness that it not only exists, but that we were made for it.

I came across a detail in my research that I can't seem to shake. The gloss of David's exterior is, in part, human skin.[34] The patina covering David's body is composed of a combination of Florentine dust and the detritus of a hundred million tourists, coughing and shuffling before him, shedding their skin to give him his. We have added to Michelangelo's work—polishing him smooth by our very presence. We who bear the image of God have taken this man of stone and given him a dusting of flesh. How much more will we, who are bound for glory, shed the limits and imperfections of these perishable frames for bodies that will forever bear up under the eternal weight of glory?[35]

Until then, we save our vacation days, plan our itineraries, and make our way across oceans, over mountains, through cities, and down the long stretches of highway that span the countryside to take our place in line to catch a glimpse of the deeper glory we know we were made for. Elaine Scarry said we make sure that we are "looking in the right direction when a comet makes its sweep through a certain patch of sky."[36] We go to the Louvre in Paris, the Met in New York City, the Rijksmuseum in Amsterdam, and the Academy in Florence. We go to the Grand Canyon of the American West, the Giant's Causeway of Northern Ireland, the forests of East Asia, and the islands of the South Pacific. We go to a pizza place in Brooklyn, a pub in Oxford, a vineyard in the Sonoma Valley, and a café in Paris.

Why? All to join the carnal to the divine. All to get closer to glory.

CHAPTER 3

THE SACRED AND
THE PROFANE

Caravaggio and the Paradox
of Corruption and Grace

Michelangelo Merisi da Caravaggio, *The Calling of St. Matthew*,
1600, oil on canvas, 322 × 340 cm, San Luigi dei Francesi, Rome

> In a very real sense not one of us is qualified, but
> it seems that God continually chooses the most
> unqualified to do his work, to bear his glory.

Madeleine L'Engle

Throughout the Gospels, Jesus met social outcasts with compassion and reserved some of his strongest language for those who regarded "tax collectors and sinners" as people beneath the basic dignity of kindness. We dare not romanticize this part of Jesus' ministry by regarding those folks on the fringe as merely misunderstood. For many of them, the ways they lived their lives added pain upon pain to those who loved them. They chose self and the satisfaction of appetites at the cost of relationships and honor. They lived every day in the misery their choices brought. Those who loved them lived in the sorrow of grieving the loss of a prodigal, which is one of the sorest kinds of grief because the prodigal is at the same time gone yet still here.

It is important to remember this if we want to understand the way Jesus loved sinful people. He loved them knowing their lives were riddled with problems. And the way he welcomed them did not always immediately deliver those people he loved from the complications of their choices. With the rich young ruler,[1] the woman at the well,[2] or the woman caught in adultery,[3] Jesus' initial encounters with them, which consisted of an invitation to leave their lives of sin and follow him, did not automatically reset their lives. Rather, it complicated them. The rich young ruler would have to rethink his adoration of the material world. The woman at the well would have to allow Jesus' words of confrontation to shine light on broken areas of her life she had become accustomed to defending. The woman caught in adultery would have to sever some relationships and seek to rebuild others, and she'd have to do it in an unjust system that held women to a level of public scrutiny men didn't have to endure.

Jesus' call can sometimes be hard to see in the life of another. And it can be complicated. But what we see in Scripture is that he moved in love and welcome toward people who willfully lived lives of opposition to his word. He called the unlikeliest people to repentance. He worked through the most unqualified people in ways that, to this day, confound the wise.

Caravaggio in Rome

Michelangelo Merisi da Caravaggio (1571–1610) was one of the most influential and important painters in Italian art, a country that dominated European art throughout the Middle Ages. It is hard to overstate his significance. In 1920, the Italian art historian Roberto Longhi said, "People speak of Michelangelo de Caravaggio, calling him now a master of shadow, now a master of light. What has been forgotten is that Ribera, Vermeer, la Tour, and Rembrandt could never have existed without him. And the art of Delacroix, Courbet, and Manet would have been utterly different."[4]

Biographer Andrew Graham-Dixon said, "He was a thunderstroke. There is art before Caravaggio and art after Caravaggio, and they aren't the same thing. The whole of Rembrandt's career is a response to the thunderstrike of seeing Caravaggio's art."[5]

Caravaggio was born in Milan on September 29, 1571. In 1576, his family moved to the nearby village of Caravaggio to escape a plague. He later took the town's name as his own. The following year, both his father and grandfather died on the same day, leaving the six-year-old boy without any other men in his family. His mother died seven years after that. As a thirteen-year-old orphan, he signed on for a four-year apprenticeship to study art under Simone Peterzano, a student of Titian. It's questionable whether he actually went through with the apprenticeship because during those years he never learned to paint fresco, which would have been standard for any art student of that era. It's possible he spent those years "auditing" his formal education while developing a style and talent all his own.

At eighteen, he moved to Rome, the cultural capital of the world. Rome had everything, and that's what Caravaggio wanted. One scholar said he arrived "naked and extremely needy . . . without fixed address and without provision . . . short of money."[6] What he did have was a marketable skill. The boy could paint.

Rome in those days drew a distinction between the sacred and the profane. The sacred encompassed things set apart for a holy purpose; the profane, by contrast, involved mundane individual concerns. The profane world was composed of what people could know through their senses—the natural world of everyday life that we experience as comprehensible.[7] The sacred world was everything beyond the world we experience with our senses. If knowability was the mark of the profane, then awe and wonder belonged to the sacred.

Though sacred themes were most common among the artists of Rome, Caravaggio was drawn to the profane—scenes of everyday life with common people doing ordinary things. On the street he sold canvases depicting bouquets of flowers and bowls of fruit. These still lifes bored him, but he put in the work because, as an unknown, he needed to develop his reputation if he wanted his career to go anywhere.

In 1596, at the age of twenty-five, he painted the profane composition *The Card Sharps*, which depicts two hustlers ripping off a rube. Word of the painting spread around town, and people came from all over to see it. One of the things that made the painting so popular was that it featured humor, an uncommon element in most of the art of that era. The young card sharp in the foreground, no older than his naive opponent, has extra cards tucked into his belt, which we can see. The visible handle of his dagger telegraphs that he is ready to deal with whatever disputes may arise. The older hustler in the background, the mentor, signals to his protégé what cards their dupe is holding. The fingertips of his gloves are worn away—a trick used by seasoned swindlers to feel for the cards they marked in their decks. The target has no idea what he's gotten himself into. That's the joke.

Caravaggio, *The Card Sharps*, ca. 1596, oil on canvas, 94 × 131 cm, Kimbell Art Museum, Fort Worth

But the painting was more than a joke. It was a commentary on life on the streets of Rome; as one young man's innocence is exploited, another's is being corrupted as he learns the ways of the cheat. Both boys are losing something here. Caravaggio was drawn to scenes like this because they depicted the kind of people he lived among. He lived in violent times, and Rome was a violent place populated largely by unmarried, out-of-work soldiers and the gambling halls and brothels that serviced them.

Caravaggio was not merely fascinated by the seedy underbelly of

Rome. He was part of it. Over the course of his life, he got into many fights, which included several brushes with the law and stretches in jail. In fact, much of what we know about him apart from his art comes from court documents, of which there are many. He is a man known not only for his art but also for his criminal record.

The Card Sharps caught the eye of Cardinal Francesco del Monte, who admired it so much that he purchased it and became one of Caravaggio's first patrons in Rome. The cardinal purchased several other paintings by Caravaggio, including *The Musicians*, *The Lute Player*, and *Boy Bitten by a Lizard*—each profane in subject matter. Del Monte also let Caravaggio share his quarters near the center of the city and introduced the young painter to many of his wealthy, influential friends in the church, which led to other commissions and greater exposure.

Though Caravaggio had a gift when it came to painting profane subject matter, and though he was able to sell what he produced, the real money was in religious art. There were, of course, altruistic reasons for this. The church knew these works helped illustrate biblical narratives and religious principles for people who didn't own Bibles or couldn't read. Art was a form of evangelism—a pictorial welcome into the faith with the goal of inspiring devotion to God and the church. This is why so much of the art from Europe in the Middle Ages, before photography or widespread travel, depicted biblical narratives in a European context. Much of the architecture, clothing, technology, and even skin tones of biblical characters— Jesus included—looked European to emphasize that the story of Scripture applied to people in their context. Depicting Jesus as he actually was—a Middle Eastern, dark-skinned Jew—wasn't a value at that time because the goal of art wasn't historical accuracy; it was accessibility. This is why so many European paintings of biblical stories from that time are so unflinchingly European in appearance.

Sacred art in the church developed a rich system of symbol-ism that people learned to "read." Paintings often featured tells to help the viewer understand the story being told—halos and gold leaf surrounded holiness, a dove represented the Holy Spirit, a serpent pointed to the devil, contrasting light and dark illustrated the tension between good and evil, and more. As viewers developed their visual vocabulary, they could stand in front of a painting and read an entire sermon in a single frame.

But another reason for the abundance of biblical art was that art required patronage, and one of the leading patrons of that time, which also happened to be the most public and therefore the most likely place for an artist's work to be seen by others, was the church. The highest-paying commissions of the day came from religious institutions.[8] Patrons of religious art sought to commission the top artists, and artists sought to outdo each other in order to get the best jobs.

Caravaggio was born soon after the Reformation, when Protestant leaders distanced themselves from narrative art based on biblical texts and banned certain imagery—particularly images of the Godhead—from their churches. The Catholic Church took another position, incorporating imagery and iconography in a governed way. Caravaggio scholar Gilles Lambert said, "Popes and Jesuits countered the austerity of Luther and Calvin, who banished paintings and sculptures from the church, with a great outpouring of imagery, ornament, colours, contrasts, and theatrical decors, fit to dazzle the believer and reaffirm the predominance of Rome."[9]

Rome wasn't playing around either. The use of imagery in Catholic worship was under the control of the bishops, who ultimately reported to the pope. Caravaggio biographer Sebastian Schütze wrote:

> Sacred images were to convey theological subjects in a clear and unequivocal fashion and win over the viewer by appealing to the emotions. The accuracy of the representation and its correspondence with Biblical sources and

church doctrine were to be ensured by theological advisors, and established iconographical traditions and their artistic interpretations were to remain strictly subordinate to the authority of the written word.[10]

For the artists, the stakes were high. Schütze continued, "Artists were expressly obligated to submit for approval design drawings . . . of the histories to be portrayed. Infringements of these regulations were punishable by fines of up to 50 gold scudi or by prison, exile, and 'other capital punishments.'"[11] Defying Rome was dangerous. In 1600, an author named Giordano Bruno wrote some essays critical of the church. When confronted, he refused to recant and was burned at the stake.[12]

Most religious art of Caravaggio's time followed the conventions of the church, which included a certain serenity and uniformity, even in the most dramatic scenes. Religious work up until this point was idealized, depicting godly, proper characters with soft edges and perfect features. Caravaggio scholar Wolfgang Kallab said, "Young artists arriving in Rome in the late 16th century were in danger not only of being bound to servile imitation of the Old Masters but of throwing off their idealism and technical expertise in favour of a hollow, superficial manner: paintings were made rather to be glanced at than studied."[13]

Early in his career, Caravaggio had no choice but to comply and paint according to convention. But he found the approach to be academic and constrained. Over time, he began exploring the edges of what was acceptable, "breaking down the conventions that maintained painting as a plausible fiction rather than an extension of everyday experience."[14] Caravaggio is one of the fathers of the Baroque period, which used a darker, richer color palette to impart energy and animation to otherwise impersonal subjects. Artists who preceded him, like Raphael and Titian, used a painting technique called *chiaroscuro*, which conveys drama through the contrast of darkness and light. Caravaggio developed an exaggerated form of chiaroscuro called *tenebrism*, which moved beyond drama to provocation. He forced viewers to focus onto the reality of his scenes, which were often more graphic and suspenseful than people were accustomed to seeing. He developed an unflinching realism with close physical observation that was at the same time approachable yet substantive, grotesque yet emotionally appealing, and energetic yet contemplative. For many, Caravaggio's combination of drama and realism came across as vulgar.

In *The Sacrifice of Isaac* (1598), for example, Abraham clutches a knife in one hand while his other hand grips a fistful of his son's hair. We can practically feel the pain and aggression in the tightness of Isaac's scalp. The patriarch's body is turned toward his son, indicating this was the precise moment when he was about to go through with his unthinkable task.[15] But his head is turned, as if suddenly, toward the angel, who is presented more in human terms than divine. Only his feathered wings give away his identity. Abraham's face is racked with anguish—he is already grieving, already feeling the weight of what he is doing to his only son. But the angel's expression is calm and deescalating as he caresses with his right hand a ram whose chin rests peacefully near Isaac's knee.

By setting the divine rescue in the context of the human agony of the whole situation, Caravaggio tells the sacred story by way of emphasizing the profane, stunning viewers with his intensity and directness. He didn't want to make art that was only meant to be glanced at. He wanted to create a visceral experience for his viewers—something that would stop them, trouble them, or arouse whatever might be sleeping in their souls. He used real-life models—often prostitutes and peasants—to emphasize the intersection between heaven and earth. He didn't like the idealized image of humanity and much preferred to paint people as they were, with their flaws and defects on display. He was a painter for the poor, whose mission was to emphasize that the gospel was for poor people. He wanted to leave room for ambiguity, doubt, and sorrow. He wanted the simple difficulty of living in this world to be written on his subjects' faces.

Many in Rome regarded Caravaggio's work as scandalous. His French contemporary in the Baroque style, Nicholas Poussin, went so far as to say Caravaggio "came to destroy painting."[16] One cardinal's secretary said of his painting *Madonna and Child with Saint Anne* (1605), depicting Mary with her skirt rolled up holding a naked Jesus as they step together on a serpent's head, "In this painting there are but vulgarity, sacrilege, impiousness, and disgust . . . One would say it is a work made by a painter that can paint well, but of a dark spirit."[17]

Perhaps combining the sacred with the profane was autobiographical. Perhaps it was all Caravaggio knew. One thing is certain: Caravaggio's art resonated with people, and he was soon revered for his ability. In 1599, Cardinal del Monte secured Caravaggio's crucial first public commission, consisting of two canvases: *The Calling of St. Matthew* and *The Martyrdom of St. Matthew* for the Contarelli Chapel in San Luigi dei Francesi.

The Martyrdom of St. Matthew shows the apostle dying at the altar by the sword of a soldier sent by the king of Ethiopia. The traditional account parallels John the Baptist's story; the king of Ethiopia sought an illicit relationship with his own niece. Matthew publicly criticized his immorality, so the king had him put to death. Caravaggio painted himself into the scene as one of the fellow worshipers looking on in shock and disbelief.

In *The Calling of St. Matthew*, tax collectors sit at a table counting money. To their right, Jesus stands in the shadows, with Peter at his side. Jesus' arm is outstretched, pointing at one of the men. One tax collector, wearing a look of surprise, responds by pointing, possibly to himself, identifying himself as Matthew.

Or he may be pointing at the younger man at the end of the table who is so engrossed in counting coins that he is as yet unaware that he has been called to follow Jesus. Either way, Matthew will leave that room united to Christ forever, which, for many, was hard to comprehend or accept. The window between the tax collectors and Jesus is covered in vellum. The light comes through darkly.[18] Over the vellum, Caravaggio places the clarity of a cross. The light illuminating the scene comes from the direction of Christ. Matthew will rise from that table and follow Jesus, and his life will change in such a way that he will come to be the subject of masterworks that will be displayed in churches and museums around the world.

After people saw *The Calling of St. Matthew* and *The Martyrdom of St. Matthew*, Caravaggio never again lacked patrons or opportunities to paint on commission.

The Calling of St. Matthew

One day, while in Capernaum, Jesus went for a walk.[19] He passed by a man everyone knew, though few liked—Matthew. A Hebrew by birth, Matthew made his living collecting taxes for Rome. When he chose this career, he knew what it would mean for his place in the community. Most of his countrymen viewed tax collectors as traitors who weakened Israel and strengthened Rome while making themselves rich in the process by taking more than they needed to live off the surplus. Over the years, Matthew had grown accustomed to the scorn of his neighbors. The money coming in eased the pain of the community he lost. But he was never fully at peace with the life he had chosen.

As with the rest of the Capernaum residents, Matthew was fascinated by Jesus of Nazareth. So when he saw Jesus passing by his tax-collecting booth, he paused what he was doing to watch. Jesus stopped and looked at Matthew.

"Follow me," Jesus said to him.

Matthew came out from behind his table, and the two men faced each other. Matthew searched Jesus' face for scorn but found none—only a sincere invitation to go with him. Matthew left everything as it was and walked alongside Jesus through the streets of Capernaum.

"Let's have dinner together tonight," Jesus said.

Matthew let the words register. *Dinner? Tonight?*

"Yes. Let's," said Matthew, and he immediately began to pull together a feast. He invited everyone he thought might come—mostly other tax collectors, along with a few friends who lived on the fringes of society. When the Pharisees saw that Jesus was sharing a meal with Matthew's friends, reclining as though this was a comfortable visit, they asked his disciples, "Why does your teacher eat with such people?"

When their question reached Jesus, he stiffened. "By what rule do you think God measures out his favor? Do you think what he wants is religious precision? Do you think because you have made for yourselves rules and then kept them that God prefers you to those who know their lives have fallen apart? It's the sick, not the healthy, who need a doctor. But you despise the sin-sick among you. Didn't God say through Hosea, 'I desire mercy, not sacrifice?'[20] Will you ever learn what this means? I draw near to the broken so they might hear the voice of mercy. I'm not here to change their minds; I'm here to heal their hearts."

As he listened to Jesus and the Pharisees argue over him and his friends, Matthew quietly decided he would follow Jesus from then on. No one had ever defended his dignity like this before. Jesus knew the ugly truth—he knew Matthew had chosen money over God. Yet here stood Jesus in his home, defending his right to befriend the marginalized and outcast. Wherever it took him, whatever it cost, he would follow Jesus, even if it meant following him all the way to the end of his life.[21]

The Calling of St. Matthew was one of Caravaggio's most important paintings because it established him as a master. Matthew was a paradox—a sinner who made his living taking from others and also a man who left everything to follow Jesus. Caravaggio was drawn to these life-changing moments in Scripture, like when the risen Jesus guided Thomas's dirty finger into the open wound in his side; or when Saul fell off his horse, struck by the power and presence of Christ converting him without warning; or when Peter denied knowing Jesus in the very moment his Lord was being handed over to die.[22]

Caravaggio gravitated toward situations where the sacred confronted the profane, and he was moved by the power of Christ to change people's heart. The theme of the sinner's need for rescue and Christ's power to give it runs throughout his entire body of work. It was a story he told over and over again throughout his entire life, presumably because he kept needing to hear it.

Carnival and Lent, with Nothing in Between

Biographer Andrew Graham-Dixon said, "Caravaggio lived his life as if there were only Carnival and Lent, with nothing in between."[23] When he was painting, he worked with a laser focus. But when he was finished and the commission had come in, he would drink, carouse, and brawl for months at a time. One report said, "After a fortnight's work he will swagger about for a month or two with a sword at his side and a servant following him, from one ball-court to the next, ever ready to engage in a fight or an argument, with the result that it is most awkward to get along with him."[24] This pattern was never tamed.

On July 29, 1605, a young notary named Mariano Pasqualone staggered into a legal office, bleeding from a stab wound. In a rather lengthy statement, he said:

I am here in the office because I have been assaulted by Michelangelo da Caravaggio, the painter ... As Messer Galeazzo and I ... were strolling in Piazza Navona in front of the palace of the Spanish ambassador, I suddenly felt a blow on the back of my head. I fell to the ground at once and realized that I had been wounded in the head by what I believe to have been the stroke of a sword ...

I didn't see who wounded me, but I never had disputes with anybody but the said Michelangelo. A few nights ago he and I had words on the Corso on account of a woman called Lena ... She is Michelangelo's woman. Please, excuse me quickly, that I may dress my wounds.[25]

Caravaggio was taken into custody but was soon bailed out by his patrons.[26] Not long after, "to complicate matters, there was now a new 'affair': during a hard-drinking dinner at the Albergo del Moro, Caravaggio considered himself illtreated and hurled a plate of scalding hot artichokes in the face of a waiter, causing a fight which spread through the inn. The Corte again arrested the malefactor, and his patrons again obtained his liberation."[27]

During the period when these altercations occurred, Caravaggio painted *John the Baptist in the Wilderness* (1604), which now hangs in the Nelson-Atkins Museum in Kansas City. Caravaggio's John the Baptist is not the triumphant prophet vehemently denouncing the sins of the world and calling people to repentance. He displays no swagger. Instead, he is a man cloaked in privacy. We can discern almost nothing about him from his appearance, except that whatever is on his mind is heavy. The plaque on the gallery wall reads:

The conception of the image is itself remarkable, for the Baptist had hardly ever before been portrayed as an isolated, seated figure who lacks, moreover, his usual attributes of halo, lamb, and banderole. Stark contrasts of light and dark accentuate the perception that the figure leans forward, out of the deep shadows of the background and into the lighter realm of the viewer's own space . . . It seems, indeed, as if Caravaggio instilled in this image an element of the essential pessimism of the Baptist's preaching, of the senseless tragedy of his early martyrdom, and perhaps even some measure of the artist's own troubled psyche.[28]

Perhaps the work is meant to convey Caravaggio leaning out of his shadowed existence to ask the question, "Can the proclamation of the coming of Christ actually penetrate the heart in a way that would lead to repentance?" It is as though to the drunken brawler with the sword in his hand, John the Baptist's mission to prepare the way for Christ's ministry was an isolating burden, one that perhaps felt at times like a futile one.

In 1605, after another night of heavy drinking, Caravaggio was stopped and questioned by a police sergeant. The officer died that night from a mysterious blow that crushed his skull. Caravaggio testified that, yes, the officer questioned him, but during the interrogation, a stone fell from the rooftops and struck the constable on the head. Caravaggio's friends backed his story, but the Corte found the coincidence too impossible. They arrested Caravaggio and put him in prison, where he was tortured for his suspected crime—bound to the rack and lashed. His friends feared that he would be killed in jail, so they coordinated his escape; two guards were bribed to unlock his chains, and one of Caravaggio's patrons, Scipione Borghese, who happened to be the head of the papal justice system, looked the other way—this time. But Caravaggio's escape came at a cost. Though he managed to slip away in the night, he was now a fugitive, which drove him even deeper into the dark heart of Rome.

Soon after his torture in the Roman prison, Caravaggio

painted *Ecce Homo*, Latin for "Behold the Man," a reference to Pontius Pilate's declaration when he presented a beaten Christ to the crowd for crucifixion.[29] The light is dramatic. The figures fill the frame. The beaten Jesus wears a crown of thorns as one of his tormentors mockingly places on his shoulders a royal robe. The image expresses both the brutality of the soldiers and the pitiful state of their prisoner. Jesus looks fragile, yet single-minded in his mission. His wrists are bound. He holds in one hand a bamboo switch, presumably the tool they used to lash him. Pilate looks at the viewers of the painting, as if to ask us the question he put to the crowd in the gospel: "Is this what you wanted?"

Caravaggio continued brawling and drinking, without a hint that he had any plans to stop. On May 29, 1606, a quarrel involving four men over what appears to be gambling on a tennis game spilled over into a more ignoble matter of honor settled by swords.[30] The police report of the incident survived, indicating that Caravaggio and his opponent, Ranuccio Tomassoni, had both tried to woo the same woman, and their fight was "fueled by constant provocations, superior behavior, arrogance, and jealousy."[31] Caravaggio stabbed Tomassoni in the femoral artery, leading some to speculate that he was actually trying to castrate his enemy, who bled out and died later that night. Caravaggio was also wounded in the exchange but managed to slip away again, evading arrest. After Tomassoni's death, Rome charged Caravaggio with murder.

Around that time, as a fugitive now wanted for murder, Caravaggio painted *The Death of the Virgin*. Here Mary has died, and those who knew her and loved her—Mary Magdalene and the apostles—gather around her body to mourn. Caravaggio put aside all symbolic and conventional standards for depicting Jesus' mother except for the thread of a halo adorning her head, rendering her simply and starkly as a dead body, swollen and limp. The grief over the tragedy of their loss is palpable as her friends look on, weeping. In the Louvre in Paris, the gallery label for this painting reads, "In some ways this is a silent grief, this is no wake for wailers. The sobbing occurs in faceless emotional silence. Suppressing all anecdotal detail, Caravaggio invests this subdued scene with extraordinary monumentality through the sole presence of these figures and the intensity of their emotions."[32]

The apostle John is the figure closest to Mary, leaning over her, pressing his fists into his eyes to wring his tears. We presume this is John, because as Jesus was dying on the cross, "he said to his mother, 'Woman, behold your son!' Then he said to [John], 'Behold, your mother!' And from that hour the disciple took her to his own home."[33] John is as a son weeping for his mother. To this day, many who pass before this painting weep as well.[34]

After Tomassoni's death, Caravaggio's former patron, Scipione Borghese, placed a death warrant on his head, meaning any officer of the law could kill Caravaggio on sight. If they couldn't bring the criminal's body to Borghese, just his head would do. Caravaggio had no choice but to flee Rome. He was thirty-five when he went on the run, and he fled as one of the most famous painters the city had ever known.

Chased by His Enemies

In October 1606, wanted for murder, Caravaggio fled to Naples, one of the most populous cities in Europe at the time and outside the legal jurisdiction of Rome. He took refuge in the home of an old friend of his father, Costanza Colonna Sforza. The Colonna family was well connected and able to give him protection. The artist's reputation preceded him, and Caravaggio the criminal was welcomed in as Caravaggio the master painter. Commissions came quickly, and the most famous painter in Rome soon became the most famous painter in Naples as well.

Michelangelo Merisi da Caravaggio, *The Seven Works of Mercy*, 1607, oil on canvas, 390 x 260 cm, Pio Monte della Misericordia, Naples

Caravaggio's eight months in Naples were prolific. He painted two *Flagellation of Christ* scenes, drawing on his experience of torture while in the Roman prison. He also painted the masterpiece *The Seven Works of Mercy*, which illustrates the six mercies listed in Matthew 25:35–46, with the traditional burial of the dead included as the seventh. In a single frame, a woman gives milk from her breast to an old man at the prison gate (*I was hungry and you gave me food; I was in prison and you came to me*), a man cuts his robe in half to share it with a naked, sickly beggar (*I was naked and you clothed me; I was sick and you visited me*), an innkeeper gives a man water (*I was thirsty and you gave me drink*), another welcomes a pilgrim covered in the dust of the road (*I was a stranger and you welcomed me*), and finally two men tend to the burial of a dead man, who is shown simply as a pair of feet.

In a single frame, Caravaggio depicts mercy as a costly endeavor, something that cannot be done without fully entering into the misery and need of another. Angels observe from above with a kind of astonishment that calls to mind the words of Peter, who described living out the gospel as something "into which angels long to look."[35]

In July 1607, Caravaggio left Naples for Malta. The reason for his departure is unclear. Some suggest he learned that Roman mercenaries had come to Naples looking for him, but it's more likely he went to Malta to become a knight, which would go a long way to securing a papal pardon following Tomassoni's death.[36] Caravaggio presented himself to Alof de Wignacourt, the grand master of the Knights of Malta, who offered Caravaggio knighthood in exchange for an altar piece for his church. Caravaggio produced *The Beheading of St. John the Baptist*—his largest, and the only painting of his to bear his name—for St. John's Co-Cathedral in Valletta Malta, where it remains to this day. Before his name is the letter "f", for "Fra," which indicated he was a knight.[37] Wignacourt's coat of arms was painted onto the frame. The fame and reputation of the painting were almost instantaneous. European painters came from all over to Valletta to see it.[38]

But Caravaggio's rhythm of Carnival and Lent continued, and in August 1608, he started another brawl during which he shot a fellow knight named Giovanni Rodomonte Roero. The Knights of Valletta threw him in the prison at Castel Sant'Angelo to await trial and most likely execution. He managed to escape yet again by climbing down 200 feet from the prison wall to the shore below, swimming three miles around the island, and boarding a boat for Sicily.

Fleeing the island was considered abandonment and high treason by the order. That December, he was labeled a "corrupt and stinking member" and stripped of his knighthood, making the most famous painter in Rome, Naples, and now Malta a criminal who was not only wanted by the pope but also hunted by the Knights of Valletta.[39]

In Sicily, Caravaggio stayed with his old friend Mario Minniti. The two of them traveled around the island to Syracuse, Messina, and Palermo. Caravaggio was not well mentally or physically. He was possibly fighting an infection from the beatings he received in the Maltese prison. His behavior was erratic and volatile. Before long, Minniti couldn't take any more of his friend's mania and returned home. Caravaggio moved around from city to city in constant fear that he was being hunted. He spoke of being "chased by his enemy," likely a reference to the friends of the knight he shot.[40]

During his time in Sicily, Caravaggio painted *The Adoration of the Shepherds*, which presents the mystery of the birth of the Savior in royal color and confident light, and *The Raising of Lazarus*, which shows the infant now grown, commanding death with authority, to the wonder and terror of those who bore witness. When he was in the throes of despair, desperate, and afraid for his life, he created these two works that tell the story of the birth of the tender Savior who grew into a man who wept over suffering, sickness, and loss while demonstrating his power over death itself. This is the paradox of Caravaggio—he brought so much suffering on himself, with such bravado and acrimony, yet when he picked up his brush, the Christ he rendered was the Redeemer of the vulnerable.

In late summer of 1609, after only nine months in Sicily, he returned to Naples to elude the Knights of Malta and lobby Rome for a pardon. Not long after his arrival, he was attacked and left to die in the streets. His attacker—likely a friend of the Order—slashed his face, leaving him grossly disfigured. Reports spread that he had died, but he survived, though he was gravely ill.

During his convalescence, he painted two paintings of note: *Salome with the Head of St. John the Baptist* and *David with the Head of Goliath*. He sent *Salome with the Head of St. John the Baptist* to Wignacourt. Andrew Graham-Dixon said, "The picture is a plea bargain."[41] Roberto Longhi wrote, "The turbulent and dramatic lighting here reach new intensity, as if it were the artist's last, feral lament."[42] The head on the platter is Caravaggio's own, as if to acknowledge the fate he believed he deserved, or at least couldn't escape.

The second painting—and likely his last—was *David with the Head of Goliath*. Here also the severed head is Caravaggio's. David the conqueror looks despondent and dejected, as though the utter brokenness of this world was so overwhelming that even the victor found little consolation in his triumph. Goliath's face—Caravaggio's—wears a stare of astonishment over his defeat, anxiety over his demise, and resignation to his fate. Caravaggio sent this one to his former patron, Scipione Borghese, the man who held the authority to grant and withhold papal pardons, in the hope that it might earn him some mercy there.[43]

It seems his appeal to Rome worked, because in July 1610, he took a boat north from Naples to Rome. Traveling by sea seemed safer than on land.[44] On his way, he stopped off in Porto Ercole, one day's journey to Rome, to await news that his pardon had gone through. When he got off the boat in Porto Ercole, he was immediately arrested for reasons that are unclear. He was stripped of his possessions. His protests that he was a knight fell on deaf ears, suggesting his arrest was coordinated by the Order of Malta. Or perhaps it was the work of the friends of the slain Tomassoni.

Caravaggio managed to get released. How he did is unclear. Perhaps it was to set up what followed. Though the details of what happened to Caravaggio after his release are incomplete, Lambert writes, "One account has him haggard, hungry, ill, and worn out, looking for the felucca he had hired, or for another boat. His wounds, it is said, had become infected and brought fever in their wake. In another account, he entrusted himself to prowlers on the beach and was assassinated."[45]

Caravaggio's Travels
Designed by Brad Davis

Whatever happened that night, Caravaggio never made it to Rome. In July 1610, he was found lying fatally ill on the beach at Porto Ercole. He was taken to the hospital, where he died a few days later on July 18. The painter's body was buried in a common grave on the hospital grounds.[46] He was thirty-eight years old.

Soon after his death, Pope Paul V granted Caravaggio's pardon.

What Begins in the Work of Caravaggio

American art critic Bernard Berenson said of Caravaggio, "With the exception of Michelangelo, no other Italian painter exercised so great an influence."[47] Early in his career, when Caravaggio's style was beginning to depart from popular convention but his subject matter was still mostly aligned with the expectations of a religious painter, younger artists hailed him as a visionary. Just a few decades after his death, Giovanni Bellori said, "The painters then in Rome were greatly impressed by his novelty and the young ones especially gathered around him and praised him as the only true imitator of nature. Looking upon his works as miracles, they outdid each other in following his methods."[48]

But when he died, that reverence vanished. The records of his life—many of them criminal records—presented a troubled, corrupt murderer. His hard living and early death, along with his provocative style, cast a pall over him in the eyes of his contemporaries. His reputation was too much to overcome. It would take nearly three hundred years for his name to return and his work to be esteemed.

Still, historian Giuliano Briganti said, "After him, painting would never be the same again. His revolution was a profound and irreversible modification of the emotional and intellectual relation between the artist and his subject."[49] How is this possible if "immediately after his death, he was all but forgotten, written off as a wasted talent?"[50]

Though his name was forgotten, his influence was carried forward by other painters whose lives were shaped by his art—Rembrandt, Vermeer, Delacroix, Manet, and countless others. Art historian Andre Berne-Joffrey said, "What begins in the work of Caravaggio is, quite simply, modern painting."[51]

Why did his influence carry on? Because his art is made of darkness and light. It is glorious yet grotesque, divine yet close to the earth, highly intelligent yet easy to understand. It presents a gospel to the poor. In spite of what the records show, Caravaggio understood that the gospel was not just a story but a power vital for the languishing. It was a message of grit and hope for the vile and desperate. It was the promise of a God at work in a world of prostitutes and magistrates and murderers and those chased by the hounds of heaven.

Caravaggio knew what it meant to be pursued—to live so violent an existence that this world would come to give no quarter to one like him. He knew what it was to have the ability to render beauty that could bring a person to tears and yet remain unable to live free from his own destructive behavior. He was able to tap into something transcendent, to render a familiar scene in a way that compelled millions to come from all over the world just to stand before it and weep. He became the inspiration of some of the greatest names in the history of art, who aspired not only to match his skill but to somehow tap into his vision, intelligence, and spiritual insight.

The prostitutes and vagrants who stood in as his models were the woman at the well, the rich young ruler, the young virgin mother herself—common people living hard lives drawn into the too-good-to-be-true story of salvation.

Did Caravaggio know the love of Christ? When Jesus stood before Pontius Pilate, about to go to the cross, Pilate asked him if he was a king. Jesus said, "For this purpose I was born and for this purpose I have come into the world—to bear witness to the truth.

Everyone who is of the truth listens to my voice."[52] Caravaggio's art reveals a man who seemed to listen to Jesus in some way. It reveals someone who embodied a poverty of spirit. It reveals a rich young ruler—wealthy in raw talent and a discerning eye—who, according to his criminal records, may have walked away from Jesus, but according to his art, seems to have known the hope of grace that comes from Christ alone.

As with the rich young ruler who walked away from Jesus sad,[53] the outcome of Caravaggio's spiritual journey is not known to us. We don't know what was in his heart as he lay dying on the beach at Porto Ercole. But we know the gospel he painted. We know that while he was yet sinning, he was producing some of the most profoundly merciful and eloquent commentaries on Scripture ever painted. Based on the content of his art, along with the biblical truth that God's mercy is a product of his love and not our conduct,[54] we cannot dismiss Caravaggio from the kingdom of God. We cannot conclude that his behavior was so destructive that it shattered the grace of the Lord he painted with such reverence.

Martin Luther described Christians as *simul justus et peccator*—at the same time sinner and justified. Throughout Scripture, the Lord worked through tragically flawed people: Moses the murderer,[55] Jacob the liar,[56] David the adulterer,[57] Solomon the philanderer,[58] and Jonah who resented that God would show mercy to his enemies, let alone ask him to deliver the news.[59] In the New Testament, Jesus welcomed prostitutes,[60] ate with tax collectors and sinners,[61] and called future deniers to be his disciples.[62] Saul of Tarsus was converted while in the process of trying to destroy the church.[63] The pattern in Scripture is that of God working through unlikely servants for the glory of his name and the spread of the gospel.

Caravaggio's life reminds us that we who embody the sacred and the profane have an enormous capacity to hurt each other.

Caravaggio lived a destructive life. But his art shouts into that chaos that just as Christ could call the tax collector to follow him or draw from the recesses of the hardest heart the beauty and wonder that poured out of Caravaggio between his seasons of Carnival, our Lord's capacity to extend grace is greater still. And grace transforms even the hardest hearts.

CHAPTER 4

REMBRANDT IS
IN THE WIND

The Tragedy of Desecration and
the Hope of Redemption

Rembrandt van Rijn, *The Storm on the Sea of Galilee*,
1633, oil on canvas, 160 × 128 cm, stolen from the
Isabella Stewart Gardner Museum in March 1990

Life etches itself onto our faces as we grow older,
showing our violence, excesses or kindnesses.

Rembrandt van Rijn

The security guard sitting behind the main desk of the Isabella Stewart Gardner Museum looked up from his homework when he heard the buzzer for the Palace Road entrance. On the monitor, he saw two uniformed police officers standing outside. The officers told him through the intercom they had received a report of a disturbance in the museum's courtyard and needed to check it out.[1]

It was 1:24 a.m. on March 18, 1990. Though midnight officially marked the end of Saint Patrick's Day, the pubs in Boston's Fenway neighborhood were still pouring pints and spilling their staggering celebrants into the streets when, against protocol, the guard buzzed the officers in.

Once inside, the officer in charge asked the guard if he had noticed anything unusual and if there was anyone else on duty that night.

The guard told them yes, he had a partner upstairs, and no, they had not seen anything out of the ordinary.

The lead officer said, "Go ahead and call your partner down here."

The second officer studied the guard's face as he made the call.

"You look familiar," the second officer said to the guard. "Is there a warrant out for your arrest?"

The security guard looked surprised and insisted there wasn't, but the question itself set him on edge, and his denial seemed only to deepen the officer's suspicion. "Please come over here and show me your ID," the lead officer ordered.

The security guard stepped out from behind the desk and away from the only silent alarm button in the museum. He handed his driver's license and Berklee College of Music ID to the officer. After studying the license for a second, the officer cuffed the guard and said, "You are under arrest. We need to take you in."

Just then the second watchman on duty that night, an aspiring musician, came around the corner, and the officers immediately put him in handcuffs too.

Surprised, the second guard asked, "Why are you arresting me?"

The officers said, "You are not being arrested. You are being robbed. Don't give us any problems and you won't get hurt."

The thieves then bound the guards, covered their eyes and mouths with tape, and chained them to pipes on opposite ends of the basement. After this, the thieves spent the next 81 minutes selecting and loading thirteen irreplaceable pieces of art into a vehicle waiting outside. Then they drove off quietly past the homes and businesses of Fenway, never to be heard from again.

The Storm

The sea surges and swells. The little fishing boat has no hope of holding on to the churning foam below. The bow rides up the back of one white breaker, while the stern dips into the valley beneath it. Waves break over the sides. The half dozen men to Rembrandt's right shout and strain at the sails, struggling to keep the ship from capsizing. The five men to his left plead with Jesus of Nazareth to save them. Rembrandt stands in the middle of the boat, his right hand tightly clutching a rope and his left pinning his hat to his head. His name is scrawled across the useless rudder, as though this is his boat on his sea, and they are all caught in his storm. He and everyone else in the ship are soon to be lost unless their leader intervenes.[2]

We don't think much about our mortality, but the question is never far away. It comes in an instant and often brings with it an inherent sense of reverence. Life is a fragile, sacred thing. This sacred fragility has played a central role in the creation of much of the world's great art. We marvel at the lithe physical perfection of youth in Michelangelo's *David*. We wonder what sort of burden has Rodin's *Thinker* so bent over.[3] We avert our eyes from death in Reuben's *The Lamentation Over the Dead Christ*, as Joseph of Arimathea and Nicodemus lay Jesus' lifeless body on a stone slab.

When our seas are calm, we regard them as safe. We say, "I know these waters like the back of my hand." But what we mean is, *We know these waters when they are still and when our boats are sound and when the sun is out and when our supplies are in order.* And that, as it turns out, has nothing to do with actually knowing what churns in the depths or what gathers in the heavens. When the storm breaks out, we have much to learn.

For the men in the boat with Rembrandt, this storm was not their first encounter with their mortality. Early in Jesus' ministry, he and his disciples came to a town called Nain in the foothills of Mount Tabor southeast of Nazareth.[4] As they drew near to the village, they heard the unmistakable cries of mourning coming from just inside the gate. This community's tragedy, whatever it was, was recent and the wounds were fresh.

The disciples watched as mourners trickled out like tears from the town's gate. Behind the mourners came four men carrying a dead man on a stretcher. The dead man's mother followed behind, weeping. The disciples looked for the dead man's father or brothers. There were none. People from the procession said his mother was a widow and this was her only son. A loss like this meant the widow would have no one to care for her in her old age. Those who knew her situation all felt the same sting. No mother should have to bury her own child.

In those days, people looked to their religious leaders to make sense of death and the grief it caused. But when Jesus' disciples looked at their teacher, they didn't see a man composing a speech. Instead, they saw a man dealing with his own grief. Jesus watched the dead son's mother weeping into her hands. He walked over and stood in front of her until she regarded him.

"Do not weep," he said. His words were tender, but words alone would not stop these tears. They both knew this. Still, Jesus interrupted her mourning long enough for her to look up and see his compassion for her.

Jesus went over to the funeral bier and touched the pall. The bearers stopped. In fact, in that moment, everything seemed to stop. When Jesus touched the board bearing the dead man, several people gasped, because touching the dead defiled a rabbi's ceremonial purity. *What was he thinking? Had he sunk so deep into his own empathy that he had forgotten himself?*

Jesus whispered, "Young man."

The dead man's mother's sorrow changed to confusion. Did the rabbi just whisper something to her son?

Jesus said, "Young man, listen to my voice. Get up."

A huge gasp came from the stretcher as the body jerked like someone startled awake by a clap of thunder. The young man sat up and asked why he was on that board and why everyone looked so terrified. Jesus helped him down and returned him to his mother. Fear seized the crowd of mourners. They weren't sure how to feel. Some wept even more. Others laughed in disbelief. One said what they were all feeling: "God has visited his people and he has given us a great prophet. Jesus of Nazareth speaks and the dead live again."⁵

The disciples were no strangers to matters of mortality, but the ways Jesus responded to it were unlike anything they, or the rest of the world, had ever seen. Reports of that miracle spread all around Judea and the surrounding countryside. Great crowds flocked to Jesus. As those crowds continued to grow, Jesus stayed on the move to manage them the best he could.

It was a world with no shortage of need, and people continued to bring theirs to him in droves. After one particularly intense day of ministry by the Sea of Galilee, Jesus asked his disciples to set off in a boat to get some peace and quiet. Weary, Jesus went to the bow of the boat and lay down. Rocking in the gentle swells of the sea, he fell asleep.

He awoke to a dripping, desperate face inches from his own shouting over the noise of a sudden storm, "Wake up! Don't you care that we are perishing?"[6]

A canyon wind had whipped the lake into such a torrent that the waves were beginning to break over the sides of the boat. She was sinking. Most of the souls on board were experienced seafarers, and all of them, in fact, except Jesus were working furiously to keep their boat afloat and so also their lives.

"Jesus, we're dying! Don't you care?" screamed Peter.

It was an ironic question. The reason Jesus and his disciples were in the boat in the first place was to escape the crowds that continually pressed in around Jesus because he had come to be known as a healer who could raise the dead.[7] The masses sought him because he not only cared about their perishing; he stopped it. He even *reversed* it.

But there in the boat, paralyzed on a leprous-white sea, they knew this could only end in one of two ways: in death or in a miracle. In spite of their best efforts, they were headed for death, and they were desperate. Did Jesus have anything for them like he had for the widow from Nain's son? Even if it was only words, they needed something.

The Master

The Storm on the Sea of Galilee, Rembrandt Harmenszoon van Rijn's (1606–1669) only known seascape, is one of his most dramatic paintings, capturing that moment just after the disciples knew they would die if Jesus didn't save them and just before he did. The 5-foot by 4-foot canvas hung in the Dutch Room on the second floor of the Isabella Stewart Gardner Museum for close to one hundred years. Everyone who looked at it saw the same thing: Rembrandt looking out through the frame to us—looking us dead in the eye. The terror on his face asked us what the disciples were asking Jesus: "Don't you care that we're perishing here?"

Rembrandt, who was known even to his own contemporaries as "The Master," was as much a storyteller as he was a painter.[8] He cared about the narratives behind his paintings and painted them to tell as much of the story as he could in a single frame. One way he did this was by painting himself into several biblical scenes. He did this not for vanity but for the sake of the story. He wanted to draw us in, capture our imaginations, instruct us on how we should relate to what was happening on the canvas, and bear witness to what he believed to be true about the world he painted and his place in it.

For example, in *The Raising of the Cross,* Rembrandt strains with three other men to lift the cross of Jesus into its base on Golgotha. He and Jesus are the only two men not draped in shadow. The contrast between them is stark. Jesus is naked, pale, and bloody; Rembrandt is wearing a rich man's clean, blue robe and matching beret. Rembrandt wants us to know that while he believed all people had a hand in Jesus' crucifixion (as seen in the array of soldiers, peasants, politicians, and faceless figures hidden in the background), as far as he is concerned, the one whose guilt shines brightest in that affair is his own.

In his painting *The Prodigal Son in the Tavern,* Rembrandt

is the glassy-eyed, drunk younger brother looking at us over his left shoulder as he holds a pint in one hand and a woman in the other. The woman in the painting is his wife, Saskia. By painting himself into this scene, Rembrandt confesses his great capacity for folly as well as his imminent need for mercy. We look on with a mix of pity and compassion. We know what the man in the story has squandered and what he has left behind. We know how his world is about to crumble. But we also know that his father loves him and is probably scanning the horizon for the young man's return even at that very moment. And we know that the prodigal will return to his father's love, but not before he breaks.

By painting himself into the boat in *The Storm on the Sea of Galilee*, Rembrandt wants us to know that he believes his life will either be lost in a sea of chaos or preserved by the Son of God. Those are his only two options. And by peering through the storm and out of the frame to us, he asks if we are not in the same boat.

The Collector

America's first great art collector, Isabella Stewart Gardner (1840–1924), came to know this perishing all too well when her two-year-old son died in 1865. Heartbroken, she and her husband, Jack, began traveling the world in an effort to assuage their grief. Both Jack and Isabella came from wealthy families, so they were never wanting financially. This freed them to venture as far and wide as they pleased. And that they did. In their travels they began to collect art, both folk and fine, from around the globe.[9]

Though their grief over the loss of their son eventually subsided, their appetite for art did not. In 1890, after twenty-five years of gathering, they realized they had assembled the makings of a world-class permanent collection of fine art that any museum would have been eager to call their own. So they set the folk art aside and focused on obtaining works from many of the world's greatest artists: Botticelli, Titian, Raphael, Manet, Degas, Vermeer, and Rembrandt. Their collection, Isabella said, "ought to have only a few, and all of them *A. No 1's.*"[10]

Before long, Isabella and Jack's collection grew so large that she felt it would be improper to keep it to themselves. She wanted to create a permanent home for their art, "a museum for the education and enjoyment of the public forever."[11] She and Jack purchased a plot of land in Boston's Fenway neighborhood and began to dream.

Then in 1898, tragedy struck again. Jack died. Once again Isabella was thrown into grief, and as she had done when she lost her son, she turned to art to lead her through. Only this time, instead of gathering more art others had created, she wanted to make something of her own—her own masterpiece, *her* museum: Fenway Court.

Isabella poured herself into the project. She was not content to simply meet with her builders and pay her contractors. She designed every aspect of the museum herself. Her architect, William Sears, joked that on this particular job he was little more than a carpenter and mechanical engineer carrying out the true architect's vision. Isabella designed an Italian Renaissance palazzo with great halls framing a grand courtyard in the center, just like the ones in Venice she and Jack used to stay in when they were younger and had the world by the tail.

Over the next few years, the four-story Fenway Court rose from the marshlands as one of the finer things many of its neighbors had ever seen. Once the structure was completed in 1902, Isabella spent an entire year working on the interior design. Unimpressed with traditional gallery-style museums, which, to her, were boring, bare rooms with pictures hanging on the walls, she arranged her collection to overwhelm her guests with the sense that they were getting a truly intimate experience with some of the world's most magnificent creations.

Each room would be its own living diorama featuring paintings, tapestries, furniture, and sculptures, all arranged to immerse the patron in the experience of a culture and era they would never be able to find anywhere other than her museum. "Love of art, not knowledge about the history of art, was her aim,"[12] the museum's official history explained.

From the pieces in her collection to where she placed them in the palazzo to the architecture to the furniture to the floor plan, Fenway Court was just as Isabella wanted it. She was adamant that it remain that way, so much so that in her last will and testament she stipulated that if any changes were made to her collection after her death—if future trustees allowed anything to either be brought in or taken out—the entire collection would have to be turned over to Harvard for liquidation.[13] Adding anything to her collection would be like adding length to the Mona Lisa's hair, just as removing anything would be tantamount to cutting it.

Isabella Stewart Gardner, a woman of sorrows and acquainted with grief, wanted to bring something into this world that would not perish. She chose art. At the time of her death in 1924, Isabella had accumulated more than 2,500 tapestries, manuscripts, rare books, sculptures, pieces of furniture, and masterworks from Titian, Vermeer, Flinck, Michelangelo, Raphael, Whistler, Degas, Manet, Sargent, Botticelli, and the Dutch master himself, Rembrandt. She had given them a home. More than that, she had given them places of honor to be savored by the "rapt glad faces of those who love art."[14]

When asked why she was so protective of keeping Fenway Court just as she had made it, the widow who buried her son all those years earlier said, "My museum will live."[15]

The Take

The sensors on the security door revealed that the thieves had to make two trips. The thirteen stolen works included Johannes Vermeer's *The Concert* (one of only thirty-four confirmed Vermeers in existence), a Flinck landscape, a three-thousand-year-old Chinese vase from the Shang Dynasty, one Manet painting, five works of Degas, a bronze eagle finial, and three Rembrandts—one, a postage stamp–sized self-portrait etching; one, his formal *Lady and Gentleman in Black*; and last, one of the museum's most prominently displayed works, *The Storm on the Sea of Galilee*. Together, the thirteen stolen pieces of art amounted to the largest property theft in America's history, with an estimated value of more than $500 million.

The most valuable works were taken from the museum's Dutch Room on the second floor. "Strong personalities dominate this room," the museum guide says. "Looking down from the walls are a queen, a doctor, an archduchess, a lawyer, an artist, and even a collector."[16] Even in the elite company of Isabella's other Dutch and Flemish masterpieces, there was no disputing that Rembrandt's *The Storm on the Sea of Galilee* ruled the room.

Rembrandt painted *The Storm on the Sea of Galilee* in 1633, shortly after moving from his home in Leiden to Amsterdam. He wanted to establish himself as one of the city's masters of biblical and geopolitical portraiture and historical scenes. Rembrandt's fine brushwork and bright palette were characteristic of his early style, which featured detail as intricate as the braid of a rope or the crow's-feet around a man's eyes.

Rembrandt's "ability not only to represent a sacred history, but also to seize our attention and immerse us in an unfolding pictorial drama"[17] makes *The Storm on the Sea of Galilee* transcend the scene itself. The story here is about so much more than one group of men getting caught up in that one storm on that one afternoon.

This painting is about all of us. Rembrandt retraces the old story that pits humanity against nature as the angry sea tosses that fully rigged boat with her terrified passengers around like a toy. And he pits the vulgar against the divine as one disciple vomits over the leeward rail while another, only two feet away, holds on to the second person of the Blessed Trinity, pleading for him to save them.

The crime scene revealed that while the thieves had plenty of time to handle the art with care, they chose not to. One Rembrandt was left behind, bent and scuffed on the floor. Vermeer's *The Concert* had been knocked out of its frame, as had Manet's *Chez Tortoni*. In what could only be seen as an act of mockery, the thieves left Manet's empty frame in a chair in the security supervisor's office.

Rembrandt's *The Storm on the Sea of Galilee* fared even worse. Rather than risk getting caught with the 5-foot canvas, the thieves took a knife and cut the painting out of its stretcher boards. The frame, complete with its tiny brass plaque at the bottom that read, simply, "Rembrandt," was left hanging empty on the wall.

The Market

Anthony Amore, the Gardner Museum's security director, said, "Art is not stolen by master criminals, but by common criminals . . . This is less like *The Thomas Crown Affair* and more like a Coen brothers movie."[18] Art thieves are rarely art collectors. Collectors want to show others what they have. Criminals want to keep their cache hidden and turn it into money as soon as possible. Because art thieves are not often collectors, they don't always know what they are taking. In 2003, one thief made off with Leonardo da Vinci's *The Madonna of the Yarnwinder*, not realizing he had stolen one of the most famous and valuable paintings in the world. When he tried to sell it, no one would touch it because it was too famous.[19]

Stolen art is a burden few can manage. What can a thief do with half a billion dollars in stolen art when the paintings taken in the heist are featured in every newspaper, magazine, and news show around the world? The average law-abiding citizen gets stuck on this question because they assume the point is for the thief to try to get something close to what the art is worth. A 100 million dollars stolen Vermeer, even at a discount, should fetch the thief 50 million dollars, right?

Wrong. Thieves in possession of well-known works of art—Vermeers, Rembrandts, Monets, da Vincis—know that attempting to sell the art outright almost guarantees their arrest. So what happens to art once it is taken? Typically, especially in the days before the internet, a stolen piece of art would meet one of four fates: it would either be destroyed, held for ransom, used as a black market currency, or sold as a high-quality replica of itself.

Of course, there are instances where thieves steal art because they want to keep it for themselves, but that seldom turns out well. Stéphane Breitwieser, a thirty-two-year-old waiter who lived with his mother in eastern France, stole hundreds of pieces of art from museums in Germany, Switzerland, and France. He stole them because he liked them; he displayed them in his mother's home. When he was arrested for stealing a bugle, of all things, his mother, in an effort to hide his crimes, burned many of the pieces in his collection. At the time of Breitwieser's arrest, he had gathered close to two billion dollars in stolen art.[20]

Investigators estimate that 20 percent of all stolen art meets a similar fate. The stress and inconvenience of holding such precious public treasures ends up being more than the thieves bargained for. With nowhere to turn and no way to give it back, they destroy their prize.

The FBI says only 5 percent of the world's stolen art is ever recovered. Often, these pieces were stolen for the purpose of being returned for a ransom. This art tends to end up back on the museum wall. For some thieves, this is the plan all along—steal a painting, cut out letters from a newspaper, glue them together into a ransom note, and hope for the best.

For others, they're after a ransom of a different kind. Some criminals have the foresight to know that, due to their unlawful lifestyle, they will likely one day be arrested for something. This is a question of when, not if. Facilitating the return of a stolen treasure becomes a strategic bargaining chip when they go to plead down their charges. Criminals know that law enforcement agencies look great in the public eye when they recover stolen art, and there is no such thing as too much goodwill between these agencies and the communities they serve.

This leaves approximately 75 percent of the world's stolen art unaccounted for—in the wind. Once the Gardner art trundled away from the museum in the back of a panel van, it took on a completely new purpose. It ceased to exist, as Gardner intended, "for the education and enjoyment of the public forever" and most likely became a form of currency. Black market paintings and sculptures end up traveling the world like a twenty dollar bill.

How does this work? Suppose someone drives off with a Monet worth 10 million dollars. That painting might be traded right away for one million dollars' worth of high-quality cocaine. The cocaine dealer then sits on the painting for a year while the buzz around it dies down. Then he trades it to an arms dealer for a cache of weapons for his cartel. Another year passes, and the arms dealer trades the Monet to a weapons supplier, who knows a black market art dealer. Now the painting has been off the grid for a few years and is five people removed from the thief and his crime, without one dollar actually exchanging hands. The black market has laundered the painting and the memory of its theft to a point where it can begin to appear in unscrupulous deals and move from private sale to private sale for years, even decades, before ever emerging on the open market or being discovered in an attic at some estate sale. Stolen art fetches roughly 10 percent of its actual value in that first sale. But the further it travels from the crime, the greater the buyer's plausible deniability and thus the safer the purchase and the higher the price tag.

The laws surrounding art theft don't exactly deter thieves. They know how the system works. In the United States, the National Stolen Property Act protects collectors from going to jail for owning stolen art unless it can be proven that they knew they were buying stolen merchandise, which is almost impossible to demonstrate with laundered art since one of the hallmarks of the black market is secrecy. In the Netherlands, the law says that after twenty years, a piece of stolen art becomes the legal property of whoever possesses it.

In 2004, six men stole Edvard Munch's *The Scream* (worth more than 100 million dollars) from a museum wall in Oslo. They were arrested, but only three were convicted and only two served any jail time; one man got six years, and the other got four. Stéphane Breitwieser, the French waiter, spent just four years in jail for stealing close to 2 billion dollars' worth of art.

One former art thief said in an interview that criminals know if they steal a Rembrandt, they might get three to five years, but if they steal the equivalent of what that Rembrandt is worth in cash or commodities, they might face twenty-five years to life.[21] Stolen art has long been prized as a low-risk, high-reward currency for funding criminal activity.

If those pieces of the Gardner art haven't been destroyed, held for ransom, or passed around like a briefcase full of cash, they likely fall into one other grim scenario—one that would have been much easier to pull off in the pre-internet world of the Gardner heist. They may have been sold as high-quality replicas of themselves.

Say, for example, a thief steals a lesser-known Rembrandt. Rembrandt had many pupils over the years, young painters who studied in his studio alongside the master himself. These students learned to mimic Rembrandt's technique and style. Many of his protégés became so skilled in the art of imitation that historians have been debating the authenticity of hundreds of canvases and etchings attributed to him. German art historian Wilhelm von Bode quipped, "Rembrandt painted 700 pictures. Of these, 3,000 are still in existence."[22]

A savvy con man with a gullible target could convince his potential buyer that the painting he had to sell came from one of Rembrandt's own students. All he needed to do to make his case was turn to the painting itself. The detail in the unknown artist's copy would have required unobstructed access to the original. See how the light hits the woman's nose in the exact way Rembrandt would have painted it. Look at the details in the tassels on the man's coat. Take a sample of the paint to a lab if you like. You will discover it is, in fact, paint from the seventeenth century—Dutch in origin. It may not be a true Rembrandt, the con explains, but it comes from the brush of the master's protégé. The palette, the scale, the detail, and even the signature all say that this is a rare work in its own right—easily worth a percentage of the masterwork it apes. For a mere $100,000, you could own an actual seventeenth-century painting from Rembrandt's studio. Perhaps it was even painted on the same easel that held the original.

This has to be the most insidious option of the four. Rather than reduce a work of art to ash, the thief burns it from our memory. Rather than holding it for a ransom worthy of its pedigree, it endures the indignity of being sold for a pittance. Rather than circulate the painting among art lovers, corrupt though they may be, the thief removes the painting from circulation and banishes it to a fate worse than fire—a life of obscurity where it continues to exist in a world that will never find it. Its new owner doesn't know it is real, and the seller is praying he never finds out.

Rembrandt's *The Storm on the Sea of Galilee* has been in the wind for close to thirty years now. There is a 5 million dollar reward for the recovery of the Gardner art. So far no one has stepped forward to claim that reward. There have been no arrests. No demands for ransom. No legitimate sightings. Despite thousands of tips, leads, and suspects shared among the FBI, the U.S. Attorney's Office for the District of Massachusetts, and local, federal, and international law enforcement, no one knows who stole the art or where it is.

Ron Gollobin, a Boston crime beat reporter, said, "There's a 5 million dollar reward. That's a pretty powerful statement. Absolute silence. Not one peep as to who might have done this."[23] While it may be in the possession of someone who is simply biding their time, the silence suggests the sober probability that we have seen the last of *The Storm on the Sea of Galilee.*

Still, every year on the anniversary of the theft, the Gardner Museum issues a press release asking for its return. In the release, like the parent of a diabetic kidnapped child going on television to describe how to properly use an EpiPen, the museum explains that the missing art should be kept at 68 degrees Fahrenheit with 50 percent humidity.

The Frame

The Dutch Room's brownish gray fleur-de-lis wall covering now fills Rembrandt's frame like an eerie calm after a violent storm. Aside from perhaps a few canvas fibers and paint chips from the seventeenth century embedded in the cracks of the museum floor, there remains no sign of Rembrandt's boat or any of the souls on board. All are lost.

Museumgoers visit the Dutch Room like mourners passing the grave of a loved one. They describe Rembrandt's empty frame as "an unholy tragedy, a monstrous corruption of beauty."[24] Some refuse to even set foot in the room. Those who know how that museum came to be are offended by the theft—not because of how much the stolen art was worth, but because what the thieves did was rude. It was disrespectful of Isabella's gift and inconsiderate of her grief.

Isabella Stewart Gardner walked in the way of the widow from Nain and had carried her sorrows to this place in the hope of finding some rest. When she lost her baby in a sea of grief, she turned to beauty for healing. When she lost her husband, she determined to create something that would not die—a museum that would live forever. And she would give it to the world.

Isabella was one person in a long line of many who have, in their own way, tried to arrest the decay of a dying creation. She wanted to give us something beautiful, something lasting, something whole born out of a groaning too deep for words.[25] It was a defiant act of war against death, using beauty as her weapon.

Whoever cut *The Storm on the Sea of Galilee* from its frame did so with Rembrandt looking straight at him. Did the two men make eye contact? Did the man disguised as a Boston police officer understand what Rembrandt was trying to say?

This is a hard world, where children die and widows grieve. This is the nature of the storm we are all painted into. The same sea that lures us in with its beauty and bounty surges with a power that can destroy us without warning. And eventually there comes a reckoning. Rembrandt knew this well. So did Isabella Stewart Gardner. So did every man in the boat.

Has the thief learned this yet? Or is he still glassy-eyed at the tavern bar in a distant country, unaware that he has now painted himself into Isabella's storm. His workmanship now hangs in Rembrandt's place, leaving behind a frame that has become something like the location of a dead drop, a place where messages are exchanged between people who are not meant to see each other.

The empty frame is a note from the thief that tells Isabella that though she may want to create something beyond the reach of death, that is not something this world affords. She can dress up the pain all she likes, but nothing she has made will last forever. This is a world where thieves break in and steal.[26] It is a place where beautiful things are destroyed, where precious treasures are sold for a pittance, where talents are buried in the ground, never to be seen again. This is a world where we are constantly trying to tell each other that we are not what we truly are. The gloom of criminality enshrouds us. The thief knew this well. So did Rembrandt. So did every man in the boat.

Does Isabella?

Things will not always be this way. Sad things such as these will one day come untrue.[27] The apostle Paul said those who put their faith in Jesus are like earthen vessels with glory inside—frames that hold masterpieces:

> We are afflicted in every way, but not crushed; perplexed, but not driven to despair; persecuted, but not forsaken; struck down, but not destroyed; always carrying in the body the death of Jesus, so that the life of Jesus may also be manifested in our bodies. . . .
>
> So we do not lose heart. Though our outer self is wasting away, our inner self is being renewed day by day. For this light momentary affliction is preparing for us an eternal weight of glory beyond all comparison.[28]

The disciple's question reverberates down through the ages—does God care about our perishing? Jesus came treading on our roughest seas, speaking peace into the gale. And he will do it again. His triumph over the grave calls those who are perishing to be born again into a new and living hope. The peace he has brought by his resurrection is neither myth nor fantasy. It is an inheritance that will never perish, kept for those who believe, world without end.[29] His is a kingdom that will live. But it is the only one of its kind.

If *The Storm on the Sea of Galilee* still exists, Rembrandt, in all his glory, is tucked away in some closet, attic, or vault, hidden from the world. He is still clutching that rope, still trying to keep his hat from flying off his head. And he is looking out into our world for anyone who will make eye contact. If he still exists, it is quite a storm he is caught in.

Someday soon, if the Bible is true, Jesus will stand and say to widows and thieves alike, "Peace! Be still!"[30] His words will be followed by an unprecedented, eternal calm.[31] Knowing this helps us now. Whatever we suffer, we need not grieve as those who have no hope.[32] So we learn to hope in a coming kingdom. But we do so, knowing that in this one, at least for now, Rembrandt is in the wind.

Isabella Stewart Gardner Museum, Dutch Room,
the frame once containing Rembrandt's
The Storm on the Sea of Galilee
Photo by Kate Charlton, used by permission.

BORROWED LIGHT

Johannes Vermeer and the
Mystery of Creation

Johannes Vermeer, *The Milkmaid*, ca. 1658–1660,
oil on canvas, 46 × 41 cm, Rijksmuseum, Amsterdam

A great deal of light falls on everything.

Vincent van Gogh

In the beginning, God created the heavens and the earth. The earth was without form and void, and darkness was over the face of the deep. And the Spirit of God was hovering over the face of the waters.

And God said, "Let there be light," and there was light. And God saw that the light was good. And God separated the light from the darkness. God called the light Day, and the darkness he called Night. And there was evening and there was morning, the first day.

Genesis 1:1–5

The first sentence in the Bible is about creation—bringing into being something that did not previously exist. God created the heavens and the earth from nothing—*ex nihilo*. Then God spoke into the darkness, "Let there be light," and in a moment, creation went from a formless void to a place of discernable definition. Whatever existed would now be visible to all creatures blessed with the faculties of sight, because light would fall on it.

Though we're told that God made the world, we're not really told how. He spoke, and things came into being. Surely that sentence spreads out like an umbrella over an unfathomable amount of specificity. We study the expansion of the universe and the behavior of objects in space; we put some details together and draw some conclusions as best we can. But as long as we are tethered by gravity to the vantage point of the earthbound, even the best attempts of our brightest minds can only venture so far back in time and so deep into the reaches of space before we have to concede that much of what there is to know about how God made the cosmos is, and shall remain, shrouded in mystery.

In reference to the world, Isaiah reminds us that God "did not create it empty, he formed it to be inhabited!"[1] The crowning achievement of his inhabiting creation was humanity—those who bear his image and are made according to his likeness.[2] We reflect God in ways no other created thing does. And our call as human beings reflecting a Creator is to imitate him, not only in his moral ethic but also in his creative work. We were created to create. When human beings do the work of creation—bringing something into being that did not previously exist—we reflect that part of God as Creator.

When God made the world, he created it *ex nihilo*, out of nothing. While we don't possess that ability, nevertheless we are created to make things out of what we find scattered on the floor of creation. So we do. But we never truly work alone.

The Vermeer Estate

Johannes Vermeer died suddenly at the age of forty-three. Though he always listed his profession as "painter," Vermeer made his living as an art dealer. He sold his own paintings, but the bulk of his income came from selling the work of other artists. To build his inventory, Vermeer first had to purchase those works on credit, which he could repay upon their sale. His livelihood relied on his ability to move the art he bought or painted.

In 1672, three years before Vermeer's death, the Dutch Republic was attacked by England and France. Vermeer joined the Delft militia and spent the last years of his life serving in the military, which restricted his ability not only to paint, but also to sell. The stock he had purchased on credit sat idle. With an inventory he could not move, he maintained a debt he could not repay. His widow, Catharina, whom he left with eleven children, ten of whom were still living at home, believed he died from the stress of struggling to provide for his family.[3] In a petition to Vermeer's creditors, Catharina wrote of her husband's death:

> During the ruinous war with France he not only was unable to sell any of his art but also, to his great detriment, was left sitting with the paintings of other masters that he was dealing in. As a result and owing to the great burden of his children having no means of his own, he lapsed into such decay and decadence, which he had so taken to heart that, as if he had fallen into a frenzy, in a day and a half he went from being healthy to being dead.[4]

Catharina had never been involved in her family's finances, and the Vermeer estate was complicated. They owed a lot and owned only a little. After Johannes died, Catharina did her best to get out in front of her creditors before the auditors could come in and sell what remained. With the help of her mother, Maria Thins, she inventoried her family's possessions, assigning ownership to every item. As the notary clerk later went from room to room, noting which objects could be sold, half of Catharina's possessions were listed as belonging solely to herself, and the other half were listed as jointly owned by her and her mother. Those items could not legally be auctioned. Other possessions not inventoried were deeded entirely to Maria, and still others were presumably hidden so they could not be sold to pay off creditors.

Possessions Catharina listed as her own were items like worn-out clothing and furniture, some old kitchen crockery, and around thirty books. She listed some paintings by other artists that were worth some money, but not much. She also listed her late husband's art supplies as assets: "an easel, three palettes, a maulstick with an ivory knob, six wood panels, ten canvases, and three bundles of prints."[5]

Catharina's list was curious. Her husband's paintings feature many valuable items—a gilded pitcher, ornate curtains and rugs, musical instruments, and maps. But none of the valuable items that appeared in Vermeer's works were included in her inventory, and the list of tools he used for his studio was much too basic for an artist of his caliber. Vermeer may have sold some of those items during his lifetime to cover his cost of living, but there are no records of that. And as a painter in his early forties, it is hard to imagine he would have liquidated the tools he relied on to produce income.

Sorting out Vermeer's estate would be a complicated process, but Catharina was bleeding money. She had to find a way to settle her debts as quickly and officially as possible. In the same petition in which she described Johannes's death, she also asked the court to relieve her of her own debts. The petition read:

> She, supplicant, charged with the care of eleven children, because her aforementioned husband during the recent war with the King of France, a few years ago now, had been able to earn very little or hardly anything at all, but also the art that he had bought and with which he was trading had to be sold at great loss in order to feed his . . . children, owing to which he had then so far run into debts . . . she is not able to pay all her creditors.[6]

Mercifully, the court declared Catharina Vermeer bankrupt and assigned an executor to handle the estate—a lens maker from Delft named Antonie van Leeuwenhoek. He would decide what of the remaining assets would be sold, which creditors would be repaid, and how much they would receive. Van Leeuwenhoek's charge was to represent the Vermeer family, reconcile Catharina

and her children to their community, and relieve them from
Johannes's debt.

Finding Vermeer

I discovered the works of Johannes Vermeer in the way people
often come upon unfamiliar artists—by paying attention to a different one. Back when I was a teen, I found myself drawn to the
works of Rembrandt. My art teacher showed our class *The Storm
on the Sea of Galilee*, and I felt as though I fell into that painting
when I saw it. It stirred something deep inside me, and from that
time forward, Rembrandt has held my attention.

Later, I learned that *The Storm on the Sea of Galilee* had been
stolen in an art heist in Boston in 1990. I read as many articles
and books as I could about the theft and discovered that one of
the thirteen works stolen that night accounted for about half of
the total estimated loss. That piece was Johannes Vermeer's *The
Concert*, said to be worth more than 200 million dollars.

Until I read that, I had never even heard Vermeer's name.
But I couldn't think of any single item in this world worth 200
million dollars, so I looked him up. I discovered that one of
the reasons I had not known about Vermeer is that there isn't
much to know. Official records about his life are scant. There
are only thirty-four verified Vermeer paintings in existence, of
a presumed forty-five total. We do not know who taught him
to paint. He was virtually unrecognized for his work during
his lifetime. And though his work was praised by some in the
seventeenth and eighteenth centuries, it wasn't until the rise of
impressionism in the nineteenth century, some two hundred
years after his death, that Vermeer came to be revered within the
artistic community.[7]

I purchased Norbert Schneider's thin volume *Vermeer: The
Complete Paintings* from a used bookstore and took a cursory

look at his entire portfolio. This only took about thirty minutes, but that experience was unlike any other I'd known when discovering a new artist. It wasn't that his paintings stood out to me as better or more moving than the work of others. It was that as I took in his compositions, I felt that something was amiss. I couldn't have told you then what it was, but there was something strange about his work. I could feel it in my gut.

Consider a selection of those works, created over a span of about ten years, from 1660 to 1670. Perhaps as you look them up, you too will sense something unusual.

- *Girl Interrupted at Her Music,* 1660
- *Woman with a Lute,* 1663
- *The Music Lesson,* 1664 ·
- *The Concert,* 1665
- *The Allegory of Painting,* 1666
- *Girl Reading a Letter at an Open Window,* 1667
- *The Astronomer,* 1668
- *The Geographer,* 1669
  These images appear in color in the photo insert.

The more I looked into Vermeer's work, the more I discovered I was not the only one who felt there was something strange about his paintings. Many have been perplexed by this artist. Acknowledging the mystery of Vermeer, one of his own biographers referred to him as "the sphinx of Delft."[8]

In his book *Blink,* Malcolm Gladwell talks about how our instincts will often tell us the truth even when a mountain of data seems to point in another direction.[9] He gives the example of an art dealer who approached the Getty Museum in 1983 with a sculpture thought to date back to the sixth century BC. Everything about the statue was right—the marble, the technique, the subject matter, the size, the patina, its provenance.

After fourteen months of researching the piece, the museum made an offer to purchase it.

After the offer was made but before the purchase was complete, the Getty brought in Thomas Hoving, the former director of The MET in New York City, to see the statue. Hoving took one look at it, found the word *fresh* popping into his mind, and said to the Getty curator, "Have you paid for this? If you have, try to get your money back. If you haven't, don't."[10] In an instant, he knew the piece was not authentic. He couldn't explain why. It just wasn't right. He turned out to be correct. Concerned, the Getty arranged for a special symposium in Athens to discuss the sculpture, and one of the attendees, Angelos Delivorrias, director of a museum in Athens, said he felt a wave of "intuitive repulsion" when he first saw it.[11] The repulsion is not dislike as much as a visceral sense that the story being told doesn't add up.

I felt this intuitive repulsion when I looked at Vermeer's catalog for the first time. It wasn't that I disliked what I was seeing, or that I thought what I was seeing was somehow fraudulent. On the contrary, I thought Vermeer was amazing and was glad then, as I still am now, to have discovered his work. No, my reaction was based on the sense that the narrative I had formed in my own mind about how master painters produced their work did not fit Vermeer. My narrative was that master painters were set apart by their ability to render by hand with precision anything they saw with their eyes. A master, I presumed, was able to create impeccable compositions by way of direct observation alone. But some of what Vermeer rendered in his work doesn't seem humanly possible, and it doesn't look like what other painters of his era painted. I could not understand how a man with a brush at an easel could achieve what Vermeer accomplished.

What if my narrative about how great art comes into being is not the full story? What if my presumptions are flawed? What if there is more going on than I can see? What if Vermeer was seeing something his contemporaries could not see?

The Sphinx of Delft

The thirty-four existing works of Johannes Vermeer were painted in the span of about twenty years, from 1655 to 1675. The first few years include a combination of indoor and outdoor scenes, ranging from biblical and mythological subjects to social gatherings to views of his city. But in the late 1650s, he moved his entire operation indoors and painted almost exclusively contemporary scenes, mostly featuring women doing ordinary things like preparing food, playing music, and reading letters.

It was not that unusual for an artist of his era to work out of an established indoor studio. Vermeer painted before the "plein air" era of the 1800s, when the impressionists took John Goffe Rand's revolutionary invention—the compressible tin paint tube—outdoors. Before the invention of the paint tube, much of the world's art—like Vermeer's—was created in artists' studios, with their equipment set up and close at hand. In those days, artists had to make their own paints with linseed oil, varnish, and pigment. Colors were limited to what artists could mix themselves or buy locally.

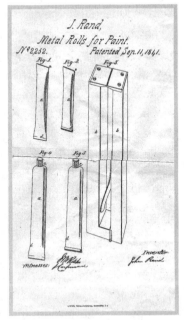

John Goffe Rand's sketch of his tin tube, submitted to the patent office

The invention of the tin paint tube changed the landscape of art, quite literally. You can see it on the walls of museums everywhere. Sometime around the mid-1800s, outdoor scenes went from darkened affairs painted indoors to color-filled fields ablaze in the light of the sun. This happened because technological innovation changed how artists worked. The portability and manufactured consistency of paint in a metal tube made it easy for them to do something that was difficult for the generations before—stand outside in a field and paint under the light of the sun.

To understand Vermeer, we must understand this: technology shapes art. What used to be stationary becomes portable. What once was expensive becomes affordable. What used to take hours to load in an analog world takes seconds to process digitally. Every generation of artists borrows technological progress from the generations before. And every generation advances technology for those who come after them. This reflects the concept of borrowed light—light that filters from one room into another that would be otherwise dark. Rembrandt produced what he did because he studied Caravaggio. Van Gogh studied Rembrandt. And nearly every artist of note in the last hundred years has studied all three.

We borrow the light of others to illuminate the places where we're doing our own work, and then our work lights the way for others. This doesn't only apply to artists borrowing from other artists. We borrow light across disciplines. The guitar player borrows light from the guitar maker. The chef borrows light from the forger who casts the iron skillet. The builder borrows light from the architect, and the architect from the surveyor.

One of the things that makes Vermeer such a mystery is that we know very little about his inspirations or training. He didn't leave a written record, so most of what we know about him comes from secondary references. Even his artistic journey is unclear.

It was common for artists of his era to apprentice under a master and then later to run a workshop of their own for other young aspiring painters. There are no records indicating Vermeer did any of this. In fact, the evidence suggests he did not. Martin Bailey noted that Vermeer's "low output and the fact that so few pictures have been found in a style close enough to be his pupils suggest that he worked very much by himself."[12]

Another oddity about his work is that all we have are paintings—no drawings. It was common for painters to sketch studies of their compositions and work off those drawings as they painted. No such drawings by Vermeer exist. It was also common for painters to sketch some of the rudimentary outlines of their compositions onto their canvases to guide their work. Scans of Vermeer's canvases reveal no such markings.[13] Lawrence Gowing said, "There has been no correction, nor is there evidence of line or design . . . No other artist's method reveals this immediate and perfect objectivity."[14] It appears Vermeer worked from hand to brush to canvas without any guiding lines. If this is true, then some of the detail in his work defies explanation. Consider the map on the wall in *Officer and Laughing Girl*, the detail of the virginal in *The Music Lesson*, or the intricacy of the oriental rug in the same painting.

Vermeer scholar Laura Snyder said, "The experience of viewing Vermeer's pictures in the prephotographic age would have been like that of viewing motion pictures for the first time: unsettling, strange, and even perhaps (as for the audiences said to have fled from the 1895 film of an oncoming locomotive) a bit frightening."[15]

It isn't uncommon for an artist's style and ability to develop over time. But the paintings from the last fifteen years or so of Vermeer's life—the indoor studio works—look like they could have come from a completely different artist than the ones that come before. For example, the brushwork in his early painting

Christ in the House of Martha and Mary (1655) was somewhat flat, but *The Milkmaid*, done only three years later (1658), takes on an almost photographic quality. The light glistens and pearls like the sun shining on dew. Ten years after *Christ in the House of Martha and Mary*, he painted *The Allegory of Painting*. When one looks at these two side by side, with only ten years between them, it is clear that something significant changed.

Vermeer changed. The paintings from the last fifteen years of his life are what initially caught my attention. They are all carefully staged; Vermeer was a master of composition. But they are also curiously *alike*.

A black-and-white tile floor features prominently in at least twelve different works. The leaded window in that room, with its distinctive pattern, appears in three others. Some of these compositions reveal that the room is skirted with distinctive Delft tiles, and heavy wood beams run the length of the ceiling. Martin Bailey also notes Vermeer's furnishings:

> Equally familiar are the distinctive chairs with lion-head finials, the oriental rug covering a table and the white ceramic wine pitcher. Even the clothing of the figures seems likely to have come from the family wardrobe; the "elegant yellow mantle trimmed with white fur," listed in the 1676 inventory of Catharina's possessions, appears in no less than six paintings.[16]

And Vermeer's paintings don't just feature the same room and furnishings; they are all painted from the same basic vantage point—the painter at six o'clock, the window (and source of light) at nine o'clock, and the subject at twelve o'clock.

What is unusual about Vermeer's paintings is not that they were painted in the same room, but that they were paintings *of* the same room from the same vantage point. Of all the things he could have chosen to paint, why would he keep painting the same room from the same position? And why do those later paintings, without a hint of either sketch marks or correction, stand as some of the greatest technical achievements in the history of art?

Perhaps the answer lies with someone else, someone hiding in plain sight: Antonie van Leeuwenhoek, the lens maker from Delft who became the executor of the Vermeer estate.

Jan Verkolje, *Antoni van Leeuwenhoek*, ca. 1686, oil on canvas, 56 × 47.5 cm, Museum Boerhaave, Leiden

Antonie van Leeuwenhoek

Antonie van Leeuwenhoek was no ordinary man about town. He was a true Renaissance man—a student of both science and art. Leeuwenhoek is considered the father of microbiology, doing his work a full two hundred years before Louis Pasteur came on the scene. He was an expert in the field of making and using lenses and mirrors and controlling light to render the microscopic world visible to the human eye. He examined everything from semen, blood, and saliva to the anatomy of the organisms that lived in them.

Leeuwenhoek also surrounded himself with artists and employed them to illustrate his scientific observations. He wanted other scientists to see what appeared in his lenses, so he hired artists to come into his lab to paint what they saw through his microscopes. He also sat for several portraits, possibly even two for Vermeer—*The Astronomer* and *The Geographer*—which would have been fitting, since they each depicted a scientist. These are the only two existing works by Vermeer featuring a solitary male as his subject. A later painting of Leeuwenhoek by Jan Verkolje shows a man who might well have been Vermeer's *Geographer* twenty years earlier.

Though he was largely self-taught, Leeuwenhoek was well respected in the scientific community, made evident by his appointment to the Royal Society of London for his scientific achievements. He devised a single-lens microscope that intensified light and enhanced magnification through the incorporation of a concave mirror, the focused light of a single candle in a dark room, and water on the microscope lens. A member of the Royal Society who visited Leeuwenhoek in 1685 was amazed at the quality of Leeuwenhoek's microscope, marveling over its "extreme clearness and . . . representing all objects so extraordinarily distinctly."[17]

At the time of his death, Leeuwenhoek had 247 microscopes in his personal collection—many of which he made himself. Anthony Bailey wrote, "To look through a microscope Leeuwenhoek had first to make one. He had to get the materials for the glass, blow it, grind and polish it, and then fix the lens in a silver or brass mounting. He learned glass-blowing from a professional glass-blower whom he met at a fair in Delft, and then practised at home."[18] In those days, scientists had to make many of the tools they used for their research. Leeuwenhoek made microscopes—very good ones.

How did a scientist like Leeuwenhoek come to be the executor of a bankrupt painter's estate? The most probable explanation is that they knew each other. Though it was routine for the courts to assign executors to handle the estates of those who had no other proxy, Leeuwenhoek only served as an executor four times during his life. In each of the other three cases, he had a personal connection to the deceased or the estate: One was his sister-in-law, another was his wine supplier (Leeuwenhoek was a wine expert, making him uniquely fit to handle a wine buyer's estate), and the third was for a family he knew through the art community in Delft, to which both he and Vermeer belonged.[19] With the thousands of deaths that occurred in Delft over his lifetime, and with the other three executorships attached to people he knew, it seems unlikely that Leeuwenhoek would become the executor for a stranger, much less a bankrupt one.

Other details strengthen the probability that these two men knew each other. They were both born in 1632 and were baptized within days of each other at the same church. They lived a few blocks apart for most of their lives. Anthony Bailey wrote, "Delft was a relatively small city. Living in the centre of town, as Vermeer did, it was impossible in the course of daily walks and errands not to run into people he recognized . . . A person he must have seen from time to time was Antony van Leeuwenhoek . . . who lived not far from the western end of the Market Place . . . and who worked part-time at the Town Hall."[20]

Leeuwenhoek and Vermeer also shared interests. Both were fascinated by science and the role scientific discovery played in the arts. Both were ambitious businessmen—Vermeer as a master artist enamored with technical and scientific advancements and Leeuwenhoek as a scientist fascinated by the wonder and beauty of the microscopic world.[21] It is hard to conceive that they never crossed paths. Perhaps the strongest clue that the two men knew each other is found in the otherwise confounding details of Vermeer's art.

Vermeer's Camera

Anthony Bailey said Vermeer "saw and painted things in a way that none of his colleagues did."[22] The fact that Vermeer painted most of his paintings from the same precise vantage point, with his works oriented the same way, tells us his workstation was fixed in place and dialed in. The most probable explanation for this is that, when he painted, he used an optical device—some sort of a lens—that was also fixed in place and dialed in. In fact, nearly every book about Johannes Vermeer devotes at least some space to discussing his use of an optical device. Several focus entirely on the matter.[23]

Artists began using optical devices in the 1600s. Still, though these devices were known, they were neither common nor sophisticated. The quality and precision of Vermeer's work suggests his device was on another level—something achieved by a master of lenses, mirrors, and light; someone with a fascination for fine detail; someone with the ability to manufacture an apparatus powerful enough to capture Vermeer's room but small enough to be out of the artist's way. Who in Vermeer's world fit that description? The father of microbiology and inventor of microscopes who lived just a few blocks away: Antonie van Leeuwenhoek, the man who would become executor of Vermeer's estate.

If Vermeer used lenses when he painted, where did he get them? These were not the sort of things one could just run to the store to pick up. He would have obtained them from a lens maker or through someone who used them in their work. In Vermeer's world, this was Leeuwenhoek. And because they were both innovators, it makes sense that the device Vermeer would have used would have been an experiment in something unique, built to achieve something extraordinary. This is certainly the result of Vermeer's work.

The most common optical device used by painters of that era was called a *camera obscura*. It worked much like modern cameras, except instead of projecting light from the lens onto film, it projected light onto the artist's canvas hanging on a wall. The most basic single-lens camera obscura projected an image that was upside down and reversed. What Vermeer used would have been more complex because the single lens setup projected a weak light, and the artist would have blocked the projected image with his brush hand when he went to paint, compromising both the accuracy of detail and color. What Vermeer used gave him *command* of accuracy and color.

In 2013, the magician team Penn and Teller released a fascinating documentary called *Tim's Vermeer* that tells of a Texas-based inventor named Tim Jenison who set out not only to re-create the optical device Vermeer used, but to then use that device to paint a replica of Vermeer's *The Music Lesson*. Jenison wagered that if he could figure out how Vermeer managed to paint photo-realistic compositions 150 years before the invention of the camera, he should be able to employ the same approach to paint a Vermeer of his own. The catch was that Jenison had no prior painting experience.

After several attempts to configure a device that would

work, he finally arrived at a setup that used a small mirror fixed at a 45-degree angle between the lens and his canvas. An article about the documentary explained his technique:

> By placing a small, fixed mirror above the canvas at a 45-degree angle, he is able to view parts of the original image and the canvas simultaneously, and obtain a precise color match by continuously comparing the reflection of the original image with what he has put on the canvas, moving from area to area by simply moving his own point-of-view slightly. When the edge of the mirror "disappears" [indicating he has successfully matched the color in the mirror with the color on the canvas], he has it right.[24]

After Jenison figured out the optical device, he then spent close to a full year reconstructing the room seen in *The Music Lesson*—building all the furniture by hand, laying the tile, staging the furnishings and mannequins, making his own paint, setting up his workstation, and positioning his canvas and lens. Then he spent the next seven months painstakingly putting onto his canvas exactly what he saw in his mirror.

Though Jenison's painting lacks the heart and depth of the original, his approach appears to be spot-on. Arthur Wheelock said, "Lenses leave no physical traces on the painting, and only when certain distortions are evident, or optical effects are present that are not seen with the naked eye, can one deduce that an optical device has been used as an artistic aid."[25] A device like the one Tim Jenison discovered explains how Vermeer was able to do what he did without sketches, studies, or corrections. Vermeer's lens left no physical trace—no markings. But it did leave all kinds of clues.

The use of a lens would have set certain parts of a painting in a sharper focus than others, a contrast noticeable, for example, between the foreground and background in *The Milkmaid*. Lenses also affect how light is perceived. Certain highlights appear on objects that don't appear naturally to the unaided eye, like the blobs of light on the rough surface of the loaf of bread in *The Milkmaid*.[26] Lenses also create a halo effect, leaving ghost-like traces of opaque color outlining a dark object, like the faint light blue line Vermeer included that runs down the back edge of the milkmaid's dress. The only reason he would have painted this ghost line—which would not have been visible to the naked eye—is because he saw it through his lens.

Vermeer was an artist whose vision was shaped by science. His use of a lens was not a shortcut, but rather an innovation—the kind that gave his work a mysterious quality, leaving his viewers a benevolent kind of "intuitive repulsion," as though something strange was happening that they couldn't quite put their finger on.

Painting is not just an art, but a science. It is an achievement not only in beauty or emotion or color, but in math and geometry and light. It is understanding the linear perspective that leads to a single vanishing point, which must first be learned and then mastered. It is understanding the geometry of a scene well enough to know when to depart from it ever so slightly to create a dramatic shift. It is employing light and shadow according to the laws of optics to lead the eyes of the viewer through a composition in a particular order.

What Vermeer chose to paint with the use of an optical aid takes us deeper into the mind of the artist. What did he want to say? What did he care about? He had the world at his fingertips. As we see with the map hanging on the wall in *Officer and Laughing Girl*, Vermeer's potential to render almost anything in the world with a kind of photo-realism unseen by those of his generation seemed limitless. So, what did he choose to paint? What would be the subject matter of his artistic vision?

He chose the most dignified thing in the world: people in a room doing ordinary things. And to what effect? Awe.

Arthur Wheelock said, "The striking luminosity of his paintings, their apparent realism, and the dignity imparted to the common man and everyday situations all struck a responsive chord."[27] One French art critic from the 1800s, Théophile Thoré-Bürger, said his desire to connect with Vermeer led him on many journeys and to many expenditures. "To view a painting by van der Meer [Vermeer]," he wrote, "I traveled far and wide: to acquire a photograph of a van der Meer, I behaved like a fool."[28]

We Never Truly Work Alone

In a letter to his brother Theo, Vincent van Gogh wrote, "A good deal of light falls on everything."[29] Seeing is as much of an art as it is a physiological ability. There is skill involved. When a person looks through a telescope or a microscope for the first time, they do not see clearly. Eyelashes flutter in the lens; finding focus involves trial and error; and the slightest movement bumps the examined object out of view. These are just some of the challenges of seeing through an optical device. Once those challenges are overcome, the viewer must then learn to understand what they're seeing through the lens, which is another matter entirely.

The same is true for the naked eye. We don't just see. We learn to see.

The concept of learning to see became a guiding principle for both science and art. The idea gained popularity in the 1700s during the scientific revolution, but the concept was certainly not new. Leonardo da Vinci's "principles for the development of a complete mind," written two hundred years earlier, stated, "Study the science of art. Study the art of science. Develop your senses—especially learn how to see. Realize that everything connects to everything else."[30]

Laura Snyder said the basic idea behind learning to see was "that there was more to nature than meets the naked eye, and that lenses, and other optical instruments, could help us see a part of nature that was otherwise hidden."[31] Scientists reasoned that if the only source for our perception comes from ancient texts, logical deduction, and visual experience, we will miss much of what there is to see, and as a consequence, much of what there is to know.

When Vermeer used his optical device, he was not pulling a trick on his viewers. He was learning to see. Snyder wrote:

> By looking through the camera obscura, Vermeer has become expert in the way that light affects how we see the world. He has seen the world as we do not normally see it, revealed in surprising new ways invisible to the naked eye. Like the microscope, the camera obscura disclosed to its seventeenth-century users truths about the natural world otherwise inaccessible to the senses . . . The sublime work that defines Vermeer's mature style was the result of his optical investigations.[32]

Though Vermeer painted scenes visible to the naked eye, he did so in a way that gave him access to the behavior of light not visible. And that is what he painted—the way the light illuminated his subjects. That light was the life of his paintings. By painting what he saw through his lens, Vermeer did not paint a hand, a vase, or a viola; instead, he painted forms of light and color as they appeared on those objects.

Philip Steadman noted that "to copy or work from an image in a camera obscura is distinctly not like taking a photograph. The process is not instantaneous, but protracted."[33] Where a camera coldly grabs, in a fraction of a second, everything in the frame exactly as it appears, Vermeer "is not indifferent to his subjects but he wants to contemplate them from a safe distance. He puts barriers between himself and his sitters—chairs, tables with heavy carpets over them, heavy tapestries. And then he retreats still further, into the darkness behind the screens of his cubicle, to become a voyeur through his lens."[34] In doing so, Lawrence Gowing said, Vermeer creates an illusion "not of closeness but of distance."[35]

This illusion of distance is what gives his work a certain sense of intimacy. His subjects behave as though no one is watching them, making this sense of intimacy one of the end results of his paintings. But Vermeer was not distant. He was deeply connected to his work. He had to be. His compositions involved constant adjustment and constant interaction. Vermeer was the architect of his compositions, from the models to the furniture to the arrangement of the scene. He was not just copying a photo; he was engaging with a live room.

With the help of a lens maker, when Vermeer sat down to paint, he captured moments frozen in time of people as we see them and know them, doing what people do. How fascinating is it that one of the most celebrated painters in history chose to confine himself to one room for the bulk of his body of work? And how amazing that from that one room, he showed us an entire world by way of a small collection of simple objects: "a few friends and members of his family, their best clothes, some of his family's collection of paintings and treasured pieces of furniture,"[36] and all of them through the borrowed light of a lens.

Philip Steadman wrote, Vermeer "disposed these simple elements, in a few pictures, to say what he wanted—however elusively—about the subjects for which he really cared: domestic routine, the love of men for women and fathers for daughters, the consolations of music, the worlds of science and scholarship, his own profession and its ambitions—all captured in his room within a room, his camera in a camera."[37]

We are created to make things, so we do. But we never truly work alone.

Consider a painter like Johannes Vermeer. He likely used Antonie van Leeuwenhoek's lens. But what had to happen before he ever put brush to canvas? Someone had to stretch that piece of canvas across a frame. Both the canvas and frame had to be made. So did the tacks that fixed the canvas to the frame and the hammer that drove them in. Consider the easel on which the canvas sat and the lumber mill from which its pieces came, with its drying racks, saw blades, aprons, and brooms, all of which were also made. Consider his paintbrushes—with their turned and sanded handles, their hammered-thin tin ferrules holding the finely trimmed bristles in place—arranged clean and neat upside down in a cup that was also made, and the mortise and pestle he used to grind his pigments and linseed oil into paint.

So many things were designed and fashioned in order for the artist to sit down and do their work—even their chair and the floor on which it rested. And so many people contributed their skills: carpenters, weavers, potters, metalsmiths, brush makers, architects, distillers, and even lens makers. When we stand before a Vermeer, we are seeing not only his work, but also the work of all these others and many more. Everything we make, in some measure, relies on the help of others. All of us rely on borrowed light. Even the blind composer sits at a piano not made in darkness.

There is only one who can make something from nothing: God. The rest of us sub-create. We work with what can be found lying around on the floor of creation and repurposed from the belly of the earth and the salvage heaps of industry. In this sense, human beings are, as a species, "found object" sculptors. Even the light we work by is borrowed. The question is, what shall we say with it?

We cannot see light, but by it we see everything else.[38] Without light there is no life. Without light there is no order. Without light there is no collaboration, no crafting of language, no planting of fields or harvesting crops.[39] Everything that followed in God's order of creation after that first day would be set to the rhythms of the cycles of day and night.

By light we do our work. By that same light others behold it. And all of the light is borrowed from God.

CHAPTER 6

CREATING IN COMMUNITY

Jean Frédéric Bazille, the Impressionists,
and the Importance of Belonging

Jean Frédéric Bazille, *Studio; 9 Rue de la Condamine*, 1870,
oil on canvas, 38-5/8 × 50-5/8 inches, Musée d'Orsay, Paris

A proper community is a commonwealth: a place, a
resource, an economy. It answers the needs, practical as well as social and spiritual, of its members—
among them the need to need one another.

Wendell Berry

The year is 1862. Paris, France.

Picture three young men, barely out of their teens. They are climbing a wall in a courtyard to spy on an old man who quietly paints at his easel in his garden studio.[1] The old man, now in his sixties, is the French romantic painter Eugène Delacroix.

Delacroix was an old soul who grew up, as most painters of his generation, influenced by the classic works of Michelangelo, da Vinci, Rembrandt, and the masters of the Renaissance. But he was particularly drawn to the brushwork of the great Peter Paul Rubens, who forsook the more subdued, carefully arranged compositions of his peers for scenes filled with motion, expression, and color. Delacroix traveled widely over the course of his life, expanding his vision beyond the classical Greek and Roman roots of design and incorporating the exotic expressions of North African culture. He studied and illustrated works by Shakespeare, Sir Walter Scott, and Goethe. The range of his art, interests, and experience combined to make him a living legend and a bridge to the past.

The young men watched in awe as the master plied his craft. His hand was steady. His composition, confident and full of life. His technique, refined and instinctual. His workspace, a finely tuned, orderly mess. His paint palette looked like a work of art itself.

Much of the work involved in being an artist lies in the discipline of practicing the fundamentals of the craft. Artists must master the rules of composition if they want to break them well. They must understand the basic elements of unity, balance, movement, rhythm, focus, contrast, pattern, and proportion. They must train their eye and their hand to render perspective, vanishing point, proper proportion of form, the visual weight of a line, and the integrity of a shadow in ways that are true to form, lest they lose their viewers in the uncanny valley.

Delacroix devoted himself to mastering the compositional precision of the masters, but he wanted to push beyond the more rigid compositions of his heroes. He wanted his work to exude passion. He was a romantic, after all. But he was also a master technician. The French poet Charles Baudelaire wrote, "Delacroix was passionately in love with passion, but coldly determined to express passion as clearly as possible."[2] Delacroix rendered this passion not through a pandering sentimentality, but through the discipline of sound technique. He learned to create works that captured onlookers with their sensuality, but also with their precision.

One of the lines of convention Delacroix mastered and then ventured beyond was in his brushwork. His steady hand could produce clean lines and precise detail, but he found that less precise, more active brushwork could render life in ways fundamental precision couldn't. The brush could render passion. For example, Delacroix discovered that one could paint a horse with fine detail and precise proportion and show the viewer a realistic representation of the animal. Or he could paint with fluid, dynamic, unrestrained brushstrokes and give the viewer the impression of a horse in the wild, coiled in fear. The impression of the horse seemed more alive—a truer horse than the realistic portrait. Though he did not know it, Delacroix and others like him were inspiring the development of a new genre of art: Impressionism.

The Boys at the Courtyard Wall

One of the boys peering over the courtyard wall was a young painter named Jean Frédéric Bazille. He was taken with Delacroix's work at a young age when he and his family visited the home of an art collector named Alfred Bruyas, who lived in Bazille's hometown of Montpelier, France.[3] Two paintings in Bruyas's collections captured young Bazille's imagination: Delacroix's *Daniel and the Lions' Den* (probably for the sense of danger and adventure it depicted) and his *Women of Algiers in Their Apartment* (no doubt for the exotic sense of mystery depicted in the bedroom of a harem.)

Since the dawn of boyhood, ferocious beasts and beautiful women have been subjects of great fascination, carefully studied, committed to memory, and revisited as often as discretion allows. Bazille had not only seen Delacroix's lions and women; he had internalized them. He did what we do with art. He stored them away in his memory and carried them in his mind as a part of his own personal collection.

Delacroix made young Bazille want to become a painter. Spying on Delacroix in his studio must have been for the twenty-one-year-old Bazille what it would be like for a young musician in Austin or Nashville to hide in a closet to watch Paul Simon or Bruce Springsteen write a song. Bazille aspired to stand in the foothills of the greatness he admired in his mentor's work. The thought of developing even a fraction of the master's skill compelled him onward. Seeing Delacroix at work that day must have been nothing short of a religious experience for Bazille.

The other two young men peeking into Delacroix's window with Bazille were a twenty-one-year-old painter named Auguste Renoir and a twenty-two-year-old painter named Claude Monet. Auguste Renoir, whose work focused largely on French society and feminine sensuality, went on to become one of the fathers of

Impressionism. Claude Monet, perhaps best known for his water lilies, worked largely in plein-air landscape painting, favoring natural settings over Renoir's social situations involving people. He, too, was one of the fathers of Impressionism.

In fact, Monet was accidentally responsible for the name "Impressionism." The term came from the title of Monet's painting *Impression, Sunrise*. Monet submitted this painting of the harbor at Le Havre for inclusion in an exhibition in 1874, thirteen years after he, Bazille, and Renoir had spied on Delacroix. Compared to works typically shown at major art exhibitions in Paris, Monet's painting looked incomplete. It lacked detail. It resembled a sketch, except that it was presented in oils. Organizers of the exhibit asked Monet what they should call the painting. He wrote, "They asked me for a title for the catalogue, it couldn't really be taken for a view of [the harbor], and I said: 'Put Impression.' They turned it into Impressionism."[4]

For want of a title in an exhibition catalog, the name "Impressionism" was born. Critics did not intend the name as a compliment. Many of them used the term to describe an emerging line of art that seemed to them undisciplined and unfinished. One journalist, Louis Leroy, in a sarcastic review of *Impression, Sunrise*, wrote, "Impression . . . Since I am impressed, there must be some impressions in it."[5] Impressionism was rock and roll in a doo-wop world. As it goes with most new creative expressions, people usually need some time to warm to the idea of things being different from what they're used to. And that season of warming is often punctuated with reactions of cynicism and snark by those called upon to critique it.

But the boys at the courtyard wall were not thinking about the voices of the critics. They were watching a master push the lines of convention. Delacroix was distancing himself from the nymphs, goddesses, battles, and myths that were the darling subject matter of the dominant art exhibitions of the age, like the judiciously curated, self-important Salon in Paris. Delacroix's brushwork, his energy, his expression, his willingness to bend and even break the rules of convention inspired these young painters to pick up where he left off and to push the lines even further. Little did they know this inspiration would lead to the formation of a community of artists who would give the world what we all know now as "Impressionism." And had it not been for Jean Frédéric Bazille, none of this may have happened.

Studio; 9 Rue de la Condamine

Jean Frédéric Bazille was born in 1841 in Montpelier, France, into a wealthy Protestant family. He descended from a long line of goldsmiths, the industry that became the foundation for his family's wealth. Bazille's father, Gaston, was a wine merchant. Jean Frédéric knew from a very young age, ever since seeing the Delacroixs, that he wanted to become an artist. He declared this plan to his parents very early on. Gaston let young Frédéric attend art lectures and drawing classes and agreed to let his son study painting so long as Frédéric agreed to also study medicine. Frédéric took to drawing and quickly became a skilled and competent draftsman.

In 1862, Bazille moved to Paris and enrolled in the Faculty of Medicine to honor his father's request. There he also enrolled in the art historian Charles Gleyre's drawing workshop, where he met and became friends with fellow artists Pierre-Auguste Renoir, Alfred Sisley, Édouard Manet, and Claude Monet. This was also the year he, Renoir, and Monet spied on Delacroix.

Art held Bazille's attention, and in 1864, Bazille failed his medical exams and turned to painting full-time. Frédéric's father did not respond in anger to his son's failure. Instead, he took it as confirmation that his son should pursue the arts and agreed to support his son in this endeavor.

Frédéric's family's wealth enabled him to stay in Paris after failing medical school. He used his resources to support his fellow painters by renting studio space and purchasing art supplies for them to share.[6] Bazille and Monet shared a studio in 1865. Monet grew up in Paris. His father was a grocer. From the time he was young, Monet would draw and sell charcoal caricatures to the locals in order to support his desire to create. He knew how to make and sell art to fund his craft, but he also knew, as every working artist must learn, that his was a vocation of feast and famine.

When finances grew tight for Monet, Bazille would purchase some of Monet's work to help keep him afloat.[7] For Bazille, this was not an act of charity. It was an investment in an artist he respected. Bazille knew Monet was a rare talent, and Jean Frédéric was building his own world-class art collection.

In the late 1860s, Renoir also shared studio space with Bazille —a nice room at 9 rue de la Condamine. The studio became a hub for this fellowship of artists, which soon began to grow. Other painters, including Camille Pissarro, Paul Cézanne, Gustave Courbet, and Edgar Degas, came over to the studio to spend time with Renoir, Monet, and Manet at Bazille's place.

Bazille painted the scene. His *Studio; 9 rue de la Condamine* gives us a peek into this era of art history in Paris. In this painting, we see Bazille showing one of his new paintings to Manet and Monet. Renoir sits to the left, talking with the French novelist and playwright Émile Zola. At the piano sits one of their musician friends, Edmond Maître. Three of Bazille's known works hang on the wall—*The Fisherman with a Net*, *La Toilette*, and *Family Reunion*. Also on the wall are Renoir's *Landscape with Two People* (which has since been lost, though thankfully preserved by Bazille in this painting and in a sketch by Renoir's friend, Jules Le Coeur) and what appears to be a Monet, possibly one Bazille had purchased.

Stop for a moment to consider what was happening in this little studio. No less than seven of the world's most celebrated painters gathered to work on their craft, but even more, to be part of this community of artists. They shared a common perspective on where they believed art was going, which Bazille summarized by saying, "The big classical compositions are finished; an ordinary view of daily life would be much more interesting."[8] These artists were testing new waters, trying new techniques, hoping to introduce something new into an area of culture known for resisting and even scoffing at attempts to defy convention.

It was imperative for these artists to work in community, not in isolation. They needed one another. They needed to be around each other. They needed to be able to share a common space—a place where they could gather and speak freely. A place where they could show what they were working on to get feedback, encouragement, and pushback. They needed voices that understood what they were trying to do. They needed assurance that they were not fools. And if they were in fact fools, they needed to be a tribe of fools together. They needed a place, and that's exactly what Bazille gave them.

As Bazille and the others developed their technique, they were becoming "The Impressionists," though neither the name nor the association yet existed. Bazille is the lesser-known artist in the group (for reasons that will become apparent), but his work belongs alongside the greats like Monet, Renoir, Manet, Cézanne, Pissarro, and Degas, who have since become household names.

But before any of these painters garnered the sort of fame that would compel art galleries around the world to feature their work as the centerpieces of their collections, they were friends who created art together in community. And they needed each other because it would require a team effort if they were to break past the gatekeepers of the art industry in Paris.

The Salon and the Anonymous Society

In the early days of Impressionism, the art world in France was ruled by the Salon in Paris. The Salon was founded more than two hundred years earlier, in 1667, as France's official exhibition of the Academy of Fine Arts, established by the government as the nationally recognized venue for art patronage. The government regarded painting as a worthy profession and created a system of advancement through a series of tiered competitions. For a painter, Malcolm Gladwell noted, "at each stage of his education, there would be competition. Those who did poorly would be weeded out. Those who did well would win awards and prestigious fellowships, and at the pinnacle of the profession was the Salon, the most important art exhibition in all of Europe."[9]

The Salon was originally formed to showcase the work of graduates from the academy, but it soon expanded to show art from a wide variety of artists. It was an "invitation only" affair. The Salon became the place people would look to if they wanted to know which art was popular, and for those lacking a discerning eye, which art was good. A panel of artists, academics, and critics known as "The Jury" chose what would be shown at each year's Salon Exposition. They also chose the prominence of placement each work would receive.

The Jury did not like the Impressionists. When artists like Monet, Manet, and Renoir submitted their work, it was usually rejected or, if accepted, placed too high on the walls of the exhibition hall to be seen.

Monet summarized the challenge the Salon presented when he said, "There were a few of us, my friends and myself, who were systematically rejected by Jury. It's all very well to paint, but you have to sell, you have to live. The dealers would have nothing to do with us. And yet we had to exhibit. Where? Should we rent a hall? But when we had a whip round, we barely had enough to take a box at the Théâtre de Cluny."[10]

Édouard Joseph Dantan, *A Corner of the Salon in 1880*,
1880, oil on canvas, 97.2 × 130.2 cm

As it happened, they did not need to rent a hall. A French photographer who went by the name Nadar, who had become a fan of this community's work, offered Monet and his friends use of the second floor of his studio space to hold an exhibition of their own. In 1874, Monet, Degas, Renoir, Pissarro, and a female painter named Berthe Morisot formed a fellowship they called the Cooperative and Anonymous Society of Painters, Sculptors, and Engravers. Their distinctives were threefold:

"1. The organization of free exhibitions, without juries or prizes, where each of the associates will be able to show his work. 2. The sale of said works. 3. The publication, at the earliest opportunity, of a journal concerned exclusively with the arts." For it was not enough just to show one's work; they also had to be shown properly . . . With the works well displayed, the next step was to sell them.[11]

The Anonymous Society were the rejects of the Salon. This band of artists launched a series of eight impressionism exhibits that featured the work of thirty different artists and made the 165 collected works available for purchase. It was during this 1874 exhibit that Monet showed *Impression, Sunrise*, accidentally inventing the name "Impressionism." The Impressionists were an early version of indie artists—ditching the major labels, working their own merch tables, and trusting that together they could hold one another up and break through to earning something resembling a livable wage.

They took this seriously. If they were going to make it, there was work to be done. "The works also had to be talked about. The artist's methods explained. The public had to be won over. This was the role of the critics and the press . . . Other champions were needed."[12] They needed to not only set the table for their own success but pave the way for those who would come after them.

Émile Zola said, "They found themselves forming a homogeneous group, with all of them having a more or less similar view of nature; and so they picked up the description that had been made of them, 'Impressionists,' and used it as a banner. They were called Impressionists in a spirit of mockery; Impressionists they remained out of pluck."[13] Before long, this plucky, grass-roots community took the art world by storm. And now, museums around the globe give entire wings to their work.

Jean Frédéric Bazille, however, was not part of the Anonymous Society. The same year he completed his *Studio; 9 rue de la Condamine*, he went off to fight in the Franco-Prussian War. His friends all tried to talk him out of going, but to no avail. On November 28, 1870, when his commanding officer fell in battle, Bazille took command of what troops were left and led an assault on an enemy German position. Jean Frédéric Bazille was shot twice and died on the field of battle. He was twenty-eight years old.

Earlier that year, when Bazille painted the picture of his studio, neither he nor his fellow artists were successful or respected in Paris. But they were friends. They were a band of painters who shared ideas, supplies, and studio space to create some of the world's most beloved art. And they were at ease with one another. In Bazille's *Studio; 9 rue de la Condamine*, there is no apparent hierarchy, no apparent leader. Just people who labored together in the pursuit of using their gifts to accomplish something meaningful.

Bazille wrote in a letter to his father that it was Édouard Manet, the one in the hat holding the cane, who painted Bazille into the painting.[14] Manet placed Jean Frédéric Bazille's towering frame in front of the painting Manet and Monet were admiring, so that we, the viewers, would not be able to see it. Instead, we would only see Bazille. Manet did this because he and Bazille were friends, yes, but also out of respect. That group of painters believed greatly in their friend's talent. Camille Pissarro described Jean Frédéric Bazille as "one of the most gifted among us."[15]

Creating in Community

What happens when a person's potential can be fully realized—when things like war, sorrow, pain, and death don't stand in the way? What happens when the best parts of what we have to offer develop unencumbered? We do well to wonder about such things, because this is the hope offered in the gospel of Jesus Christ.[16]

I wonder about uninterrupted potential. We live in a world of limits. The full range of "all that could be" is not offered to any of us in this life. Michelangelo had to work from a precut stone;

Caravaggio could not balance his artistic talent with his carnal appetites; Vermeer was constrained by financial limitations and an early death; and Bazille fell in battle when he was still young.

Every one of us faces limitations of many kinds. This should not surprise us.[17] Every one of us must make certain choices in life that take other options off the table. Of course, this isn't always a negative—we choose one spouse at the exclusion of all others. We take a job east of the Mississippi, making it impractical to stay connected to what's happening on the West Coast. Work and parenthood begin to chip away at the time we were once able to devote to some creative or athletic passions, and we lay those interests down—at least in part—on the altar of personal responsibility.

Here is where community is so vitally important. Without it, we might be tempted to believe that the limitations and hardships we experience are unique to us and are therefore ours alone to navigate. That just isn't the case. Being part of a community puts us in proximity to other strugglers—people who can reassure us that we are not alone, who can offer wisdom because they're familiar with the woods we're lost in, and who can benefit from the experiences and insights we've gained through the hardships we've endured.

I wonder what might have happened had Bazille not fallen in battle that day. I wonder what more he might have given the world. I wonder how his influence would have shaped what his friends went on to create and the lives and work of those who came after, like Georges Seurat, Paul Gauguin, and Vincent van Gogh.

We will never know any of that, but we do know some of the impact Bazille's life had on the community he was part of, and the impact that community had on the world. Let's take an inventory of who played a role. Delacroix devoted himself to a craft that inspired the generation to follow, the Impressionists.

He practiced. He labored. He persevered. Gaston Bazille weighed his son's passion against the practical need for a viable trade. He guided and nurtured his son. He insisted that Jean Frédéric give medical school an honest try and responded with a nurturing wisdom and with resources when it was clear the boy was made for another path. Émile Zola gave his journalist's and poet's pen, and Nadar his second-floor studio. Camille Pissarro, Paul Cézanne, Gustave Courbet, Edgar Degas, Auguste Renoir, Claude Monet, and Edouard Manet gave one another their friendship, as complicated as that can be among artists.

We certainly can't push Jean Frédéric Bazille forward as the reason Impressionism was born. We dare not suggest he is the reason for Monet's success or anyone else's. But we should look at Bazille as a person who played a role in the development of one of the world's most celebrated schools of art. He was one of many who contributed something of value to a community striving to create something beautiful, meaningful, and lasting.

He gave friendship. He provided space. He shared supplies. He welcomed gatherings. He purchased art his friends made. And lest we forget, he fought and died for his countrymen, which is, as Jesus said, the highest form of love—laying down your life for your friends.[18]

We live in communities that need goodness, truth, and beauty. And we play a role in advancing those transcendentals that make us human. We are to curate them for others. We play a role in blowing on the embers of "whatever is noble, whatever is right, whatever is pure, whatever is lovely, whatever is admirable."[19] Whatever is excellent or praiseworthy, think about such things—and be a part of them.

Who knows what could happen?

CHAPTER 7

THE STRIVING ARTIST

Vincent van Gogh's *The Red Vineyard*
and the Elusive Nature of Contentment

Vincent van Gogh, *The Red Vineyard*, 1888, oil on canvas,
75 × 93 cm, Pushkin Museum of Fine Arts, Moscow

All streams run to the sea,
but the sea is not full;
to the place where the streams flow,
there they flow again.
All things are full of weariness.

Ecclesiastes 1:7–8

Imagine Vincent van Gogh in the last year of his life. See him buying his art supplies, mixing his colors, preening his brushes, stretching and preparing his canvases. Imagine his sketches, like recipes, lying faceup on the table next to the easel. Imagine the eternal bits of color under his fingernails, on his beard, and deep in the seams of his clothes, his person an accidental painting in the same spectrum as the canvas of the day. The pace and nature of his craft immerse him in a sensual world of color, shape, texture, scent, and composition. It is hard to tell where the man stops and his work begins.

The postman's letter, dated 15 November 1889, sat facedown on the table by the window. Octave Maus, the founder of the Brussels Art Exposition, had extended an invitation that read, "The association requests you, Sir, to kindly let us know as soon as possible if you accept its invitation, as the number of these is strictly limited, and to inform us before 15 December of the notes and comments you wish to see featured in the catalogue."[1]

The Brussels Art Exposition was formed six years earlier, in 1883. The preeminence of the Salon in Paris made it difficult for artists and styles rejected by the Salon to break into the public arena. So in response, Octave Maus, an artist and lawyer, gathered a board of ten other artists and put together an exposition of their own work, much like what the Impressionists did with the Anonymous Society. They invited nine other international artists to show their work as well. They called themselves "the Twenty."

In 1889, as the Twenty began planning the 1890 expo, they discussed which artists should round out their company. They agreed to invite Paul Cézanne, Paul Signac, Henri de Toulouse-Lautrec, Alfred Sisley, and Paul Gauguin, along with Vincent van Gogh.[2]

The Invitation

Each time Maus's letter caught Vincent's eye, he sorted out the question a little more in his mind: *The Orchard in Blossom and Sunflowers, for sure. Not the Starry Night though. It's not me. Not the Cypresses either. Perhaps The Red Vineyard, though. Yes. The Red Vineyard.*

After settling the matter, Vincent put down his brush, grabbed a piece of paper, and wrote:

> Sir,
>   I accept with pleasure your invitation to exhibit . . .
> Here is the list of canvases I intend for you:
>
> 1. Sunflowers
> 2. Sunflowers
> 3. The Ivy
> 4. Orchard in blossom (Arles)
> 5. Wheatfield. Rising sun (St.-Rémy)
> 6. The red vineyard (Montmajour)
>
> (All these canvases are no. 30 canvases.)
>   I am perhaps exceeding the 4 metres of room but as I believe that the 6 together, thus chosen, will make a rather

varied colour effect, perhaps you will find a way of placing them.

Vincent van Gogh[3]

One year before receiving Maus's invitation, on October 2, 1888, Vincent wrote a letter to his friend and fellow painter Eugène Boch. When Vincent wrote this letter, he had no idea how his seemingly passing references to Eugene's sister, Anna, and the vineyard near Montmajour would later be joined as an indelible and complicated part of his story. The letter read in part:

I'd very much like to ask you to do an exchange with me of one of your studies of the coal-mines . . .

Is your sister [Anna] also going to do miners? There's certainly work for two people there. I believe that it's very fortunate for you that the two of you both do painting in your house.

Ah well, I have to go to work in the vineyard, near Montmajour. It's all purplish yellow green under the blue sky, a beautiful colour motif. Good handshake and good luck, and much success in your work.

Ever yours,
Vincent[4]

The vineyard he mentioned became the subject of the only painting he ever sold during his lifetime: *The Red Vineyard*. And Anna, Eugene's sister, was the person who bought it. She and her brother were admirers of van Gogh's work. But even more, they were his friends. Vincent once painted a portrait of Eugène and then included that portrait as one of the paintings hanging on the wall in his well-known work *The Bedroom*. Anna was a respected Belgian Impressionist painter. In 1885, Octave Maus invited her to join as the first female board member of the Twenty.

If Anna's friendship with Vincent wasn't the reason Maus invited him to exhibit at the 1890 Brussels Art Expo, it most certainly influenced the board's decision. But it wasn't this friendship alone that got Vincent those four meters of exhibition space. It was his art. More than anything else, it was his talent as a painter, a gift the world was just beginning to notice, that opened the door for him to exhibit and then sell *The Red Vineyard*.

The Painting

Often, when people think of van Gogh, their minds go to *Sunflowers*, *Irises*, or *The Starry Night*. To understand the story of *The Red Vineyard*, we must locate it in the greater body of Vincent's work and try to understand the artist himself.

The Red Vineyard hangs in the Pushkin Museum of Fine Arts in Moscow, along with five other canvases painted by Vincent. Although *The Red Vineyard* bears all the hallmarks of the classic van Gogh style—thick application, hatched brushstrokes, geometric outlines—it does not necessarily stand out as the flagship of the fleet in the museum, or even as the best of his five works that are housed there. Many who see *The Red Vineyard* at the Pushkin Museum and neglect to read the plaque on the wall beside it might never realize they are looking at the only one of his paintings anyone ever purchased while van Gogh was alive. Their gaze might be drawn down the wall to his cryptically autobiographical *Prisoners Exercising (After Doré)*, in which he paints himself into a line of inmates walking circles in a prison yard like inchworms on the rim of a bucket. But the details we have about *The Red Vineyard* shine an interesting light on the artist's vision and process.

Vincent painted *The Red Vineyard* on November 4, 1888, from memory in the space of a few days.[5] The scene depicts the annual grape harvest in southern France known as the "vendage." Coming from Holland, Vincent was fascinated by the vendage. There was something settling about the rhythm of the ingathering—humanity and land in harmony. People worked and enjoyed a return on their labor. One scholar wrote, "These grape harvesters were people van Gogh felt he could relate to by the fact that they were working with nature in its rhythms and not against it."[6] The harvesters in this painting do not look haggard, but bathed in the warmth of the afternoon sun, fulfilled in their work, as part of the order of things. Vincent thought this was beautiful. He wished it for himself.

In 1888, when he painted *The Red Vineyard*, Vincent was experimenting with the idea that color alone could generate an aesthetic that would capture peoples' hearts and imaginations. He was studying color theory through the art and writings of Georges Seurat, who believed the scientific application of color was like any other natural law. Seurat believed knowledge of how the eye and the brain communicated with each other could be used to create a new language of art based on the arrangement of hues, color intensity, and shapes—that there was a scientific reason that art seemed to speak to the soul.[7] This resonated with Vincent, who used color not only to depict what he saw, but to make it come to life. To stand in front of one of his works today—like *The Red Vineyard* or *The Starry Night*—proves how the vibrancy and movement of the color he used seemed to give the work life beneath its skin.

When Vincent wrote about *The Red Vineyard* to Eugène Boch before he painted it, and to his brother Theo after, he spoke more of the colors he saw than of any one aspect of the harvest itself. It was the color that caught his attention. To Boch he wrote, "It's all purplish yellow green under the blue sky, a beautiful color motif."[8] And to Theo, two days after completing the painting, he wrote, "But if only you'd been with us on Sunday! We saw a red vineyard, completely red like red wine. In the distance it became yellow, and then a green sky with a sun, fields violet and sparkling yellow here and there after the rain in which the setting sun was reflected."[9]

From memory, Vincent set out to capture the way he remembered the colors of the vendage and how they lay against each other. As it goes with so many artists, his composition developed in his mind before it ever made its way onto a canvas. His correspondences show him as a man who was always studying the world before him. He was always thinking, always imagining, always planning his next work.

Ordinary scenes of everyday objects moved Vincent. He wrote, "Even though I'm often in a mess, inside me there's still a calm, pure harmony and music. In the poorest little house, in the filthiest corner, I see paintings or drawings. And my mind turns in that direction as if with an irresistible urge."[10]

Vincent didn't see the world as a collection of plain, unaffected objects. He saw the unfolding drama of the human story, which to him was a heartbreaking tale. One example of this can be seen in how he wrote about a bridge he wished to paint. To Theo, Vincent wrote:

> I have a View of the Rhône—the Trinquetaille iron bridge, where the sky and the river are the colour of absinthe—the quays a lilac tone, the people leaning on the parapet almost black, the iron bridge, an intense blue—with a bright orange note in the blue background and an intense Veronese green note. One more effort that's far from finished—but one at least where I'm attempting something more heartbroken and therefore more heartbreaking.[11]

For Vincent, the steel and stone of the bridge were alive with color, and he sensed in the people on the banks and crossing from one side to the other all the sorrows they carried. The colors he saw bore the emotion. And because the emotion was palpable, the colors were vibrant.

The Red Vineyard relies almost exclusively on the color spectrum between red and yellow. This was a deliberate challenge Vincent set for himself. In his day, the idea of painting a scene from memory based on a desire to use a particular color spectrum was backward. Many artists took their easels and paints outside and captured what they saw. Vincent wanted to capture what he felt as he tried to remember what he saw. This is the very nature of Impressionism—painting not a perfect copy of the thing in view, but an *impression* of it—the artist's impression of what he saw in it and how he felt about it.[12]

The Artist

Vincent believed that although his use of vibrant color made his paintings appear less realistic, it helped the paintings come alive. And the many people who have viewed his paintings since would agree. Somehow, color, composition, and subject matter combine to connect with people in ways that defy explanation. This is the mysterious, transcendent quality of art—something in the liniment oil and pigment breaks through the plain of the canvas and penetrates the human soul in a way that suddenly and inexplicably matters.

This transcendence is what compels a tourist in a museum to circle back to a particular painting she encountered that day for one last look before she leaves. She may not be able to say why, but she feels she must return. So she does. And feeling as though she is forcing a sort of disconnection when she at last pulls herself away, she vows to remember the piece—to carry it with her in the recesses of her heart. And she does. The work never again appears to her as an ordinary piece of art, but as part of *her own* collection. When she saw the work the first time, it belonged to the world. But by the time she leaves that initial viewing, it belongs to her.

Some people carry with them entire collections of Renaissance-era masterworks by Rembrandt and Vermeer. Others can close their eyes and revisit the Impressionists of Paris: Monet, Manet, and Bazille. For others still, line after line of Scripture or Shakespeare effortlessly unfold from the recesses of memories dating back to when they were children catechizing or strutting and fretting their first hours upon the stage.

This is the intangibility of genius—to create work that transfers from the canvas, the page, or the instrument into the heart of another person, arousing a longing for beauty and an end to sadness. This was what Vincent wanted to create—art that would transfer from his easel into someone else's soul to work as a balm of healing for the broken.

Van Gogh approached his craft as a pure artist. He cared deeply about the sacred work of creation, but he abhorred the seemingly necessary process of commercialization. He believed his unique style contributed something novel and valuable to the art world. But he also understood the tension that artists from every generation have known: commercial success facilitates the ability to continue working. It costs time and money to make art.

Vincent's motives were not solely devoted to the work he produced. He craved recognition deeply. He wrote, "I can do nothing about it if my paintings don't sell. The day will come, though, when people will see that they're worth more than the cost of the paint and my subsistence, very meagre in fact, that we put into them."[13] His lack of commercial success discouraged him, as it would anyone who worked at something for the better part of a decade, believing it was their life's calling without ever making a dime.

Vincent was prone to depression and mental illness—perhaps displayed most infamously when he cut off his own ear or most tangibly when he spent a year in an asylum in Saint-Rémy-de-Provence. His psychological and mental struggles added a layer of despondency to his commercial failure. Though no one can say precisely what was happening inside him on that July afternoon in 1890 when it seems he surrendered to despair and pulled the trigger,[14] there can be little doubt that a sense of professional futility played a role.

To add to the tragedy of his death, when Vincent shot himself, he was closer than he could have imagined to the recognition he so very much desired. He did not know his work would soon become a staple in the Brussels Art Expo. He did not know that just twenty-four years after his death, in 1914, his letters to Theo would be published in a three-volume set. He would have been in his early sixties had he lived to see this. He did not know that twenty years after that, in 1934, Irving Stone would write a bestselling biographical novel called *Lust for Life*, based on those letters, or that twenty-two years after that, in 1956, Kirk Douglas would play him in the motion picture based on Stone's book.

Perhaps none of those things would have happened had van Gogh's life not ended so tragically. But his fame was growing in the art world even during the last years of his life. An increasing number of people who encountered his work presumed they were looking at a rising star. He exhibited some of his work in 1888 and drew the attention of his fellow painter Joseph Jacob Isaacson, who wrote an article in which he applauded Vincent's work in the August 17, 1889, issue of the weekly Amsterdam paper *De Portefeuille*.[15]

Though Vincent longed to be recognized for his genius, he was a paradox when it came to receiving it. The adulation of the public proved to be more than he could bear. When Vincent read Isaacson's complimentary article, he was embarrassed by the attention and asked Isaacson never to write about him again.[16] But it was too late. Word was spreading. In January 1890, just before the Brussels Art Expo, art critic Albert Aurier wrote a lengthy essay praising Vincent's work, saying, "In the case of Vincent van Gogh, in my opinion, despite the sometimes misleading strangeness of his works, it is difficult for an unprejudiced and knowledgeable viewer to deny or question the naive truthfulness of his art, the ingeniousness of his vision."[17]

In 1891, the year after Vincent's death, art critic Octave Mirbeau compared Vincent to his Dutch predecessor, the Master himself, Rembrandt. Mirbeau wrote, "Van Gogh does not always adhere to the discipline nor to the sobriety of the Dutch master; but he often equals his eloquence and his prodigious ability to render life."[18]

That same year, both Paris and Brussels held retrospectives of Vincent's work. Other retrospectives were later shown in Denmark, Norway, Sweden, Finland, and Germany over the course of the rest of the 1890s, making van Gogh one of the most celebrated artists in Europe by the turn of the century. Had he lived just a few more years, he would have seen this happen.

But for Vincent, this was all unimaginable and deeply frustrating. The longer he went without commercial success, the more feverishly he painted. The more canvases he amassed, the more objectively measurable his failure appeared. When he held the pistol in his hand in that wheat field in 1890, gathering his nerve, he did not know that the world he wanted to leave was beginning to love him as an artist.

The Expo

In 1889, Vincent sent off his six paintings, and when the time came, the Brussels Art Expo arranged them as he requested. His canvases were displayed alongside works from Paul Cézanne, Paul Signac, Henri de Toulouse-Lautrec, and Paul Gauguin—all painters on the leading edge of Postimpressionism. Though Vincent himself would become the most celebrated Postimpressionist of all time, the fact that all these names were on the invite list together telegraphed that just as the Impressionists of the 1860s and 1870s overtook Realists and Romantics who came before them, the Postimpressionists would soon surpass the Impressionists as the darlings of European art.[19]

Vincent's growing acclaim was not happening in a vacuum. He was part of a movement. Still, he stood out. One reason he became the face of Postimpressionism was because his work most acutely displayed the characteristics of that era—thick paint application, vibrant colors, geometric compositions, and distorted details. He employed them all. And as it happens with any artist on the leading edge of a new era, many embraced his work as exciting and refreshing, but others rejected it as being inferior work born of youthful swagger with no respect for the discipline of the craft.

Belgian symbolist painter Henry de Groux, one of the members of the Twenty, felt this way about Vincent's work. In fact, de Groux found Vincent's art so distasteful that he refused to allow his own work to be hung alongside what he called the "abominable Pot of Sunflowers by Monsieur Vincent."[20] De Groux's opposition proved revealing. What seemed so obvious to him—that Vincent van Gogh was a hack—was a view the other members of the Twenty did not share. Later, at the Expo's opening dinner, when de Groux called Vincent "an ignoramus and a charlatan," all hell broke loose.[21]

Octave Maus described the scene as it unfolded: "At the other end of the table Lautrec suddenly bounced up, with his arms in the air, and shouted that it was an outrage to criticize so great an artist. De Groux retorted. Tumult. Seconds were appointed. [Paul] Signac announced coldly that if Lautrec were killed he would assume the quarrel himself."[22] That night, the Twenty expelled de Groux from the Expo. He returned the next day, cap in hand, to apologize and was allowed to resign and withdraw his work on his own volition.

Vincent had no idea any of this happened because he was not there. He did not know these artists he admired had risen to defend his honor and validate his brilliance.

Though the scandal with de Groux drew support for Vincent from other artists at the Expo, those who witnessed it could not help but wonder how his work would be received publicly. Vincent did not represent the broader commercial taste of the time.[23] But Maus and his group were interested in art that would inspire new conversations, not just satisfy commercial appetites. And Vincent's work did just that. His paintings went on to be among the most discussed at the Expo. And before the event was over, Anna Boch, a member of the Twenty and the sister of Vincent's friend Eugène, purchased *The Red Vineyard* for 400 francs— roughly $2,000 in today's economy.

The Numbers

When Vincent learned of the sale of *The Red Vineyard*, he wrote self-deprecatingly to his mother, "Theo informed me that they'd sold one of my paintings in Brussels for 400 francs. In comparison with other prices, including the Dutch ones, this isn't much, but that's why I try to be productive in order to be able to keep working at reasonable prices. And if we have to try to earn our living with our hands, I have an awful lot of expenses to make up for."[24]

A look at the output and volume of Vincent's work, especially in the last years of his life, shines a fascinating and heartbreaking light on the nature of his genius, his productivity, and the significance of the sale of *The Red Vineyard*. They tell a story of a kind of striving no person is meant to sustain.

Vincent finished around 860 complete oil paintings over

the course of his life as a painter.[25] During this same period, he also produced another 1,240 works in the form of watercolors, sketches, and prints, and he wrote more than 900 letters—650 of them to his brother and benefactor, Theo. All told, this comes to just over 3,000 individual works of art and writing that we know of from Vincent.

VINCENT VAN GOGH'S BODY OF WORK

860—Complete oil paintings

1,240—Sketches, watercolors, prints

900—Letters (650 to Theo van Gogh)

――――

3,000—Total individual works

How much time does such prolific output require? For the sake of comparison, set aside Vincent's 2,140 letters, watercolors, sketches, and prints and consider only his 860 canvases. How does that production quantity compare to other well-known painters? Rembrandt produced roughly six hundred oil paintings during his career, which spanned more than forty years. Claude Monet, van Gogh's contemporary, painted around 2,500 paintings over the course of sixty years. Paul Cézanne painted nine hundred canvases over forty years. On average Rembrandt completed fifteen canvases per year; Monet, forty-two; and Cézanne, twenty-three.

Rembrandt, Monet, Cézanne, and many others had time on their side. They worked for decades. Vincent, however, did not. His painting career lasted only nine years, from late 1881 through July 1890. That's it. He painted from age twenty-eight to thirty-seven. Before that, he worked as an art dealer in his uncle's firm and served as a missionary.

Over the first half of his painting life, from 1881 to 1884, Van Gogh averaged twenty-one paintings per year. But between 1885 and 1889, the second half of his career, that number jumps up to

130 canvases per year. That works out to one complete painting every three days for five years straight. This does not take into account the fact that during that span from 1885 to 1889, Vincent relocated a couple of times and had personal and medical crises that would take him away from his easel for weeks on end.

COMPARISON OF AVERAGE PAINTINGS BY YEAR BY REMBRANDT, MONET, CÉZANNE, AND VAN GOGH

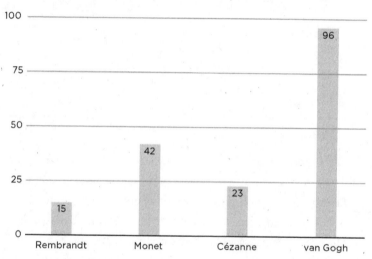

The most fascinating year of Vincent's career, in terms of not only output but also health, was the last year of his life: 1890, the year he sold *The Red Vineyard*. Vincent died midway through the year, on July 29, of complications from an apparently self-inflicted gunshot wound to the abdomen. During that half year, he produced 108 finished canvases. Although that total is sixty-one fewer than his most prolific year, 1888—the year he painted *The Red Vineyard*—and twenty-six fewer than 1889, the 108 canvases of 1890 do not represent a decline in production, but rather a stark increase. He died during the summer, which means he was on pace to finish close to two hundred paintings that year.

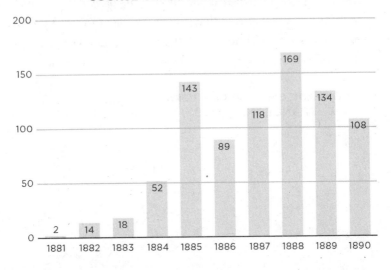

VAN GOGH'S OUTPUT BY YEAR OVER THE
COURSE OF HIS PAINTING CAREER

The monthly breakdown of his output in 1890 is even more startling. Between January and April, he painted just eighteen paintings total, which means he could not have done much the following three months besides eat, sleep, and paint. Between May and July 1890, Vincent worked at a frenetic pace, and his art bore the evidence. In the St. Louis Art Museum, in the Impressionists gallery, there is a van Gogh from June 1890 called *Vineyards with a View of Auvers*. The heavily applied paint in the lower left corner bears the distinct impression of the crosshatching of another canvas, suggesting the painting was finished and set aside in a stack with the others before it was completely dry. Of course it was. This particular canvas was one of an estimated forty-two he painted that month alone. He painted another twenty-four that May and another twenty-four that July, meaning in the three months before he died, Vincent painted ninety of that year's 108 paintings—a three-month average of one finished painting per day.

VAN GOGH'S OUTPUT DURING THE LAST YEAR OF HIS LIFE

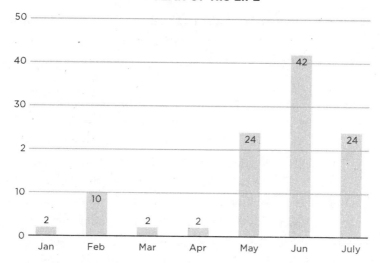

Imagine Vincent in those last months of his life. See him mixing his colors, stretching his canvases, and preening his brushes. See the eternal bits of color under his fingernails, on his beard, and in his clothes in the same spectrum as the fury of those three months, during which he completed an average of one canvas every single day.

Now add in the 2,140 other watercolors, sketches, prints, and letters he composed during those nine years, and we're left with a heartbreaking picture: Somewhere in that flurry of motion between painter and canvas was a man held captive by an insatiable appetite to capture the world he wanted while being unable to connect with the world he had. It seemed to be killing him.

Perhaps Vincent summarized his struggle best when he said, "If we're tired isn't it because we've already gone a long way, and if it's true that man's life on earth is a struggle, isn't feeling tired and having a burning head a sign that we have struggled?"[26]

The Glory

What are we to make of Vincent's story? What of the futility that seems to belong to any creative endeavor? Vincent said, "Someone has a great fire in his soul and nobody ever comes to warm themselves at it, and passers-by see nothing but a little smoke."[27] What of the great burning fires in each of us that are perceived by others as little more than wisps of smoke?

Today, Vincent's work has its place among the most celebrated and valuable art ever created. Entire wings of museums in the greatest cities in the world are devoted to his art and his influence on others who came after him. It would be obtuse to attempt to resolve Vincent's story by noting his posthumous commercial success—how his *Portrait of Dr. Gachet* sold for 82 million dollars in 1990, one hundred years after his death, or how his *Irises* went for 101 million dollars three years earlier. It would miss the point entirely to try to add up how much his collective body of work is worth now, because for Vincent, it wasn't the value of his collection that plagued him; it was the question of whether or not his time on this earth would produce beauty that would transcend his days. Would anyone ever see anything of the fire that burned within him except for the wisps of smoke?

C. S. Lewis wrote, "The sense that in this universe we are treated as strangers, the longing to be acknowledged, to meet with some response, to bridge some chasm that yawns between us and reality, is part of our inconsolable secret."[28] Though no one can say for sure why Anna Boch bought *The Red Vineyard*, it would be too simplistic to say it was because she admired the painting and wanted to own it. She certainly must have liked it well enough to lay down 400 francs. But she also knew Vincent's story. She knew his friendship with her brother and his friendship with her. She knew his struggles with mental health. She knew his ongoing fight to break into the world of artists who were taken seriously, who were acknowledged, who were met with some response. She knew his inconsolable secret. Anyone close to him knew.

His secret is ours too. It is a secret as old as time: Does my life contribute anything of value to this world? Ecclesiastes put the question to poetry:

> I turned about and gave my heart up to despair over all the toil of my labors under the sun, because sometimes a person who has toiled with wisdom and knowledge and skill must leave everything to be enjoyed by someone who did not toil for it.[29]

Vincent left his work to be enjoyed by us who did not toil for it. But we remember him not just for his art. We remember him for his words, his life, and his struggle. And we relate to him. He is the striving man from Ecclesiastes—learning firsthand about the vanity of toil under the sun while trying to live, move, breathe, and do his work under heaven. He chases after the sun and never reaches it.[30] He bears the weight of a creation "subjected to futility"[31] and longs for the renewal of all things.[32]

This is the power of art. It happens in time and space, but it points to the eternal. It takes the objects and ideas it finds lying around, the things of the here and now, and assembles them into something that belongs to a world outside of time. The trick for artists is to believe this is the true nature of their work, especially while they are in the process of making it, whether it sells or not.

Vincent was no saint, and we dare not make him into one. His relationships with people like Paul Gauguin show he could be a difficult person to befriend. And the trove of more than two thousand letters he wrote reveal that he often lashed out in anger, speaking condescendingly of other artists and people in his community, and apparently availing himself of the services of prostitutes. We should not ignore his temper, his immorality, or his pride in order to venerate him. But neither should we focus on his imperfections and iniquities and consider him damned, because for the whole of his life he never stopped speaking of his love for Christ. His life, his words, and his work show a complicated man who struggled with a lot of confusion, pain, and anger but also recognized beauty, wonder, and worth in people in ways few others ever would. He was looking for something he would never find in this life, not because he died young, but because the glory, love, beauty, and peace he hungered for were not of this world.

But they were, and still are, very real. Vincent spent his artistic life knocking on the door C. S. Lewis described as a "welcome into the heart of things." This is the door to glory. And the promise of the gospel is that for those whose faith is in Christ, as seemed to be the case with Vincent, "The door on which we have been knocking all our lives will open at last."[33] In Vincent's art, we sense the eternal glory blazing on the other side of the door, and through his art long to behold it as more than the wisps of smoke we see. This is why we are drawn to him. We have seen some of the fire that burned inside him.

As Annie Dillard said, one of the most important things we can do is to try to sense beauty and grace when they occur.[34] We stand at glory's door because we know there is wonder on the other side. We long to see it ourselves, and we want to show it to others. Sometimes this is the artist's work—to stand and knock on the door of glory and, whenever possible, siphon little wisps of smoke from those places where we catch a glimpse of the light so that others might see and believe. What can we show each other of glory anyway except light in shadow? What glory can anyone see in any of us except for wisps of smoke, traces of the great burning fire? And is that not enough for now—to show enough to prove there's more?

Vincent van Gogh, *Self-Portrait with Bandaged Ear*, 1889,
oil on canvas, 60 × 49 cm, Courtauld Gallery, London.

Paintings by Caravaggio

Michelangelo Merisi da Caravaggio, *The Calling of St. Matthew*, 1600, oil on canvas, 322 × 340 cm, San Luigi dei Francesi, Rome

Caravaggio, *Salome with the Head of John the Baptist*, 1610,
oil on canvas, 116 x 140 cm, Palacio Real de Madrid

Caravaggio, *David with the Head of Goliath*, 1609,
oil on canvas, 125 x 101 cm, Galleria Borghese, Rome

Michelangelo, *David*, 1501–1504, marble, 17 x 6-1/2 feet,
Gallery of the Academy of Florence, Florence

Photograph: TravelFlow / Getty Images

Isabella Stewart Gardner Museum, Dutch Room, the frame once
containing Rembrandt's *The Storm on the Sea of Galilee*

Photo by Kate Charlton, used by permission.

Rembrandt van Rijn, *The Storm on the Sea of Galilee*,
1633, oil on canvas, 160 × 128 cm, missing

The Music Lesson,
ca. 1662–1665, oil on canvas,
73.3 x 64.5 cm, Royal Collection,
Buckingham Palace

Woman with a Lute,
ca. 1663–1664, oil on canvas,
51.4 x 45.7 cm, Metropolitan
Museum of Art, New York

Girl Interrupted at Her Music, ca. 1660–1661, oil on canvas,
39.4 x 44.5 cm, Frick Collection, New York

Paintings by
Johannes Vermeer

The Concert, ca. 1665–1666,
oil on canvas, 72.5 x 64.7 cm, missing

The Allegory of Painting,
ca. 1666–1667, oil on canvas,
100 x 120 cm, Kunsthistorisches
Museum, Vienna

*Girl Reading a Letter at an Open
Window*, ca. 1657, oil on canvas,
83 x 64.5 cm, Gemäldegalerie
Alte Meister, Dresden

The Astronomer, ca. 1668, oil on canvas,
50.8 x 46.3 cm, The Louvre, Paris

The Geographer, ca. 1668–1669, oil on canvas,
53 x 46.6 cm, Städelsches Kunstinstitut, Frankfurt

Johannes Vermeer, *The Milkmaid*, ca. 1658–1660,
oil on canvas, 46 x 41 cm, Rijksmuseum, Amsterdam

François-Joseph Heim, *Charles X Distributing Awards
to the Artists at the Close of the Salon of 1824*, 1827,
oil on canvas, 173 x 256 cm, The Louvre, Paris

Jean Frédéric Bazille, *Studio; 9 Rue de la Condamine*, 1870,
oil on canvas, 98 x 129 cm, Musée d'Orsay, Paris

Claude Monet, *Impression, Sunrise*, 1872, oil on canvas,
48 x 63 cm, Musée Marmottan Monet, Paris

Van Gogh's Collection Submitted to the 1890 Brussels Art Expo

Sunflowers, 1888,
oil on canvas,
92.1 x 73 cm, National
Gallery, London

Sunflowers, 1888,
oil on canvas,
91 x 72 cm, Neue
Pinakothek, Munich

The Ivy, 1889,
oil on canvas,
92 x 72 cm, present
whereabouts unknown

Orchard in Blossom, 1889, oil on canvas,
72 x 92 cm, Neue Pinakothek, Munich

Wheat Field with Rising Sun, 1889, oil on canvas,
91 x 72 cm, private collection

Vincent van Gogh, *The Red Vineyard*, 1888, oil on canvas,
75 × 93 cm, Pushkin Museum of Fine Arts, Moscow

Henry Ossawa Tanner, *The Annunciation*, 1898, oil on canvas,
57 x 71-1/4 inches, Philadelphia Museum of Art, Philadelphia

Henry Ossawa Tanner, *The Thankful Poor*, 1894,
oil on canvas, 35.5 x 42.2 cm, private collection

Edward Hopper paintings featuring Josephine Nivison Hopper

Edward Hopper, *New York Movie*, 1939, oil on canvas,
81.9 × 101.9 cm, Museum of Modern Art, New York City

Edward Hopper, *Nighthawks*, 1942, oil on canvas,
84.1 × 152.4 cm, Art Institute of Chicago, Chicago

Edward Hopper's final painting, Two Comedians, 1966,
oil on canvas, 73.7 x 101.6 cm, private collection

Lilias Trotter, *Prepared as a Bride*, ca. 1888, watercolor on paper
Used by permission of Lilias Trotter Legacy.

Perhaps one of the greatest gifts Vincent gave was his conviction that this world in which we wait is not ugly or empty. This belief bore itself out in beautiful paintings of ordinary people and places. The world he knew was glorious, alive with color, texture, and wonder. He has helped us see it, and in helping us, he has nurtured the hope that a truer, greater glory lies just beyond. When we look into the night sky, Vincent taught us to see the stars swirl in the heavens. When the irises begin to rise, he gave us images to remember as we anticipate their unfolding into blooms that prove there is life in what the winter months destroyed. When the dew settles on the field of poppies, he has helped us see it as illuminated with a million little lights.[35]

And if you're ever in the south of France in the autumn, you, too, may lift your eyes and see it: "a red vineyard, completely red like red wine. In the distance it became yellow, and then a green sky with a sun, fields violet and sparkling yellow here and there after the rain in which the setting sun was reflected."[36]

Thanks to Vincent, you may find yourself confronted with a glory deeper than you expected. But even still, you will only be seeing a fraction of what's actually there. You will only see a wisp of smoke. "All things are full of weariness."[37]

BEYOND IMAGINATION

Henry O. Tanner, Race, and the
Humble Power of Curiosity

Henry Ossawa Tanner, *The Annunciation*, 1898, oil on canvas,
57 × 71-1/4 inches, Philadelphia Museum of Art, Philadelphia

Curiosity is insubordination in its purest form.

Vladimir Nabokov

While Impressionism and the Postimpressionism of Vincent van Gogh and Georges Seurat were taking root in Europe in the mid to late 1800s, America was building its own network of artists, art academies, patrons, and exhibition centers. For many, it was a land of possibility. But it was also the Civil War era, and the nation had a long way to go when it came to the idea of opportunity for all.[1] Doors that opened easily for White artists were not so welcoming to artists of color. And even when those doors opened, Black artists still had to reckon with the reality that any conversation about their work in the United States would include mention of the color of their skin.[2] When an artist of color has their work celebrated by a White majority, and the detail of that artist's race is always included in the discussion, it can frame that artist's work as an unexpected achievement in light of their race. Henry Tanner encountered this early and worked to break free from it.

An American In Paris

Henry Ossawa Tanner was born in Pittsburgh, Pennsylvania, on June 21, 1859. He was the first of nine children born to Reverend Benjamin Tucker Tanner, a minister in the African Methodist Episcopal Church, and Sarah Elizabeth Miller Tanner, a former slave and granddaughter of a White plantation owner, who had escaped through the Underground Railroad.

The Tanners were a middle-class African American family. They valued education, believing it was the best way to punch through the social ceilings of being Black. Benjamin and Sarah did all they could to make learning part of everyday life for the Tanner children. The world was not just a thing to inhabit, but a place to be discovered. They encouraged curiosity. They loved culture. Henry grew up seeing art from both White and African American artists, teaching him early that being Black and being an artist were not mutually exclusive.

In 1879, Henry enrolled in the Pennsylvania Academy of Fine Arts, where he studied under the American Realist painter Thomas Eakins. Genre painting—historical, biblical, and mythological—was once again commercially popular. Tanner's first attempt at genre painting was the myth of Androcles, the Roman slave who hid in a lion's den to escape capture. Androcles befriended the residing lion by removing a thorn from the creature's paw. Later, the story goes, Androcles was captured by the Romans and sent to face the beasts of the Colosseum in the Circus Maximus, where he would be torn limb from limb for the entertainment of the masses. The lion that emerged from the catacombs turned out to be the one he had helped, and when it recognized Androcles, it bowed before him in reverence. The audience assumed the slave was favored by the gods, and both the lion and Androcles were set free.

Artists draw on what they know and where they come from. As the son of a runaway slave, Henry grew up around the stories of evading slaveholders and countless other dangers his mother and father had to endure as Black people in America in the mid-1800s. The story of Androcles gave Henry the opportunity to convey some of the dignity of slaves, comment on the system that created them, and engender some empathy toward them. He painted two studies for the work—one of a frail, naked, imprisoned Androcles, and another of a lion licking its paw. But Henry confessed the actual painting proved "too ambitious" at his present skill level. He spent money on models and time studying, sketching, and thinking, but all that remains are his two studies. He never finished the painting.[3]

Thomas Eakins pressed the young artist to use the experience of coming to the edge of his abilities as an opportunity to grow. Henry was grateful for the prodding:

> About this time, Mr. Thomas Eakins, under whom I was studying at the Pennsylvania Academy of Fine Arts, gave me a criticism which aided me then, and ever since; it may apply to all walks of life, I will "pass it along." I had made a start on a study, which was not altogether bad, but very probably the best thing I had ever done. He encouraged but, instead of working to make it better, I became afraid I should destroy what I had done, and really did nothing the rest of the week. Well, he was disgusted. "What have you been doing? Get it, get it better, or get it worse. No middle ground of compromise."[4]

Eakins pushed Henry because he saw great promise in the young painter. He could see that Henry Tanner had something to show the world if he could find his voice. The two became lifelong friends. Eakins later painted a portrait of Tanner—a sign of respect between a teacher and student.

Henry's time in Philadelphia cultivated his skill, but the city held little for him in terms of commercial success. He didn't just want to paint; he wanted to live as a painter. In 1889, he moved to Atlanta to establish a photography studio in an attempt "to unite business with art."[5] The venture failed after a few months, but during that period, Henry met Bishop John Crane Hartzell of the Methodist Episcopal Church, who was quite taken with Tanner's work. Hartzell helped Henry get a job teaching drawing at Clark

University in Atlanta. During Tanner's time there, Hartzell arranged for him to show some of his work at an exhibition in Cincinnati. None of his paintings sold, but at the end of the show Hartzell and his wife bought the entire lot, which enabled Tanner to fulfill his lifelong dream of studying art in Europe.

In 1891, the year after van Gogh's death, Henry O. Tanner set sail for France. The plan was to head from there to Rome to study Michelangelo, Raphael, and the masters of the Renaissance. But on his way, he stopped in Paris and was so enamored by the art there that he abandoned his original plan. He said, "Strange that, after having been in Paris a week, I should find conditions so to my liking that I completely forgot that when I left New York I had made plans to study in Rome and was really on my way there when I arrived in Paris."[6]

It wasn't just the art in Paris that caught his attention; it was also the near absence of racial prejudice. Tanner was accepted in France in ways he never was in the States. For example, as his fame grew, European reviewers rarely referred to his race. He said, "In Paris, no one regards me curiously. I am simply M. Tanner, an American artist. Nobody knows or cares what was the complexion of my forebears. I live and work there on terms of absolute social equality."[7]

Henry secured lodging in Paris and enrolled in the Académie Julian, where he studied under Jean-Paul Laurens. France suited Tanner so much that he spent the rest of his life there, summering in artists colonies in Brittany and Normandy. During those early years at the academy, he completed a series of three major French genre paintings: *The Bagpipe Lesson* (1892–1893), *The Bagpipe Player* (1895), and *The Young Sabot Maker* (1895)—scenes drawn from his summers on the coast. These three paintings were shown in France and in the States. Pennsylvania retail mogul John Wanamaker admired *The Bagpipe Lesson* so much that he purchased it. Tanner's resonance with the Wanamaker family would come back to serve him well.

The Banjo Lesson

During Tanner's time at the Académie Julian, he became a member of the American Art Students Club because, as the National Gallery of Art noted, he wanted to maintain "close ties to the United States and remained concerned about the African American struggle for equality."[8] He traveled back to the States regularly, especially when he had work to show. During one of those visits, Tanner wrote and delivered a lecture titled "The American Negro in Art" at the 1893 World's Congress of Africa in Chicago. Describing his own struggle to find his place as a young student in America, he said, "No man or boy to whom this country is a land of 'equal chances' can realize what heartache this question [of finding instruction] caused me, and with what trepidation I made the rounds of the studios. The question was not, would the desired teacher have a boy who knew nothing and had little money, but would he have me, or would he keep me after he found out who I was?"[9]

Henry Tanner considered it his duty to use his voice and his art to try to reshape people's prejudices about people in the Black community. In the early 1890s, Tanner painted two African American genre works: *The Thankful Poor* and *The Banjo Lesson*. *The Banjo Lesson* was the "first recognized genre painting of blacks by an African American artist."[10] These two works complement his French paintings—*The Bagpipe Lesson* and *The Young Sabot Maker*—in that they all emphasize the importance of education in the form of the transmission of a skill from one generation to another.

What made Tanner's African American genre paintings (of which there are only two) particularly innovative was that his natural, dignified depictions of Black people stood in sharp contrast to the typical depictions of his time, which caricatured them as clownlike entertainers. Tanner wanted to show people more. He wanted to show the humanity, pathos, and quiet industry of the African American family—particularly of the men.[11]

Henry Ossawa Tanner, *The Banjo Lesson*,
1893, oil on canvas, 124.4 × 90.1 cm,
Hampton University Museum, Virginia

Writing about *The Banjo Lesson* and *The Thankful Poor* in the third person, Tanner said,

Since his return from Europe he has painted mostly Negro subjects, he feels drawn to such subjects on account of the newness of the field and because of a desire to represent the serious, and pathetic side of life among them, and it is his thought that other things being equal, he who has most sympathy with his subjects will obtain the best results. To his mind many of the artists who have represented Negro life have only seen the comic, the ludicrous side of it, and have lacked sympathy with and appreciation for the warm big heart that dwells within such a rough exterior.[12]

Popular advertisement depicting African
Americans in the late 1800s–1900s

Tanner regarded pedagogical themes, as seen in *The Bagpipe Lesson, The Banjo Lesson, The Thankful Poor,* and *The Young Sabot Maker,* as a kind of Trojan horse for getting people to reconsider prejudices. Art has always been a means of shaping hearts and minds. Paintings showing the transmission of culture and education from one generation to the next "enabled him to symbolically construct forms of kinship that were both familiar and yet strange to viewers."[13] To Tanner, the theme of teaching and learning was a touchpoint of common dignity shared by all. We are shaped by those who come before us, by those who invest in us, by those who teach us skills, by those who hand down convictions, and by those who pour love into us when we are young.

Henry wanted to stir something in his viewers by subverting the genres he painted. Marcus Bruce, professor of religious studies at Bates College in Maine, wrote:

> *The Banjo Lesson* is an example of [Tanner's] subversion of genre, as he employed black genre painting to offer a new and different way of seeing African Americans. Tanner's scene undermines the pervasive and racist stereotype of African Americans as a musically inclined people and the belief that banjo playing required little or no skill and replaces them with a representation of two figures engaged in an act of "pedagogical exchange" and transmission that requires both thought and study. But it is precisely in a painting like *The Banjo Lesson* that we can begin to see Tanner teaching his viewers how to see his work. Tanner's canvas "invites" viewers to accept, embrace, and believe in the portrayal before them, even though the surrounding visual culture and practice of their social world contradicts such knowledge, especially with regard to the abilities, skills, and intelligence of African Americans.[14]

Tanner wanted to teach people a new way to see.

When Tanner returned to Paris in 1894, he submitted both *The Bagpipe Lesson* and *The Banjo Lesson* for the Salon in Paris. Both were accepted. Art critic Dewey Mosby noted it was *The Bagpipe Lesson* "with Brittany citizens, that was given a medal, while paintings with a distinctive race influence and character were ignored."[15] Tanner couldn't help but see the irony that an African American's painting depicting the French locals was seen as not having a "distinctive race influence," while the work depicting people who were the same race as the painter did.

The Salon's response to *The Bagpipe Player* and *The Banjo Player* took Henry Tanner to a creative crossroads. As a Black painter, what kind of influence did he want to have on this world? What path would best serve other aspiring Black artists in the west? Should he work to become a recognized Black painter known for African American genre paintings? Or should he aspire to become a globally recognized painter celebrated as one of the world's finest living artists? And could he do that if he focused on African American genre paintings? Though race would always play an important role in Tanner's art, in order to expand people's view of race, he didn't want to become a niche artist focused only on race. He wanted to develop his skills in the tradition of the European masters. For this reason, he never returned to African American genre paintings.

As a man of faith, Henry believed persuading one race to regard another with equity and love was a theological endeavor, one which required a biblical view of personhood—that all people are made in the image of God and therefore share an inherent dignity and worth that transcends any human construct. With his recent successes in Paris and the United States, he was gaining some notoriety. How could he leverage his growing popularity to give voice to his principles in a way that stayed true to his convictions and was also commercially appealing? He would

offer "a powerful but now neglected alternative to racial thinking by envisioning Christ as the universal figure of humanity."[16]
He would paint Scripture.

Beyond Imagination

Tanner's shift away from French and African American genre
paintings to biblical themes was shrewd. He made this move
at a time when religious art was trending in both Europe and
America. He found a subject matter that was not only popular but
also an integral part of who he was as a man. He said, "It is not by
accident that I have chosen to be a religious painter . . . I have no
doubt an inheritance of religious feeling, and for this I am glad,
but I also have a decided and I hope an intelligent religious faith
not due to inheritance but to my own convictions."[17]

Tanner continued his pedagogical themes in his religious
paintings, which include *The Annunciation, Nicodemus, The
Pilgrims of Emmaus*, and the moving *Christ Learning to Read*,
in which a young Jesus sits with his mother Mary as they study
Scripture from a scroll. Tanner recognized that his artistic gift
was a powerful evangelistic tool. He said, "I rejoice in my ability
to give blessings to others . . . I invited the Christ spirit to manifest in me."[18] Henry wanted to invite people to see something
new in those familiar stories, to reconsider something they previously thought, and, most importantly, to have an encounter with
Scripture that moved them to a deeper faith.

Tanner's first religious painting was the now lost *Daniel in
the Lions' Den*—perhaps a harking back to his earlier attempt at
the myth of Androcles. The canvas won honorable mention at the
1896 Salon in Paris. With the Salon's official recognition, museums began to take interest in his work. The art world wanted to
hear what he had to say.

Tanner spent the summer and fall of that year painting one of his masterpieces, *The Raising of Lazarus*. He wanted to capture the humanity and intimacy of the moment when Lazarus was brought from death to life. In the painting, Jesus and a crowd are gathered inside Lazarus's cave tomb—an artistic departure from the biblical text[19] in order to take the viewer more fully into Lazarus's death. Graveclothes lay unfolded across the expanse of the floor. On Jesus' right, the introverted Mary holds her head in grief. On his left, the extroverted Martha exchanges words with her Lord and friend. Lazarus sits up as a neighbor cradles the head of this man who was once dead but now is alive, still waking and unaware of what was happening.

Rodman Wanamaker, the son of John Wanamaker who had purchased *The Bagpipe Lesson*, had a private viewing of *The Raising of Lazarus* in late 1896. He was fascinated and perplexed by what he saw. Tanner's *Lazarus* bore an uncommon sense of realism. Wanamaker said, "There is Orientalism in the 'Lazarus,' but it was a fortunate accident."[20] Tanner had captured a true sense of the Holy Land without ever having been there. The authenticity of the appearance of the people and the non-European look of the scene made Wanamaker wonder how much greater Tanner's biblical work could become if he had firsthand knowledge of Israel. Tanner said Wanamaker "thought a glimpse of the Holy Land would be beneficial, and thus it happened that in February, 1897, I saw for the first time Egypt and Palestine."[21] Wanamaker financed his trip to Cairo, Jerusalem, Port Said, Jaffa, Jericho, the Dead Sea, and Alexandria so Tanner could familiarize himself with the topography, architecture, dress, light, and customs of the biblical lands and people.

Tanner said, "Palestine always impressed me as the background for a great tragedy."[22] The stories originating from the pages of Scripture echoed the brokenness and struggle he knew as a Black man in America. The Bible is filled with stories of racial division, of people who esteem themselves as more noble than neighbors they've reduced in their minds to godless caricatures.[23] It is the story of the God of the universe telling his people to commit themselves to the well-being of the sojourner, the poor, the orphan, and the widow—descriptions of every slave to set foot on American soil—and God's people struggling to find the humility to live out that holy calling.[24]

If only people could look beyond their imagined impressions of others, if only we could see each other as we really are and not as exaggerated stereotypes, if only a genuine curiosity about the lives of others formed our pursuit to know them, then so many of the forces that divide us would be emptied of their power. We would see the common human experiences of joy and sorrow, love and loss, struggle and victory in those around us, and we would count it all sacred. Understanding would replace ignorance. Respect would overcome resistance.

Tanner didn't just want people to see the Black families in his community; as an artist and a Christian, he wanted to show them Black families as they really were. He wanted to replace the blunt resignation of prejudice with the humble power of curiosity. This is what Tanner hoped to give the world through *The Banjo Lesson* and *The Thankful Poor.*

As a painter of biblical scenes, Tanner didn't just want people to see Scripture; he wanted to show it to them. This is what artists do. He wanted to guide his viewers' eyes through familiar narratives to curate the story, to make connections, to tell it true. Seeing the Holy Land in person enabled Tanner to move beyond imagination to firsthand familiarity. He went not as a tourist but as a student. He was a disciple of the Christ who lived, died, and was raised to life there. It was where the most significant event in history—the resurrection of Jesus—shaped the direction of his life and secured his eternal destiny.

Henry Tanner wanted to "preach with his brush."[25] He believed painters should "convey to your public the relevance and elevation these subjects impart to you, which is the primary cause of their choice."[26] In other words, he wanted Scripture to stir the souls of others in the way it stirred his. He said, "My effort has been to not only put the Biblical incident in the original setting, but at the same time give the human touch 'which makes the whole kin' and which ever remains the same."[27] Showing people biblical truth would be the way he would push back against prejudice. This would be how he would proclaim the gospel.

While Tanner was in Israel, *The Raising of Lazarus* was submitted to the 1897 Salon in Paris, where it won a third-class medal. The medal was a high honor in itself, but upon winning, the French government asked to purchase the work for the Luxembourg Gallery—the country's official repository for contemporary art. Tanner didn't hear about the painting's win or France's desire to purchase it until he was on his way back to Paris. En route, he received an urgent telegram from a friend that read, "Come home, Tanner, to see the crowds before your picture."[28] Henry said, "That I should be asked to sell it to the Government, when I had no definite knowledge whether it had been even received (though I had tried to find out) was a great surprise, the greatest of my life."[29]

The Raising of Lazarus amazed critics, who likened it to a Rembrandt and called Tanner "Rembrandt's unforeseen disciple."[30] A newspaper in London described the picture as "small in size, but full of a rich Rembrandt quality, well worthy of development."[31] A newspaper in the United States said the scene "has often been painted before, from Rembrandt's time to ours, but never with more force or originality."[32] Tanner's work carried the same kind of intimate familiarity with biblical subject matter as the Dutch Renaissance master. Tanner relished the comparisons, saying, "Rembrandt, yes. Now there was a true portrayer of man."[33]

With the wind of the celebrity of *Lazarus* in his sails and stacks of journals filled with sketches and notes from his travels around the Near East at hand, Tanner began working on his next biblical scene, *The Annunciation.*

The Annunciation

Henry Tanner's *Annunciation* takes us into Mary's bedroom—a domestic setting common in his work. The arched columns, shelves, and stone tile floor were specific to what he had seen in the Holy Land. The tapestries and rugs were items he had brought back with him. The scene is authentic yet accessible. It is also familiar yet intimate, to the point that the viewer might wonder if our access to what happened there borders on indiscretion.

Marcus Bruce wrote, "Tanner's interpretation of the moment of conception, and perhaps revelation, serves as an example of how he used religious subjects to offer viewers another perspective from which to see themselves and their experiences: extraordinary events take place in the most unlikely places and among the most unlikely people."[34]

Mary was an ordinary girl when she was betrothed to a craftsman named Joseph. They lived in Nazareth. They were simple, honest people, working toward becoming a family. But all this was interrupted in a moment when the angel of the Lord appeared to Mary and told her something that would alter the course of history.

The angel said to Mary, "Greetings, you who are highly favored! The Lord is with you."[35]

Mary belonged to a people familiar with the word of God. She grew up under its teachings about Abraham, Isaac, Jacob, Joseph, Moses, David, and the prophetic foretelling of God's promised Messiah—the one sent from God who would deliver his people from suffering and sin. Everyone wondered what the Messiah's coming would lead to. Would the Lord's salvation come in a radiant rage of angelic fury? Would deliverance look like a mighty army rolling over Rome with a blazing warrior-king leading the charge? For generations the people tried to imagine it.

Then one night Gabriel, the angel who guided Daniel,[36] appeared to Mary, "an engaged virgin, signifying both purity and preparedness."[37] It must have been strange to hear this seraph dressed in light, strong and otherworldly, tell her not to be afraid. Perhaps it was even stranger for Mary to discover that God had formed an impression of her.

The Lord knew Mary. He knew the hope she scooped up like treasures and stored away in her heart.[38] Gabriel hadn't appeared merely to tell her that the Messiah was coming. He was telling her that she would be his mother. Mary was not the first person in history to receive an angelic annunciation about a coming miracle birth; it happened with Isaac's mother, Sarah;[39] the mother of Samson;[40] and Zechariah, the father of John the Baptist.[41] But Mary was the only one to be told she would bear the Christ who would rescue his people from their sins. God had already chosen his name: Jesus, which meant "the Lord is salvation." Gabriel wasn't just telling Mary that God was aware of human affairs, but that he was personally involved in them. Mary's son would come into the world with the task to redeem it.

The message of the angel did not come without consequence for Mary and Joseph. It would lead them to live as fugitives for a time, fleeing from the paranoia of a ruthless Roman ruler.[42] And as she began to show, they would have to endure the suspicious looks of friends and relatives who couldn't help questioning her purity and his character. Eventually, as an old cleric named Simeon would later predict, the anguish accompanying the consequences of this angel's news would be like a sword that would pierce through Mary's very soul.[43] All this was coming.

The angel continued with his message. Mary's boy would grow to reign over the people of God as their Savior and King.

The God who promised David so many years before that his royal line would see no end[44] would keep that ancient covenant by bringing an heir to Israel's throne through this young woman. "But how can this be, since I'm still a virgin?" she asked.[45] For her to bear this son, she must conceive. And how can a virgin conceive?

The angel explained that the laws of nature are amendable by the One who wrote them. The Holy Spirit would overshadow her, and when he pulled that shadow back, this virgin would become the mother to her Lord. *How* this would happen was incidental to the fact that it *would*. And God would be the one to do it.

The angel gave Mary a sign to help her believe. Mary's elderly cousin Elizabeth, who had been barren her entire life, was only months away from having a miracle baby of her own. "Visit her and see," Gabriel told her. This was a sign that she might understand that nothing was impossible with God.[46]

Mary responded to such an unexpected, improbable, and upsetting announcement with a profound answer of her own: "I am the servant of the Lord; let it be to me according to your word."[47]

Isaiah says Christ's coming is the story of a people walking in darkness who see a great light.[48] Darkness and light run throughout the narrative. The heavenly host appears to the shepherds watching their flocks by night.[49] The learned men from the east come following the light of a star.[50] The angel appears to Joseph in a dream. Throughout the nativity, "the light shines in the darkness, and the darkness has not overcome it."[51]

Tanner uses light and dark to subvert traditional approaches to this scene, depicting Gabriel not as the winged angel common to most artists' renderings, but as a brilliant burst of light. The genius of his tactic is that he presents one of the most majestic and terrifying portrayals of an angelic visit imaginable—an intense source of light and power, which is much more frightening than musculature—and yet manages to keep the fearsome seraph from being our focus. Rather, Gabriel's presence illuminates the room. By him we see the woman—her youth, her questioning face, her modesty, the remaining traces of the fog of sleep in her posture and expression. She has gathered her robe around her almost as though it were for protection. Her posture conveys her vulnerability. Her face reveals her uncertainty.

The art historian James Romaine noted that Tanner's composition displays two interconnected aspirations. First, he wanted "to visualize biblical subjects with an artistic integrity and spiritual accessibility that would revitalize sacred art for the modern viewer. Tanner's second purpose was to visualize the power of faith by depicting individuals, such as the virgin Mary, in moments of spiritual transformation."[52]

Transformation was his hope, so he focused not on the divinity of the moment, but on the humanity of it. He wondered what that transforming encounter must have been like for Mary—the moment when the virgin learned that she would bear the Son of God who would take away the sins of the world. Then he tried to show it to us. He wanted us to see how the Lord "looked on the humble estate of his servant," and how "from now on all generations will call [her] blessed; for he who is mighty has done great things for [her], and holy is his name. And his mercy is for those who fear him from generation to generation. He has shown strength with his arm; he has scattered the proud in the thoughts of their hearts; he has brought down the mighty from their thrones and exalted those of humble estate."[53]

The Tree in Fairmont Park

Tanner unveiled *The Annunciation* at the 1898 Salon in Paris. The following year, the Philadelphia Museum of Art bought it, making it his first work to find a home in an American museum. Since then, dozens of his works have found homes in museums around the world. Through a methodical habit of refining his skill and traveling abroad to sharpen his clarity, Tanner became a veteran.

In 1899 he married a woman from San Francisco—Jessie Macauley, an American actress of Scandinavian descent. In Paris, interracial marriage was uncommon and presented some social struggles for them to overcome, but Jessie's American friends were scandalized by their union. Interracial marriage wasn't fully legalized throughout the United States until 1967. But by that time, Henry was so immersed in the art community in Paris that he considered himself an expatriate with no plan to ever move back to America.

Henry and Jessie had a son, Jesse. Tanner's wife and son would pose for him, appearing in *Christ Learning to Read*, among many other works. Henry's artistic vision continued to develop. During the early 1900s, his style matured and became more focused. He tried to capture precise, intimate moments in his biblical scenes, experiences that would move the viewer—like *Jesus and Nicodemus*, in which the divinity of Christ is depicted as a glow emanating from the Lord's chest. In 1909, the National Academy of Design made Henry Tanner an associate member, along with the Impressionist painter Mary Cassatt.

The First World War had a traumatic effect on Tanner, leaving him often unable to work. The sacrifices endured by so many in his community paralyzed him creatively. In 1914, he wrote to a patron, "Soon you can work say some of my friends—but how can I? What right have I to do, what right to be comfortable? . . . This waiting . . . waiting, waiting, with less light each day until despair puts out all light of life—and this is why I cannot work."[54]

In 1917, the United States entered the war. Tanner offered his services at the age of fifty-eight, founding the Red Cross chapter that employed wounded and recovering soldiers to raise vegetables in hospital gardens.

In 1923, France bestowed on Tanner their highest distinction —Chevalier of the Legion of Honour. Two years after that, Jessie died, and Henry suffered serious financial loss in the Great Depression. His later years were a struggle. But he kept painting. His work was always evolving, as was his technique.

In 1927, the National Academy of Design promoted him to full membership.

In 1937, he died in his home in a village outside of Paris. He was buried beside his wife.

What sets an artist on their course? What so captures the imagination that a person would follow the path to a life of creative expression?

Picture Henry Tanner as a nine-year-old boy in Fairmont Park in Philadelphia, Pennsylvania.

There a man stands before his canvas. He is painting a picture of a tree. Young Henry comes along with his father, and when he sees the painter at work, he stops, hypnotized by the transformation of the painter's canvas.

When young Henry Tanner happened upon that painter in Fairmont Park, he had no idea where the encounter would take him. He, his father, and everyone else who walked through the park that day saw the same tree. Still, though he could see the actual tree as plainly as anyone else who happened by it, something he could not express but felt in the core of his being overcame him when he saw the painter at work.

For Henry, this encounter was a kind of annunciation. He decided then and there that he wanted to become an artist. That night, he begged his parents for money, and with the 15 cents they gave him, he purchased his first set of paints and brushes. He said, "It was this simple event that, as it were, set me on fire . . . From this time forward, I was all aglow with enthusiasm, working spare times between school hours, and it soon became the talk of school—naturally helped on by my boasting—that I was going to be an artist."[55]

And he did. Tanner became a celebrated and iconic artist in France and in the United States. His work is on display in the White House, The Louvre, The Met, and countless other repositories of the world's finest art. He had a profound influence on turn-of-the-century painters in Europe, as well as African American painters ever since.

My Confession

I discovered Henry Ossawa Tanner because I was looking for Black artists. For the most part, I am a self-taught student of art. My own fascination and curiosity have guided my lifelong quest to discover and appreciate art.

A while back, I began an online series called Art Wednesday in which I devoted my Wednesday social media feeds to sharing a series of paintings or works from a particular artist or based on a common theme. Most of the early collections I posted were of works created by White artists. I wanted to remedy that, but at the time, I didn't have much familiarity with artists of color. So I began to search, and that's how I found Tanner.

The first painting I saw was *The Thankful Poor*, followed by *The Banjo Lesson*. A surge of excitement came over me when I suspected I had discovered a Black painter who painted moving and dignified scenes of Black subjects. I was eager to discover his other works along those lines.

I confess that I was disappointed to learn he had only painted two Black genre paintings. Maybe as you read this chapter, you felt a similar feeling sneak up on you. What is that about? Why did I feel let down when I realized Henry Tanner didn't devote his career to giving the world more of his excellent Black genre paintings?

My primary vocation is ministry. I am a pastor who teaches the Bible. I discovered in Henry Tanner a painter who created some of the most moving biblical genre paintings I have ever seen, yet I felt myself wishing he had chosen other subjects— specifically Black subjects. Why?

I wrestle with this question in my own heart. The tension I feel, and what I've tried to capture in telling his story, is that the reason Tanner stopped painting Black genre paintings and switched to biblical genre scenes was, in fact, largely the result of the realities of racial prejudice. Had he continued to paint the African American genre, he would have been known only as a Black painter painting Black people and would not have been taken seriously on a global scale.

When I first discovered him, a part of me wanted him to be just that: a Black painter painting Black people. When I later decided to write a chapter about him for this book, I knew I did not want to present an easy narrative. I wanted to tell the story of a man for whom many of the major decisions he had to make as a professional artist were influenced by racial considerations— from his subject matter to where he made his home.

My intent with this chapter is to tell a complicated story. Tanner is one of my all-time favorite painters. I own more reproductions of Tanner's work than any other artist. His story is complicated, frustrating, and sad—one that challenges us to examine our own presumptions and expectations. I want to bring you into some of the unmet expectations I felt when I discovered Henry Tanner. I want to confess that expecting him to be a Black artist painting Black people made me complicit in the same stereotyping he worked his whole life to overcome. The fact that, instead, he offers scenes from the Scriptures I've given my life to teaching adds a convicting measure of irony and rebuke I have had to sit with, own, and work through.

I want you to love Henry Tanner as much as I do. I want you

to add him to your personal collection, along with every other artist mentioned in these pages. But I also want this chapter to frustrate any attempt to see his story as an easy one. Every Black artist's story includes certain and immense sacrifices most European and White American artists never had to consider. To truly know about Henry Tanner is to understand what he had to navigate, sacrifice, and choose because of his race. Anything less would risk turning him into a token.

CHAPTER 9

WHAT REMAINS UNSAID

Edward Hopper, Loneliness, and Our Longing for Connection

Edward Hopper, *New York Movie*, 1939, oil on canvas,
81.9 × 101.9 cm, Museum of Modern Art, New York City
Asar Studios / Alamy Stock Photo
© 2022 Heirs of Josephine N. Hopper / Licensed by Artists Rights Society (ARS), NY

> Great art is the outward expression of an
> inner life in the artist . . . The inner life of a
> human being is a vast and varied realm.
>
> **Edward Hopper**

Everyone has a story. And no one has a simple story.

A young usherette in a blue uniform leans against a wall, waiting, as her role requires. She is there to serve. On the other side of the little alcove where she stands, moviegoers sit in their plush red velvet seats as a story projects onto a screen in front of them. This is what they've come for. They are participating in a ritual as old as civilized society: gathering as a community to immerse themselves in the drama, comedy, and adventure of the human experience. The theater's purpose is to facilitate the shared experience of taking in the work of remembering who we are. They've made an evening of it.

A thick vertical partition separates the moviegoers from the usherette. They are all in the same room, but the reasons why they're there separate them more than the dark line on the canvas between them. The audience has come for entertainment; she has come to work. They wear nice clothes chosen for a night on the town; she wears a company uniform. They sit in the dark; she stands in the light. They are together, taking in a story written by someone else; she is alone with her own thoughts. They are unaware of her presence; she wouldn't be there if not for them.

When the movie ends and the house lights come on, she will escort them from the room and sweep up what they've left behind. This is her role. And this is also a metaphor for Edward Hopper's marriage.

Hopper's *New York Movie* hangs in a prominent location on the fifth floor of the Museum of Modern Art in New York City, next to Andrew Wyeth's *Christina's World* and down the hall from Vincent van Gogh's *The Starry Night*. Why is a painting of an usher waiting for a movie to end held in such high regard and kept in such elite company? Because, as Pulitzer Prize–winning author Mark Strand said, "we look *into* instead of *at* the painting." And in so doing, "our sympathy with the inward-looking usherette might be explained."[1]

This canvas gives us the unfolding drama of a life being lived in real time. There is nothing heroic about the scene. All we know is that she works at the theater—not as the star gracing the screen, but as the usherette preserving the order of the night, escorting people to their seats, and cleaning up after they've gone. We don't know her name. We don't know her hopes, dreams, fears, or loves. We don't know who she goes home to at night, if anyone. We don't know what's on her mind.

We do know, however, who Hopper used as his model for the young woman: his wife, Josephine Nivison Hopper. And we know some of her hopes, dreams, fears, and loves. We know that, just like the usherette, waiting was part of her work too. We know she knew what it was like to be left alone with her thoughts. We know who she lived with.

Ed and Jo

Edward Hopper met Josephine Nivison in art school in New York in the early 1900s, but it would be twenty years before they came together. Josephine was in her early twenties when she started studying under the painter Robert Henri. During this time, she became a schoolteacher in New York City, but she stayed in contact with Henri and in 1907 traveled to Europe to study art in Paris, Holland, and Italy with her teacher and some of his other students. After this, she joined an acting company in New York. Jo loved the theater—the creative collaboration, the energy of performing, the magic of the shared experience between cast and audience. Jo was a force, endlessly fascinated by and immersed in the creative process.

After a brief stint working in a hospital overseas during World War I, Jo returned home in 1918 and dug into teaching and making art.[2] She was a wonderful artist and soon became a fixture in New York's art community. She was mentioned alongside iconic names like Georgia O'Keefe and John Singer Sargent. She sold drawings to the *New York Tribune*, the *Evening Post*, and the *Chicago Herald-Examiner*. She showed oil paintings and watercolors alongside Man Ray, Modigliani, Picasso, and Magritte. She was an artist on the rise.

Edward, on the other hand, struggled. In the formative years of his twenties and thirties, he did not have a clear vision of who he was creatively. Though he made a living illustrating ad copy, he couldn't sell his own work. He was the kind of artist who lived in the privacy of his own mind and preferred it that way. Consider *Room in Brooklyn*. We stand behind a woman sitting in front of an upper-floor window. A vase of flowers basks in the sunlight. Her head is tilted down and to the left, a position that suggests by the angles, ever so subtly, that she is not looking out the windows, but is perhaps reading, or lost in thought. The fact that she is not the focal point of the room and that she is preoccupied, doing something we can't quite make out, leaves the viewer feeling we shouldn't be there and ought not linger long—as though we've walked in on her. And yet what she is doing is universally common to us all: she is living in the confines of her mind. This was Edward.

Hopper was prone to creative winters. He wrote, "It's hard

for me to decide what I want to paint. I go for months without finding it sometimes. It comes slowly."[3] One of his friends, fellow illustrator Walter Tittle, said he saw Edward struggle "from long periods of unconquerable inertia, sitting for days at a time before his easel in helpless unhappiness, unable to raise a hand to break the spell."[4]

To combat being blocked, Edward traveled and sought the creative inspiration of artist colonies around New England. It was at one of these colonies in Massachusetts in 1923 that Edward and Jo reconnected. Jo fell for Edward, describing him as a shy boy with good dancing legs. Edward would rise early and wait outside Jo's boarding house, pitching stones at her window to wake her, and the two of them would steal away into the forest to spend the mornings together drawing.

Jo thought the world of Edward's art. Though it had been a decade since Edward last sold one of his oils, Jo believed in his talent. Maybe all he needed was to shake things up a bit, so she encouraged him to try his hand at watercolor, a medium he had previously dismissed as only good for commercial work. But he took it up as a form of fine art, and when he did, something clicked. Soon he, too, began to catch the eye of the artistic community in New York. When Jo was invited that year to show some of her watercolors at the Brooklyn Museum as part of a group exhibition, she lobbied the museum to include some of Edward's watercolors too. The museum agreed to show six of his paintings, and after the show ended, they purchased one, *Mansard Roof,* for 100 dollars and added it to their permanent collection.

This was no sympathy purchase. Critics found him fascinating and began to fawn over his work, comparing him to Winslow Homer. One exclaimed, "What vitality, force, and directness! Observe what can be done with the homeliest subject."[5] Soon after selling *Mansard Roof,* the Brooklyn Museum invited Edward back for his first solo exhibit, during which he sold every piece he showed. After this, Edward left his life as an illustrator and began painting full-time, with the adoration of the critics in full bloom.

Jo's generosity in leveraging her reputation for Edward's sake was enough to cause others to see in him what she so admired—a vision she described as "a steady stare into uncertainty, a long dialog on what forever remains unsaid."[6]

Ed and Jo married the following year, in 1924. They were both forty-one.

The Elsewhere, the Missing, the Longed-For

Edward Hopper was born in 1882 in Nyack, New York, the second of two boys in a well-to-do family. Edward's great-grandfather was a Baptist minister, and his parents were churchgoers. In Sunday school, young Edward was raised to value decorum, prudence, frugality, and delayed gratification, which shaped his lifelong introversion.[7] Though he later rejected his Baptist upbringing and came to feel little beyond disdain for religion, those conservative principles he learned in the church when he was young—modesty and the denial of pleasure—remained with him over the course of his life.[8]

He was a good student with an aptitude for art. In his late teens, he enrolled in the New York School of Art and Design, where he stayed for six years, studying oil painting technique. There, like Jo, he studied under Robert Henri, who told his students, "It isn't the subject that counts but what you feel about it . . . Forget about art and paint pictures of what interests you in life."[9] Hopper buried this counsel like a seed that would germinate years later when he hit his artistic stride.

In keeping with his reclusive personality, Hopper didn't like to talk much about his art. When asked what he was trying to say, he would respond, "The whole answer is there on the canvas."[10] Concerning his compositional choices, in a letter to Charles

Sawyer, the director of the Addison Gallery of American Art, Hopper wrote, "Why I select certain subjects rather than others, I do not exactly know, unless it is that I believe them to be the best mediums for a synthesis of my inner experience."[11] Following his former teacher's advice, he was much more concerned about rendering a feeling than a subject.

Hopper did not paint on location but rather in his studio from a combination of memory, sketches, and imagination. One curious product of this approach is his application of light. Mark Strand wrote that Hopper's light is "peculiar": "it does not seem to fill the air. Instead, it seems to adhere to walls and objects, almost as if it comes from them, emanating from their carefully conceived and distributed tones . . . In Hopper's paintings, light is not applied to shape; rather, his paintings are built from the shapes that light assumes."[12] This adherence of light, which gives his work what John Updike described as "an ominous mortuary stillness,"[13] all but eliminates the drama that painters like van Gogh and Rembrandt captured through their exaggerated use of illumination. Hopper's work reflected his personality— subdued, understated, lonesome, and discreet.

Hopper's art is devoid of sentimentality. He does not capture his own era with nostalgia, nor does he seem to be making some grand statement about the world, or to it. Adrian Searle said, "There are few adverbs or adjectives, and he painted the world in simple declarative terms."[14] Hopper's compositions are generally sparse, as though his rooms have been carefully emptied and staged to only include what is absolutely necessary. Updike said Hopper "excels in making us aware of the elsewhere, the missing, the longed-for."[15]

There is nothing particularly skillful about the way Edward Hopper renders human beings. His subjects are often solitary people in impersonal places doing nothing of note—looking out a window, gazing into a half-finished cup of coffee, or sitting on the edge of a bed, thinking. His characters are at the same time the spectators of the ordinary and the subjects of our voyeurism. They don't know we're watching, which is why we find them in varying degrees of dignity and dress.

Hopper began his career as an artist in the early years of the transportation boom, as cities built public transit systems and automobiles became standard. With the number of car owners tripling every decade in the early 1900s came the infrastructure needed to support them: roads, gas stations, highways, and hotels. This advent of mobility was unprecedented. For the first time in history, a person could leave on a Friday to explore the world and still be home in time to make it to work the following Monday. People were free to roam, and roam they did.

The Hoppers loved to travel, and he focused much of his work on its infrastructure. Many of his locations were places people went to but did not live in: a movie theater, a front porch, a diner, an automat, an office at night, and a hotel lobby. Everyone is moving. No one is settled. Each person carries inside them a world of preoccupation, concern, and loyalties, but seldom do we see these things on display. If, as Hopper said, great art displays the vast and varied inner life of the artist, what he shows us about himself is a profound sense of distance from the world.

Hopper used trains to put this sense of isolation on display. He grew up near a railyard and loved trains. However, most of his railway paintings do not focus on the trains themselves but on what happens in them and around them. In *Compartment C, Car 293*, Hopper takes us inside the train, but the car's interior only serves to show the isolating experience of travel—a woman reading a book, alone. In *Chair Car*, four people sit in a compartment. No one interacts. None of them seem to be traveling together. They read or stare off. The shafts of light draw a line on the floor between the people on the right and the people on the left. No one looks out the window at the world passing by, and Hopper offers us, the viewer, no sense of what there might be to see anyway. Because it is unimportant to his subjects, it is withheld from us.

There's a certain loneliness in Hopper's work, but it's a complicated loneliness. It isn't that his characters are outcasts, destitute and unable to find community. Rather, when we see them, they are often turned inward as the world around them moves about, turned in on itself too. James Peacock said, "In Hopper's works, even a buzzing city doesn't remedy isolation, but heightens it."[16]

We see this sense of isolation in how Hopper could paint New York City so that it looked empty, in how even when he depicted people together, they often had no meaningful interaction with one another and in how access to knowledge of what's specifically happening is withheld from the viewer. Perhaps his most well-known example of all three of these is *Nighthawks*. There, Greenwich Village appears to be utterly empty, except for four people who do not interact with one another. We're at a distance too. From our angle, the diner resembles the bow of a ship, and we stand looking from the pier. There is a separation we cannot traverse. We view the people inside as though they are in a terrarium. There is no door, no point of entry.

None of these details in *Nighthawks* are overt, and yet their presence leaves us with the unsettled sense of disconnection. Mark Strand wrote, "Hopper's paintings are short, isolated moments of figuration that suggest the tone of what will follow just as they carry forward the tone of what preceded them. The tone but not the content. The implication but not the evidence. They are saturated with suggestion."[17]

John Updike said, "The silence and plainness of the best paintings by Edward Hopper repel commentary. What is said is said in a visual language that translates into fussy, strained English."[18] It is the potential of the story, not the absence of one, that draws us to Hopper's work because as human beings, if there's one thing we know instinctively, it's that there *must* be a story. Everything has a story. Everyone has a story. And every story is, in some way, sacred.

C. S. Lewis said it this way:

> There are no *ordinary* people. You have never talked to a mere mortal. Nations, cultures, arts, civilisations—these are mortal, and their life is to ours as the life of a gnat. But it is immortals whom we joke with, work with, marry, snub, and exploit—immortal horrors or everlasting splendours. This does not mean that we are to be perpetually solemn. We must play. But our merriment must be of that kind (and it is, in fact, the merriest kind) which exists between people who have, from the outset, taken each other seriously—no flippancy, no superiority, no presumption.[19]

Though Hopper only offers the suggestion of a narrative, he takes his people seriously. He takes everything seriously.

Even children pick up on this. In a *New York Times* article, Robert Coles, a former English teacher, noticed that out on the playground, his students were "marvelously forceful and vigorous storytellers. But when they were asked to write, they commonly became inarticulate, even fearfully so. 'I can't write,' became their refrain."[20] Coles decided to turn his English class into an informal art seminar and started showing slides of work by Picasso, Pissarro, Remington, Renoir, and Hopper.

Coles wrote, "I noticed that they wanted to connect what they saw to stories, which they constructed as I flashed one Hopper slide after another against the wall. It was almost as if this 20th-century American realist painter . . . somehow addressed these children, prompted in them a desire to respond to his pictures by telling of their various experiences."[21]

Coles's students picked up on the sense that something was off with Hopper's characters. They said his people seemed unhappy, lost, lonely, separated from the world around them—even from those they could reach out and touch. One student said of the man and woman in *Excursion into Philosophy*, "Those people should get out and go take a walk in the country; then they could unwind."[22]

Living with One Woman

"Isn't it nice to have a wife who paints?" Jo asked.

Edward replied, "It stinks."

The Hoppers lived restrained lives. They lived in the same coal-heated third-floor Washington Square apartment in Greenwich Village for the duration of their marriage. They did not have their own bathroom but shared a common one with other tenants on their floor. One room in their apartment was converted into studio space—half of which was Edward's, the other half Jo's. Though they took advantage of the wealth of New York City's dining and entertainment, they were homebodies. For the duration of their marriage, they spent nearly every day together, and often *only* with each other.

When the Hoppers became restless, they would get in their car and drive.[23] They took many trips out west to New Mexico and spent summers in a house in Cape Cod. They were avid moviegoers. Edward didn't just love the movies themselves; he loved the experience of going in to a theater—the formality of the rows of seats all facing the same direction, the gaudiness of the curtains and sconces and brass fixtures, the curve of the architectural arches and balconies, and the audience seated in the darkness.[24] Edward went to the cinema when he was creatively blocked. The theater was a place where he could immerse himself in culture and escape his creative immobility as a pane of flickering light told stories on a screen, engaging his imagination.

Edward's success as a celebrated artist was not meteoric, but the slow, steady culmination of doing the next thing. He practiced fundamentals and refined his technique in oils. Though he developed his craft, as all artists do, he never seemed to abandon where he had come from in an effort to reinvent himself. He said, "In every artist's development the germ of the later work is always found in the earlier. The nucleus around which the artist's intellect builds his work is himself; the central ego, personality, or whatever it may be called, and this changes little from birth to death."[25]

As Edward's star rose, so did his ego—not so much in boasting about himself to others, but in thinking of himself above others. This was especially true when it came to how he related to Jo. He was a particular man who liked having his own world in order. He did not like to share, whether it be food, art supplies, or the spotlight. In the studio in their apartment, he established which space was his and told Jo to stay out.[26] Some of Edward's apparent petulance was a product of the way men related to women in the mid-1900s. Some of it was due to the fact that they were both in their forties when they married—an age when many routines and preferences are already firmly established. But it was also true, which every Hopper biographer will confirm, that Edward could be a mean, cruel man.

Ed and Jo fought a lot—the reclusive artist who lived in his head and the vivacious woman who loved being center stage. He could be cold, selfish, and explosive, but Jo was no wilting flower. She could dish back to Edward the worst he threw at her. Edward said, "Living with one woman is like living with two or three tigers."[27] On their twenty-fifth anniversary, Jo joked that they deserved a medal for distinguished combat for making it that far. Edward responded by designing a family coat of arms featuring a ladle and a rolling pin.

Jo was not a traditional domestic housewife. She hated cooking, so they dined out often. When they did eat at home, Edward preferred canned foods over whatever his wife prepared. Jo hated housework too. Edward made fun of her domestic shortcomings, drawing condescending sketches and leaving them on the kitchen table for her to find—one depicting an upside-down house with Jo standing on top watering a garden, under which were the words, "The house that Jo built." These sketches were never intended for the public. They were messages Edward meant only for her.

Edward captured his frustration with their marriage in another sketch depicting Jo, leaning over him wagging her fingers in his face as he reclines with his head back and hands pressed together, pleading in prayer. Beneath the drawing, he wrote, "He can not choose but hear." But Jo didn't always feel heard. She said, "Sometimes talking to Eddie is just like dropping a stone in a well, except that it doesn't thump when it hits bottom."[28]

Ed and Jo never had children. Instead, Jo took on the role of parenting Edward's career. As his work began to sell, she tracked his sales, clipped newspaper articles, and even gave interviews on his behalf because he didn't want to do them. Over the course of their marriage, she kept diaries detailing Edward's work and creative process. These diaries were to Edward Hopper what Vincent van Gogh's letters were to his brother Theo—an intimate chronicle of the life of a brilliant, yet insufferable artist.

Along with managing his business, she continued to help shape Edward's artistic vision. She talked through his compositional ideas, bought props, and speculated on the backstories of his scenes. *New York Post* columnist Raquel Laneri wrote, "In Hopper's 1930 painting "Tables for Ladies," for instance, she posed as the waitress, bought the costumes, picked out the fruit and food props, and arranged them all."[29] Jo even named some of his characters. "Night Hawk" was the name she gave to the man with the beaklike nose sitting at the counter in *Nighthawks*.

Though she didn't know it in those early years, Jo was gradually stepping into the role she would occupy for the rest of their marriage (and life): support for Edward. He did not reciprocate her support. Laneri wrote, "Edward . . . disparaged Josephine's art, condescendingly calling it a 'pleasant little talent' and telling her nobody liked her work. When he sat as a juror for group exhibitions, he would reject his own wife's submissions, fearing accusations of nepotism (or, perhaps, competition)."[30]

Gaby Wood of *The Guardian* wrote, "Jo repeatedly referred to her husband's paintings as their 'children.' She wrote that one of his canvases, *New York Movie*, was shown to his gallerist and 'greeted like a newborn heir.' She referred to her own paintings as 'poor little stillborn infants,' 'too nice to have been such friendless little Cinderellas.'"[31] Many dismissed Jo's work as an inferior derivative of Edward's masterpieces. Hopper's foremost biographer, Gail Levin, said Jo "was slow to realize the depth of his ingratitude and hostility. Eventually, she managed to place her work in occasional group shows at institutions as important as the Art Institute of Chicago, the Corcoran Gallery of Art in Washington, and the Metropolitan Museum of Art. But by then her identity had shifted: it was no longer as Jo Nivison but as Jo Hopper, Edward's wife, that she received the occasional crumb."[32] Jo said, "There are several things I've been clean pushed out of by his strutting superiority . . . Painting too—I've been crowded out of that too—almost."[33]

Designer Abe Lerner, who knew the Hoppers, said, "They were like many couples who have lived together a long time, emotionally dependent but sniping. He didn't look directly at you when he spoke. He looked stern; I don't think I ever saw him smile. Jo was a very nervous person. I never remember her being relaxed. Edward was nervous under his mask of taciturnity."[34]

Jo was committed to her marriage. She told a friend, "Marriage is difficult, but the thing has to be gone through."[35] Even though Jo's artistic career all but stalled once the two of them were married, she insisted she did not resent Edward. She said, "If there can be room for only one of us, it must undoubtedly be he. I can be glad and grateful for that."[36] Jo was devoted to her husband, and if that meant living in his shadow and putting up with his cruelty, she would endure.

Eddie's World

After Edward died, Josephine entrusted his paintings, along with her entire body of work, to the Whitney Museum in New York—more than three thousand works in total. The Whitney Museum proudly displayed his work and set hers aside. Many assumed the museum simply discarded her art, but in early 2000, two hundred of her paintings were found in the basement. In recent years, galleries and organizations devoted to promoting women in the arts have begun to exhibit Josephine Nivison Hopper's paintings.

Still, Josephine Hopper is best known not as an artist, nor even as Edward's manager, but as the woman in her husband's paintings. She was his model. Scholars differ on whether this was born of her desire to keep him away from other women or his frugal unwillingness to hire them to pose for him when he was married to a trained actress who could do it for free. Out of a likely combination of both, Jo is the woman Edward painted over and over again, from the year they married until the year he died. She is the woman in the sun in *Summertime*. She sits with her hands around the coffee cup in *The Automat*. She is the woman at the counter in *Nighthawks*. She leans into the sunlight in *Cape Cod Morning*. She waits as though ready to leave in *Western Motel*. She dines with a friend in *Chop Suey*. She sits reading on the edge of her bed in *Hotel Room*. She opens a letter in *New York Office*. She plinks a key on her piano in *Room in New York*. She stands in the entryway of a lonesome house in *High Noon*. She travels alone in *Compartment C, Car 293*. She is the usherette waiting in *New York Movie*.

If Edward Hopper's paintings are meant to convey what he felt, as he said they were, and if everything he was trying to say was all there on the canvas, which he said it was, then we know he felt alone and found the world to be an isolating place. It is the most pervasive theme running through his work. And in that world—*his* world—stands Jo, usually looking lonely, almost as if he understood what sort of a world he had created for her as his wife. She epitomizes what Mark Strand said of Edward's characters: "Hopper's people seem to have nothing to do. They are like characters whose parts have deserted them and now, trapped in the space of their waiting, must keep themselves company, with no clear place to go, no future."[37] Jo seemed to understand this when she lamented, "What has become of my world? It's evaporated—I just trudge around in Eddie's."[38]

Loneliness creates a vicious cycle. When it nurses contempt, we end up creating an even greater distance from people. We're angry that we feel so alone, and we focus that anger on those who get close because they're the only ones we can reach. Our anger drives them away, and we feel even more alone, which leads to an even deeper anger. Frederick Buechner wrote, "You do not just live in a world but a world lives in you."[39] When we're caught in this cycle where the world we want—one where we're known and loved and safe and able to grow—stays out of reach, we lash out at those people who try to help us see what's true. We lack the capacity to see beyond our anger and pain, and, as Jesus said, we kill our own prophets.

Jesus' last words to the nation of Israel before going to the cross for them were, "O Jerusalem, Jerusalem, the city that kills the prophets and stones those who are sent to it! How often would I have gathered your children together as a hen gathers her brood under her wings, and you were not willing! See, your house is left to you desolate."[40]

These words to Israel give us a picture of a people living out of their loneliness—which, for them, is a feeling of being left alone by God after he had promised to be with them. They feel they are on their own now, adrift in the world, and have to make the best out of a difficult situation.

Jesus' lament over Israel's unwillingness to receive him is complicated by the fact that these people had good reason to be discouraged. The prior centuries had not been kind to them. They had suffered much. Life in this world was not easy. After they were carried away into exile, they didn't know if they'd ever come home again. So when they did return, rebuilding, reorganizing, and holding on to whatever they could occupied more of their hope than waiting for the Messiah. They were so spiritually, emotionally, and culturally beat-up that Jesus said, "O Jerusalem, you kill your own prophets—that's how unwilling you are to hear from God right now."

There is discord between the world we have and the one we were made for. When Jesus says, "I have longed to gather you under my wings, like a mother hen with her brood," he affectionately affirms Israel's sense of isolation. It's not meant to be this way. God knows the distance they feel, and he doesn't want it either. The great irony here is that the God they believed abandoned them had actually taken on flesh and dwelt among them for the purpose of eliminating this distance forever. He doesn't just see our loneliness; he does something about it.

Loneliness tells us something true. It doesn't grow from an evil root. It comes from a God-given desire buried deep inside us all to know we're not alone. It comes from a hunger for fulfillment, peace, and belonging, and it affirms our desire for love and acceptance. Loneliness awakens in us a passionate protest against isolation.

As much as Hopper's works are an expression of loneliness, they are also a protest against it. Jo's presence is the protest. Though Ed and Jo's relational struggles, the rise of his career at the expense of hers, and their biting repartee are all matters of public record, they shared a deep, inscrutable bond. They navigated their volatile marriage, not as people estranged from each other, but more as people bound to one another—like escapees from a chain gang still shackled together as they try to traverse an unfamiliar wood. And both are wounded.

Columnist Gaby Wood relayed a story that author and art historian Barbara Novak told her about a party she hosted in the 1960s, near the end of the Hoppers' lives:

> Edward and Jo were the first to arrive. They sat down next to each other on a settee, and as the other guests— many of whom were the most successful artists of that new generation—piled in, they thought the Hoppers seemed happy and left them alone. Halfway through the party Novak turned to look at them and saw that a large empty space had been left around the Hoppers' sofa. It was an image straight out of one of his paintings: even in a crowded room, they radiated isolation—together.[41]

It would be easy to romanticize the image of the two of them there in that living room, alone together in a crowd, counterparts to the single entity that was "Ed and Jo." But Jo's part in that story had become a supporting role—a smaller part giving context, tragedy, and curiosity to Ed's turn as the lead. It is such a common story. Somewhere along the way, Ed and Jo had become the bard and the muse of American loneliness.

The Two Comedians

There is an old black-and-white film of Ed and Jo shot the year before he died. They are elderly and frail. He is stooped over. They shuffle out of their Washington Square apartment, down the stairs, and across the street to a bench in the park. They sit. He unfolds a newspaper. He reads the page on the left; she reads the page on the right. They are one.

Without Jo, we would not have Edward Hopper—not as the artist he became. Had she not urged him to try his hand at watercolors when he was creatively blocked, and had she not lobbied the Brooklyn Museum to include his work in an exhibit they invited her to be part of, who knows what would have come of his career.

With Edward's final painting, *The Two Comedians*, he seemed to understand and accept this. The painting depicts Ed and Jo dressed as French clowns, taking a final bow together side by side. The scene pays homage to their long-lived partnership and shared love of the theater. But more than that, it acknowledges that she is no longer the usherette in the wings tending to the order of his life. She is his co-conspirator, his collaborator, his partner.

Gail Levin wrote:

> As Hopper explored his idea [of *The Two Comedians*], he drew the male figure leaping into the air while the other figure clambered up onto a small stage. In another drawing, he imagined the male gracefully handing the female through an exit, with spectators appearing behind a low barrier. In the canvas, he raises both figures up to the solid stage, with its border of artificial woods, where they link hands and prepare to bow, their free hands poised as if about to gesture in deference to each other.[42]

After forty-three years of marriage, Ed and Jo were bowing out. He depicted them as a unit. As equals even. Though in life he often wanted to be left alone, in death he wanted Jo by his side. The French historian and novelist Bernard Chambaz poignantly noted, "So often a painter of absence, here he depicts a presence, but it is the presence of those who are about to disappear."[43]

Edward Hopper died in his Manhattan apartment on May 15, 1967, at the age of eighty-four. Jo was there when it happened. She wrote, "And when the hour struck he was home, here in his big chair in big studio—and took one minute to die. No pain, no sound, and eyes serene and even happy and very beautiful in death, like an El Greco."[44] Hopper's obituary made the front page of the *New York Times*. *Life* magazine said, "Hopper distilled, more masterfully than any other artist of his time, a haunting look and mood of America."[45]

Though Jo's life with Ed was difficult, after he died, she said she felt like an amputee. She said life with Edward was "perfection (of its own snappy kind)," and "what was perfection together is a heart break alone."[46] Josephine Nivison Hopper died ten months later.

On the night of Edward Hopper's death, somewhere in the city, a young usherette in a company uniform reported for work. She waited under a sconce for the third act to wind down and the house lights to come up so she could escort the people from the room and clean up after them. We do not know her name. We don't know her hopes, dreams, fears, or loves. We don't know who she goes home to at night, if anyone. We don't know what's on her mind.

What we do know is that there are millions of her.

MEASURING A LIFE

Lilias Trotter and the Joys and
Sorrows of Sacrificial Obedience

Lilias Trotter, *Prepared as a Bride*,
ca. 1888, watercolor on paper
Used by permission of Lilias Trotter Legacy.

> "Truly, truly, I say to you. Unless a grain of wheat falls into the earth and dies, it remains alone; but if it dies, it bears much fruit. Whoever loves his life loses it, and whoever hates his life in this world will keep it for eternal life."
>
> **John 12:24–25**

Let's go back a few decades to the era just before Edward Hopper. 1888 was the year of Renoir's *The Daughters of Catulle Mendès*, Monet's series of *Haystacks*, Pissarro's *L'île Lacroix, Rouen (The Effect of Fog)*, Degas's *Dancers at The Bar*, and Gauguin's *The Painter of Sunflowers*, which depicted his new housemate, Vincent van Gogh, who that same year painted *The Red Vineyard*. It is hard to overstate the significance of what was happening in the world of art in Europe that year. Impressionism was at its peak, and the artistic conventions that had for so long favored commercial appeal were relaxing to allow artists to explore the reaches of their creative range. It was an exciting time to be an artist, as the eyes of the world were on London and Paris.

On March 6, 1888, a thirty-five-year-old woman named Lilias Trotter, who was just four months younger than Vincent van Gogh, boarded a train that cut through France, where all of these painters were hard at work. When Lilias passed through Arles, only miles from where Vincent lived, on her way to the Port of Marseilles, his painting *The Langlois Bridge at Arles with Women Washing* was underway, still wet on the easel. Both Lilias and Vincent lived in relative obscurity up to that point, but they were both chasing after the same thing: fulfillment of a calling to see and create beautiful things.

Had Lilias chosen a path other than the one she was on, she might well have been making that journey to meet Vincent and perhaps discuss the artist colony he was trying to form that year in the south of France. But the reason she passed him by that day all but guaranteed that their paths would never cross.

We Are Made to Give

From the time she was a child, Lilias Trotter had an aptitude for art. Her family noticed in her an amazing ability to capture on paper what she saw with technical instincts that were inexplicably correct. Hers was a natural talent. She had an innate sense for beauty; she could see it and savor it. When she saw the Alps for the first time as a child, she wept.

Lilias was born in London on July 14, 1853, to Alexander and Isabella Trotter during a time when the world was changing. The mid-1800s saw the establishment of the Penny Post mail system and the invention of the telegraph, making communication easier and more widespread. In the 1840s alone, more than 6,000 miles of railroad track were laid in England, moving the kingdom from horse and stagecoach to rail.[1]

Lilias was born into wealth. Every year, her family toured the continent of Europe. She grew up in a luxurious home, waking most mornings to a servant with a cup of tea. She never opened her own drapes. She had governesses in the home teaching her French and German. Biographer Patricia St. John wrote, "The Alexander Trotter family lived the happy, disciplined life of the Victorian upper classes: godly, serious, kind to the poor from a distance, sheltered from all that was offensive. So Lilias grew, beloved and loving, in the sheltered atmosphere of a stable home surrounded by beauty and culture."[2]

Lily's father, Alexander, was a wealthy stockbroker. He met Isabella after the death of his first wife. Lilias was their first child together, the seventh of nine for her father. Alexander was a large man with an even temperament, principled conviction, and endearing charm. Letters about him "show also that Alexander had a great respect for the dignity of all individuals, regardless of their station or rank in society, and he sought to understand divergent points of view."[3] He was a man of deep faith—expressed in his philanthropic and humanitarian endeavors. He was a devoted father, seeking to instill in his children the same sense of wonder and interest he felt in the world. He encouraged their curiosity and challenged their thinking. Lilias adored her father and thrived under her parents' care.

In 1864, tragedy struck. Alexander fell ill with a sickness he battled until he finally succumbed the following year. Lilias was twelve when her father died. She was devastated. This young woman on the verge of adolescence took on a seriousness of heart—a gravity in the form of an ever-deepening desire to know and follow God. Years later, family members recalled times when they thought Lily was off playing somewhere only to find her kneeling in her room, deep in prayer. Biographer Miriam Rockness wrote, "One can only speculate as to the nature of those prayers in one so new to suffering as well as to the faith. Was there anger? Despair over the loss of her beloved father? Fear of what the future would hold without his strong presence? Or did she simply go to her heavenly Father crying out her need and loneliness, and letting him hold her close to his heart, speaking to her pain with his love?"[4]

What is certain is that Lily developed into a warmhearted person with a gift of love and empathy that seemed to know no bounds. Her sister said, "She simply shed a constant light in and over our home. Through the very hardest life, God brought her soul to blossom."[5] Hardship often softens the heart.

At nineteen, Lilias got involved in the Higher Life movement—a sort of spiritual revival that made its way through Britain in the mid-1800s, attracting both the wealthy and the poor. The movement sought to deepen the Christian life during a time in England when religion was often formal and cold. The movement instilled in people an intimacy and zeal for God.

Through her involvement in the Higher Life movement, Lily came to believe that God's gifts were not meant to be an end in themselves but were intended to prepare followers of Jesus for a life of service to others. She wrote, "We ourselves are saved to save. We are made to give, to let everything go if only we may have more to give. The pebble takes in the rays of light that fall upon it, but the diamond flashes them out again. Every facet is means, not simply for drinking more in, but for giving more out. A flower that stops short of its flowering misses its purpose."[6] When she came to believe that her gifts were not her own, she said the rudder of her life was set for the purposes of God.[7]

Meeting John Ruskin

When Lilias was twenty-three, she and her mother took a trip to Venice. Upon arrival, they discovered that the artist and philosopher John Ruskin, the first Slade Professor of Fine Arts at the University of Oxford,[8] was staying in the same hotel. Ruskin was a true celebrity of the nineteenth century—the leading arbiter of art from the Victorian era. Stephen Wildman, director of the John Ruskin Library at Lancaster University, said Ruskin was regarded as "one of the most famous people in the English-speaking world, which is what he was. Ruskin is enormously important to the history of culture in the nineteenth century. His writing and prose is some of the greatest in the English language."[9] Ruskin wrote about art, literature, architecture, and the natural world, influencing culture makers in Europe and throughout the West. When it came to matters of art, John Ruskin was an authority whose opinion was taken seriously.

As was her habit, Lilias traveled with her sketchbooks and art supplies. Her mother, seeing an opportunity to encourage her daughter, sent Ruskin a note, asking if he might look over a few of her daughter's watercolors and perhaps offer a word or two of analysis. Ruskin recounted the encounter later in a lecture to his students:

> When I was in Venice in 1876 . . . two English ladies, mother and daughter, were staying in the same hotel, the Europa. One day the mother sent me a pretty little note asking if I would look at the young lady's drawings.
>
> On my somewhat sulky permission, a few drawings were sent, in which I perceived extremely right-minded and careful work almost totally without knowledge.[10]

Ruskin was near the heights of his powers as one of the most respected artists and philosophers in the world. He wore the part well—high-minded, brilliant, and impatient. By the time he met Lilias, he had encountered hundreds of aspiring idealists who believed that if they could only get their work in front of him, he would surely recognize their genius. Most of what he saw left him uninspired. But when he saw Lilias's work, it wasn't just her artistic ability, but also the intangible instincts of simplicity, restraint, and integrity that caught his attention. Ruskin saw incredible potential in the young woman. He continued:

> I requested that the young lady might come sketching with me and I took her to the Abbey of San Gregorio; there I set her, for the first time in her life, to draw a little piece of gray marble with the sun on it, rightly. She may have had one lesson after that, or she may have had two or three; but she seemed to learn everything the instant she was shown it—and ever so much more than she was taught.[11]

Ruskin believed he could shape Lilias into one of the world's great artists. Though many coveted Ruskin as a teacher, he coveted Lilias Trotter as a pupil. He pleaded with her to study with him:

> Of all the dainty bits of clay in the hand of the potter that ever were fashioned, I think you have the least grit in you . . . I pause to think how I can convince you of the marvelous gift that is in you. The not seeing or feeling the power that is in you is the most sure and precious sign of it.[12]

No one had ever pursued Lilias for her artistic talent, and suddenly one of the most famous voices in art wanted to train her. She accepted his offer and began to study with him. Initially, they spent a lot of time together. She came and stayed at his home on occasion, where she worked alongside other painters.

Ruskin's esteem for Lilias's work was not contrived. When he saw her watercolor book from a trip to Norway in which she depicted peasant life, he begged her for some of the pages. He framed six of them and used them as examples when he lectured his students in Oxford, saying, "You will in examining them, beyond all telling, feel that they are exactly what we should all like to be able to do, and in the plainest and frankest manner shew us how to do it—more modestly speaking, how, if heaven help us, it can be done."[13]

Ruskin believed "the greatest thing a human soul ever does in this world is to *see* something and tell what it *saw* in a plain way . . . To see clearly is poetry, prophecy, and religion—all in one."[14] He and Lilias shared the ability to look and see what was there and convey to others what they saw.

When Lily looked at the world, she saw suffering. Her heart broke for the destitute women in her city. At that time, the YWCA was just getting started, ministering to the needs of poor women in London, and Lilias got involved. She started working for a hostel that brought the prostitutes of Victoria Station in off the street to give them a place to live while teaching them marketable skills. She also helped start the first restaurant for women only in London. Most restaurants then were for wealthy people. Working women would have to bring food from home and often eat while sitting on the sidewalks. She opened a place that would serve them hot meals and provide shelter—both physical and spiritual.

As she served the women of London, she kept drawing and painting, sending Ruskin her work. He kept speaking into it—noting strengths and offering advice. But over time, their correspondence became less frequent, and he worried he was losing her. Ruskin had established a track record for developing women artists. He had done it many times before Lilias. The way it worked was if he could find someone with natural talent, he would take them under his wing and push them in the direction he wanted them to go, using his insight and experience to form them and set them up for success. But they had to be willing, and they had to be single-minded.[15]

He wrote to her, "All very fine helping the station girls, but what will you think of yourself someday, I wonder, for your neglect and contempt and defiance and tormenting and disappointing and ignoring and abjuring of me?"[16] Lily shared some new paintings with Ruskin, watercolor flowers on brown paper. When he saw them, he lamented, "The sense of color is gradually getting debased under the conditions of your life—the grays and the browns in which you now habitually work. Technically, you are losing yourself . . . There is a real vulgarity in the way you put light things against dark to bring them out."[17]

Ruskin's pursuit of Lilias was not just about her art, but of her singularity of focus. The potential he recognized in her could only come to fruition if she devoted herself wholly to her craft. But he felt Lilias's ministry was competing with her art, and in truth it was. He told Lilias if she would devote herself to art, "she would be the greatest living painter in Europe and do things that would be immortal."[18] He wanted her to choose between her ministry and her art—forcing her to face the crisis of her life: What role would her art play?

She understood what Ruskin was offering her, and it was something she loved. But her attention fell beyond the confines of art. She cared about other people. Lilias wrote to a friend about the decision before her: "I felt I had lived years during those few days."[19] She loved the thought of giving her life to her craft. She wrestled with her decision. She prayed. She took long walks, feeling the weight continuously. She couldn't eat or sleep without prayer.

British novelist and philosopher Iris Murdoch said, "At crucial moments of choice most of the business of choosing is already over."[20] As Lilias prayed about what to do, she remembered a time when she was young. She was in church, about to put her offering into the offering plate. Carved into the middle of the plate was the pierced hand of Christ. Seeing it, she emptied her entire purse into the dish. What else could she do? If the hand of Christ asks for what she possessed, what could she possibly withhold?

Ruskin's insistence that she make a choice felt the same—the hand of Christ asking for her life in response to a world in need. She wrote, "I see clear as daylight now, that I cannot dedicate myself to painting in the way that he means and continue to seek first the kingdom of God and his righteousness."[21] Lilias made up her mind—she would give herself to serving the poor, and in whatever role her art played, she would use her creative instinct and imagination to create places where the downtrodden would find respect, support, and, if God allowed, Christ himself.

Lilias remained friends with John Ruskin and continued to visit him when time allowed. But after she made her decision, she gave herself to service with a renewed zeal. She said, "And a like independence is the characteristic of the new flood of resurrection life that comes to our souls as we learn this fresh lesson of dying . . . the liberty of those who have nothing to lose, because they have nothing to keep. We can do without *anything* while we have God."[22] She felt a burden had been lifted.

Algeria

For the next ten years Lilias ministered in London, integrating her teaching, training, and art to serve the women there. She had a knack for combining image and text to convey a message deeper than either could deliver on its own. But in her early thirties, she felt God was calling her to something deeper—specifically to the people of a faraway land. World missions was a relatively new concept, but when Lilias heard about it, she felt called to the work. When she prayed about God's calling on her life in particular, the words "North Africa" resounded as a voice calling to her. In May 1887, she attended a lecture about missions in Algeria, and the presenter made the comment that "they have a people of whom no knowledge of Christ exists."[23]

Lilias recalled, "In that first sentence God's calling had sounded. If Algeria was so near that I could spend half a year there and the other half at home, then it was for me, and before the morning there remained no shadow of a doubt that it was his plan."[24]

On July 14, 1887, Lilias sent an application to the North African mission board and was rejected due to health reasons. Lilias had a weak heart and would tire easily. The board feared this Victorian woman of means would not be able to endure the harsh conditions of the African Sahara.

Lilias decided to go to Algeria anyway, using her own resources to get there. Seven months later, on March 5, 1888, she left the Waterloo Station with her friend Lisa Lewis, singing

"Crown Him with Many Crowns." At Southampton, they met up with her friend Blanche Hayworth, who would serve alongside her for more than thirty years. Then they passed through France—past van Gogh, Pissarro, Monet, and Degas, all hard at work—and on March 9, the three women, all of whom had been rejected by mission boards, sailed into the Algiers harbor. They didn't know a single person in the country. They didn't know a single sentence of Arabic. They had no church leaders to meet up with. They had no cross-cultural training. Yet they came, asking God to open doors and hearts and to bring forth a harvest.

Lilias was thirty-four when she stepped off the boat. She and her companions' first ministry contact came through ministering to the women and children in the slums of Algiers. They were the first European women many of the Algerian women had ever seen. The place women occupied in that country at that time was not pretty. Many were married off when they were ten to twelve years old, taken into a harem, and then discarded for younger wives once they bore some children and got a little older. These women, many in their early twenties and with their whole lives ahead of them, became destitute.[25] Lilias would gather them and teach them stories from the Bible and help care for their children. She wanted to help these women develop some kind of economic independence so they could live on their own, apart from their fathers' and former husbands' homes. So Lilias provided classes to teach them marketable skills, much like her work with the women of London. In her mind, she wasn't trying to start a movement; she was just trying to respond to a need she saw that was happening right in front of her.

Lilias's aesthetic eye served her well in those early months. She regarded the country and people of Algeria as utterly beautiful. She wrote in her diary, "Oh how good it is that I have been sent here to such beauty."[26] She loved the place. Her journals soon filled with small paintings of people and places, put down for no one's sake but her own. She wanted to capture the beauty of those she had come to serve.

Something Good for Something Better

Lilias and John Ruskin corresponded for the rest of his life, and she even sent him an occasional painting or sketch. Her decision to choose mission work over art wasn't simple, nor was it painless. For the rest of her life, she carried in her heart the ache of not having developed her art. It was the burden many artists, athletes, musicians, and craftspeople come to know when they must set to the side what they once hoped might be their primary calling in order to pursue another path. It is a sacred, lonesome kind of sorrow—always imagining what could have been, always questioning the present, always asking whether the chosen path was the way of wisdom or folly.

Artists are drawn to depicting human suffering and struggle. Caravaggio showed it in *The Sacrifice of Isaac*, in which the God of the universe intervenes for the redemption that humanity so desperately needs but cannot supply for themselves. Michelangelo carved *David* to remind us that nations rise up against each other, often provoked by the bravado and injustice of just a few crucially placed voices in power. Edward Hopper painted *New York Movie* to suggest human suffering is a product of an innate isolation we all share that no amount of community can resolve. Henry O. Tanner created *The Annunciation* to show how the Lord would complete the redemption he promised to Abraham as the patriarch held the knife above his son. Rembrandt gave us *The Storm on the Sea of Galilee*, in which the disciples look into the eyes of the thief that cut him from the frame, pleading in his expression, "Do you feel the world is broken?"[27] Even Isabella Stewart Gardner spoke to it when she built her museum, wanting to give the world something that would never die.

As for Lilias, she responded to the suffering she saw with a ministry of presence. And yet, she bore in her character many qualities that made so many of the artists who came before her so great. Like Michelangelo, she was captured by beauty. She instinctively knew there was such a thing as glory and that we were made for it, to be part of it. Michelangelo and Lilias both sought that glory by trying to make from stone hearts of flesh.[28]

Like Vermeer, she borrowed the light of others who had gone before her to create something new for those who came after. Innovation is a form of art in itself. We learn to see. Part of the artist's job is to see and then take what they see to say something true about the world. Vermeer developed a technique using optics; Lilias used innovative techniques to blaze a new trail for world missions. And just as Vermeer's subjects behaved as though no one was watching, so did Lilias, relatively unseen until recent years when people like Miriam Rockness and Elisabeth Elliot began to study her life and tell her story.

Like Henry O. Tanner, Lilias valued the transmission of a skill from one generation to another as a means of preserving truth. Tanner used his voice to shape people's thinking and respond to the needs of a people he loved. So did Lilias. They both used their art to illustrate light for a people walking in darkness,[29] submitting themselves to the humble process of learning about other people, places, and cultures. Part of learning to see involves the humility to have things shown to us.

Like Vincent, beauty flooded her heart and pushed her forward. Lilias carried in her heart the inconsolable secret that Vincent and so many other artists shared—knowledge that she could spend herself for a future with no guarantees. Vincent responded to this possibility with productivity and despair. Michelangelo turned to anger and pride. Caravaggio set his world on fire and ran from justice. Hopper used cruelty to keep others at a distance. But Lilias chose a different path altogether.

She laid down her life and felt the weight of the cost for the rest of her life.

Lilias's friend Constance Padwick said, "The ache of desire was with her to the end, not so much on the days when she did no drawing, as on the days when she took up her brush to make a cover for an Arabic tract. That when fellow-Christians spoke, with joy, of 'the consecration of her beautiful gift' was she most conscious of the pain of the artist who takes up an unpracticed tool and knows full well to what beauty he might bend it if he could but give to it his strength and life."[30] Her biographer, Miriam Rockness, said, "The pain of which Lily spoke was the inevitable sense of loss any human being experiences when recognizing the toll of giving up something good for something he or she deems better."[31]

And yet on the other side of that sorrow lay her belief that success in God's kingdom comes by losing, not gaining. Quoting the nineteenth-century priest Ugo Bassi, Lilias wrote in her diary, "Measure thy life by loss, not by gain; not by the wine drunk, but by the wine poured forth. For love's strength standeth in love's sacrifice, and he who suffers most has most to give."[32]

Lilias served the Algerian people for forty years. She died in 1928 at the age of seventy-five, after a period of two years confined to her bed. During that time, she kept a map of Algeria taped to the ceiling above where she lay so she could see it and pray for the people she had given her life to serve. As she lay dying, friends gathered around her. One asked what she saw. She said, "I see a chariot with six horses." A friend asked, "Are you seeing beautiful things, Lily?" She said, "Yes, I see many, many beautiful things."[33]

Had Lilias chosen a career as an artist, who knows what she might have produced. And it wouldn't have been a wrong choice if her conscience before God permitted her to give herself to her painting. She could have given the world the gospel she so loved in a different way.

Instead, she chose the desert. She immersed herself in the culture in a way that showed deep respect for those she encountered. She longed to learn their language, so she got to work. She studied and trained every day, establishing a routine that would have vaulted her to the top of the art world, had painting been her focus:[34]

Arabic—9:30–11:00 a.m.
Breakfast—11:30 a.m.
Arabic—12:30–2:00 p.m.
Tea—2:00 p.m.
Visiting—2:30–6:00 p.m.
Dinner—6:30 p.m.
Arabic—7:00–8:00 p.m.

Over time, Lilias and her friends were accepted into the Algerian culture by men and women alike. But Lilias chose a hard road, and she suffered for her choice. She left behind everything that was familiar to live in a French colony that resented the English and a Muslim country that resented Christians. Since she arrived without any official affiliations with the church, she struggled to gain the support of local congregations. She had a weak heart and a frail frame. Some of the people she led to Christ were killed for converting. Others would come to faith but then abandon it when opposition arose. All of this happened while she labored in relative obscurity. But recognition didn't seem to matter. She said, "The results need not end with our earthly days. God may use, by the wonderful solidarity of the church, the things he has wrought in us for the blessings of souls unknown to us."[35] After establishing a mission in Algiers, she and her companions planted a few more stations along the coast before moving into the interior, the Sahara Desert.

Lilias Trotter revolutionized mission work as we know it. She began her ministry before learning the language, using art to paint the gospel in pictures—effectively inventing wordless evangelism. The innovative approach of engaging women and children as a way to build trust among a people, which she pioneered, is used all over the world in missions today. She trained nationals to serve alongside her. The work she began grew to include thirty different missionaries with fifteen stations around the country of Algeria. And her work continues on even still.

Service to the Lord is never wasted, even if people don't see it. God sees it and uses it. This wasn't just Lilias's hope; it was her confidence. She said, "Let us dare to test God's resources. Let us ask him to kindle in us, and to keep aflame that passion for the impossible, that God might make us delight in it with him, because God doesn't find anything impossible. Nor should we. And we delight in it with him until the day we shall see it by his grace transformed into fact."[36]

She saw beauty everywhere. To read her journals and see her sketches and paintings is to see the overflow of a heart enamored with the world she inhabited. Even in the toughest conditions, she marveled at the lilies that grew from the desert floor and saw the kindness and grace of God in every petal. The natural beauty happening around her reminded her that the Lord was at work. The thought that he was working through her filled her heart with joy.

During one particularly difficult time in her work in Algiers, Lilias took her diary into her garden to pray. She wrote, "A bee comforted me very much this morning. He was hovering above some blackberry sprays just touching flowers here and there, yet all unconsciously life, life, life was left behind at every touch."[37]

A WORLD SHORT
ON MASTERS

Rembrandt van Rijn, *Artist in His Studio*, ca. 1628, oil on panel,
9.75 × 12.5 inches, Museum of Fine Arts, Boston

W hat is your craft? What art or skill are you developing? Painting? Writing? Cooking? Raising children? Teaching? Leading a team? Organizing data? You may not develop at the rate you want, and you will certainly always run across others who are better in some way. But don't quit. Lilias Trotter didn't give up art. She may have stepped away from pursuing art as a career, but she didn't step away from art. Give yourself to a craft, even if you only have a little time, even if you sometimes step away from it for a year or two. Don't consider yourself to be someone who *used to do something*. If you've learned guitar but haven't picked one up in a while, don't say you used to play. Say you play. It's been a while, but you do play.

Learn to contribute beauty to this world—modest though your part may be. It's okay to be a slow learner. Just don't bow out of the work of beautifying the gardens you tend. The world benefits from your voice, your touch, your vision.

Rembrandt knew he was a great artist, but he also knew he wasn't limitless. He wrestled with his inability to satisfy what other people wanted him to be, if you can imagine. He said once, "I can't paint the way they want me to paint and they know that too. Of course you will say that I ought to be practical and ought to try and paint the way they want me to paint. Well, I will tell you a secret. I have tried and I have tried very hard, but I can't do it. I just can't do it!"[1] The Dutch master was astonishingly gifted, but when he tried to train his hands to create another person's vision, he just couldn't do it. Neither can I. Neither can you.

For Rembrandt to become who he was, he had to train his hands to paint as he alone was made to paint. But in doing that, he had to learn the fundamentals. He had to practice. This means he must have started somewhere. It's hard to imagine, but there had to have existed some pretty terrible Rembrandts—early charcoal works hung on the wall by his mother. What's not hard to imagine is a solitary figure in a lamp-lit room, mixing his oils, preening his brushes, thinking and painting and thinking and painting.

The mastery of something leads to a greater enjoyment of it. Singers, musicians, painters, writers, athletes, and artists of all stripes know this. The harder we work at something, the more we are able to enjoy it. Rembrandt knew it too. Later he would advise, "Try to put well in practice what you already know; and in so doing, you will, in good time, discover the hidden things which you now inquire about. Practice what you know, and it will help to make clear what now you do not know."[2] Annie Dillard said it another way: "Who will teach me to write? The page, the page, that eternal blankness."[3]

All Rembrandt could do was paint and paint and paint. He couldn't be a different painter. He could only be Rembrandt. And this is what he sought to master: how to be Rembrandt. When I stand before a Rembrandt, every fiber of my being knows I am in the presence of greatness. Sure, we're talking about something human hands have made, but those hands are so distinct, refined, and meaningful that I'm a fool if I don't at least try to understand the joy that comes from mastery. And I'm also a fool if I don't regard myself as his student in those moments when we're in the room together.

A couple hundred years after Rembrandt's death, there came another student of the Dutch master—the poor and lovely Vincent van Gogh—who said, "Rembrandt goes so deep into the mysterious that he says things for which there are no words in any language. It is with justice that they call Rembrandt—*magician*—that's no easy occupation."[4]

Mastery doesn't just produce stories. It considers how to tell them and occasionally even provides new language when there are no words. The canvases Rembrandt left us do so much more than illustrate scenes from the Bible. They are like the picture of the Dawn Treader that sucked the Pevensies and Eustace into an adventure whose goal was to reach the end of everything in the hopes that Aslan would be all that remained.[5]

What are you mastering? What are you practicing in order to make clear what you don't yet know? If you're anything like me, I'm sure you reach points where you begin to wonder if it might just be easier to plateau. And if not plateau, then quit altogether.

Don't. Please. This world is short on masters, and consequently, it's a world short on joy too.

APPENDICES

Giovanni Paolo Panini, *Ancient Rome*, 1757, oil on canvas,
172.1 × 229.9 cm, Metropolitan Museum of Art, New York

HOW TO VISIT AN ART MUSEUM

et's go to the art museum." How do those words make you feel? Many of us might admit to some measure of apprehension. Why is this? Art museums are affordable, if not free (except for the suggested donation), so it's not the money. There's no requirement to spend time with every work of art in the building, so it's not the time investment. And they're often situated in cities or towns filled with history, culture, and lots to explore, so it's not the location either.

What restrains our excitement about a day in a building full of art? May I suggest it is the art itself? The apprehension many of us feel is due to the fact that art is demanding. It hangs on the wall or stands on its pedestal, calling, "Look up here!" A day in an art gallery will wear you out, and you'll wonder how the simple act of looking could be so exhausting. There's nothing simple about really looking at art. If you let it, a great painting will demand as much from you as reading *War and Peace* in one sitting.

Let me tell you how to walk into an art museum like you own the place.

In high school, I had the good fortune of having an art teacher who loved art. She wanted us to love it too, so she introduced us not only to great works of art but, more importantly, to the people who created them. She broke out the old projector and filmstrips so we could tour Frank Lloyd Wright's *Falling Water* from our classroom in Tipton, Indiana. She impressed on us the role of math and dimension by taking us on the trip that is M. C. Escher. She broke our hearts with the sad and beautiful story of Vincent van Gogh by making us watch the wonderful Technicolor Kirk Douglas film from the 1960s, *Lust for Life*, which is based on Irving Stone's book by the same name—a great place to start with van Gogh.

One year, she took us to the Art Institute of Chicago. That was where I learned how exhausting art can be. She turned us loose for the afternoon. I meandered from room to room, and that's when I saw him for the first time: Vincent van Gogh. I'll never forget that moment. His canvases struck me in such a way that I had to sit down and just look. In fact, I spent most of my time in that room that day, just looking at van Gogh. I checked the dates: he painted *this one* in 1887, earlier in his career when he was trying to find a way to be a commercial success, and he painted *that one* in 1890, the same year he painted close to a canvas a day, the same year he shot himself in the abdomen and died. These late paintings, with their thick, vibrant colors looked urgent, desperate.

That day with van Gogh shaped the way I would approach art museums thereafter. I developed a strategy that was simple: Find van Gogh, look long, and if there's any time left, wander around and look at other things.

That's how I found Rembrandt. When I was younger, I looked down on Renaissance art. I didn't get it. I had no idea what went into those paintings. But then I found myself in front of a Rembrandt, and the figure in the painting was looking harder at me than I was at him. It grabbed hold of me and drew me in.

I discovered that Rembrandt's peers regarded him as The Master even while he lived. And I learned he was a man who loved the gospel. That opened up a new wing of the museum for me: Dutch Renaissance. Now I was looking for van Gogh and

Rembrandt. Before long, Rembrandt introduced me to Caravaggio and Vermeer, and van Gogh introduced me to Gauguin, Seurat, and Cézanne.

In more recent years, I've come to think of visual artists like artists in my music library. I have my favorite musicians, and they have a body of work that I return to over and over again. For those I like most, I welcome every new song they release.

I think about the visual artists I love in much the same way. I regard their works like songs. I'm not interested in hits. I'm interested in the body of work. Vincent's *The Starry Night* is great, but I don't love van Gogh because of that canvas. I love that canvas because it came from van Gogh. I love the story he told through that work—the tragic tale of his hope of glory locking horns with his disillusionment toward the church, the only building whose windows are dark and lifeless in *The Starry Night*. You could argue it's as much a painting of a church as it is the glorious sky above it.

I want to see anything Rembrandt etched, drew, or painted. Each new piece is a part of the puzzle of his life and a window into his vision, theology, artistry, and burdens. The same is true with van Gogh. And now, all these years later, the same goes for Rodin, Caravaggio, Chagall, Hopper, Rockwell (as in Norman), Delacroix, and Picasso.

When I go into an art museum now, I have a plan. I know it will wear me out. Art is a lot to take in, and it takes a lot out. So I find my friends. I don't try to reach too far. It's not a race. I have whatever time the Lord has ordained for me to be a lifelong patron of the arts. So I'm taking it slow, returning as often as I can. When I do, all I need is a map and time, and both are free.

See? I own the place.

HOW TO LOOK AT
A WORK OF ART

S o you've managed to get yourself to an art museum. Now what? Developing a love for art is a lifelong venture, and one of life's great and simple joys. The key is not to master all there is to know overnight, but to grow over time. This starts by looking. How do you look at a work of art? Here are some strategies that have helped me.

- **Gravitate toward what you like.** Pay the most attention to works that catch your eye. Saying "I like this one" is one of the purest and most legitimate forms of art criticism. In a museum gallery, stand in the middle of the room, take in the collection as a whole, and go to what moves you. Do the same with art books or online content.
- **Look.** Now that you're in front of something you like, look at it. Give yourself time to examine the piece in its entirety. Let your imagination and intuition form your first impression. If you carry a notebook, jot down a few notes, along with the artist's name and title.
- **Read the plaque.** Do this *after* you've looked, not before. Read what the gallery wall or page provides. Not only will this information help you understand what you're looking at, but it will deepen your overall understanding of art in a cumulative way over time.

- **Think.** As you absorb information, think about what you're seeing and how it connects. What do you think the artist wants you to take away from the piece? What questions does it raise? What does it answer?

- **Grow your vocabulary.** As you read the plaques, take note of words or references that are new to you. Learn what Impressionism is and who the Impressionists were. Build a visual vocabulary too. Often everything you see in a painting was deliberately put there by the artist. Assume everything you see has some meaning or purpose. For examples, dogs, which appear surprisingly often in Renaissance art, represent loyalty. Rabbits symbolize sexual desire. Peacocks symbolize immortality.

- **Notice technique.** An artist's goal is to connect with the viewer. This is often done through technique. Get as close as you safely can and study the brushwork or chisel patterns. Try to get a sense of what it was like to make the piece. This will get you into the mind of the artist and help you understand the process used to create the piece.

- **Follow the visual path.** Great paintings train your eye to look at the composition in a certain sequence. Where does your eye go first? Second? Often when we look at art, our eye follows a path intended by the artist. We look at paintings a bit at a time. We take in bits of information in sequence. Using composition to lead the eye allows the artist to tell a story in a single frame.

- **Read the room.** What are other people looking at? Look for what draws a crowd but also for what draws the focus of a single person. If you see someone really examining a particular work, drift over to see what's the big deal. Maybe even ask the person what has their attention.

- **Allow yourself to dislike things.** Nothing is for everyone. You will see art you love. You will see art you like well enough. You will see art that does nothing for you. And you will see art you dislike. If art draws a visceral response from you, ask why.

- **Spend your life looking at art.** You don't have to become an art expert before you leave the museum. Just keep your eyes open. Pay attention. Follow social media accounts based on artists you like—there are hundreds of them. Over time, you will expand your base of knowledge, and you'll develop a deeper familiarity with art, which will lead to a deeper enjoyment.

OVERVIEW OF WESTERN ART: RENAISSANCE TO MODERN

Renaissance: ca. 1300–1602

Origin: Italy

Description: The rebirth of classical culture. Applied developments in philosophy, literature, music, science, and technology into art. Disciplined, built around linear perspective. Marked the transition of Europe from the medieval period to the early modern period.

Subgenres

- Italian Renaissance: Late thirteenth century to late fifteenth century
- Venetian Renaissance: 1430–1550

Major Artists and Works

- Donatello (1386–1466), *St. John the Evangelist* (1409–1411, sculpture)
- Jan van Eyck (ca. 1390–1441), *Crucifixion and Last Judgement diptych* (ca. 1430–1440)
- Giovanni Bellini (1430–1516), *Christ Blessing* (1500)
- Leonardo da Vinci (1452–1519), *Mona Lisa* (1503–1516)

- Sandro Botticelli (1455–1510), *The Birth of Venus* (1484–1486)
- Michelangelo (1475–1564), *David* (1504, statue)
- Raphael (1483–1520), *Madonna of the Pinks* (1506–07)
- Titian (1488–1576), *The Rape of Europa* (1560–1562)
- Pieter Bruegel the Elder (1525–1569), *The Tower of Babel* (1563)

Mannerism: 1527–1580

Origin: Rome, Italy

Description: Also known as Late Renaissance. Broke many of the rules of classical Renaissance painting, reacting to the proportion, balance, and idealized beauty of the Renaissance masters by exaggerating those values, which resulted in asymmetry and elongated and twisted forms to convey motion and life. Prefers tension over clarity and instability over balance.

Major Artists and Works
- Benvenuto Cellini (1500–1571), *Perseus with the Head of Medusa* (ca. 1545–1554)
- Tintoretto (1518–1594), *Paradise* (1588)
- El Greco (1541–1614), *The Assumption of the Virgin* (1577–1579)

Baroque: 1600–1730

Origin: Rome, Italy

Description: Majesty and flourish focused on divine themes. Leveraged to solidify the base within the Roman Church during the Protestant Reformation. Used movement, detail, deep color, suspense, and heavy contrast between light and dark to achieve a sense of wonder.

Subgenres

- Dutch Golden Age: 1585–1702
- Flemish Baroque: 1585–1700
- Caravaggisti: 1590–1650

Major Artists and Works

- Michelangelo Merisi da Caravaggio (1571–1610), *The Calling of St. Matthew* (1599–1600)
- Peter Paul Rubens (1577–1640), *The Elevation of the Cross* (1610)
- Rembrandt Harmenszoon van Rijn (1606–1669), *The Storm on the Sea of Galilee* (1633)
- Johannes Vermeer (1632–1675), *The Music Lesson* (ca. 1662–1665)

Neoclassicism: 1750–1830

Origin: Rome, Italy

Description: Recapturing Greco-Roman beauty and scope, based on principles of simplicity and symmetry. Reaction against the excesses of previously popular styles. Grand portraiture.

Major Artists and Works

- Jacques-Louis David (1748–1825), *Oath of the Horatii* (1786)
- Jean-Auguste-Dominique Ingres (1780–1867), *The Source* (1856)

Romanticism: 1780–1850

Origin: Florence, Italy

Description: Emphasized emotion and individualism. Celebrated the artist's imagination and originality. Glorified the past and nature in reaction to the Industrial Revolution. Lots of landscape and history paintings.

Subgenres
- Nazarene Movement: ca. 1820–1845
- Purismo: ca. 1820–1860

Major Artists and Works
- Francisco Goya (1746–1828), *The Third of May, 1808* (1814)
- J. M. W. Turner (1775–1851), *The Fighting Temeraire* (1838)
- Eugène Delacroix (1798–1863), *Liberty Leading the People* (1830)

Realism: 1830–1870

Origin: France
Description: Depicted working-class people in everyday situations. Valued presenting scenes accurately, without stylization or commentary. Facilitated by the plein air movement after the invention of the tin tube, when painting moved outdoors.

Major Artists and Works
- Honoré Daumier (1808–1879), *Don Quixote and Sancho Panza* (1868)
- Jean-François Millet (1814–1875), *The Gleaners* (1857)
- Gustave Courbet (1819–1877), *The Desperate Man* (1844–1845)
- Winslow Homer (American, 1836–1910), *The Gulf Stream* (1899
- Thomas Eakins (American, 1844–1916), *Max Schmitt in a Single Scull* (1871

Impressionism: 1860–1890

Origin: France

Description: Characterized largely by painting technique—thin, short brushstrokes. Often painted outdoors. Emphasized effects of light and color to form impressions of scenes. Initial public response was hostile but soon became celebrated for its originality.

Subgenres

* American Impressionism

Major Artists and Works

* Claude Monet (1840–1926), *Impression Sunrise* (1872)
* Édouard Manet (1832–1883), *The Luncheon on the Grass* (1863)
* Pierre-Auguste Renoir (1841–1919), *Dance at Le Moulin de la Galette* (1876)
* Camille Pissarro (1830–1903), *Boulevard Montmartre, morning, cloudy weather* (1897)
* Mary Cassatt (1844–1926), *The Boating Party* (1893–1894)
* Edgar Degas (1834–1917), *Musicians in the Orchestra* (1872)

Postimpressionism: 1886–1905

Origin: France

Description: Reaction against the Impressionists' naturalistic depiction of light and color, apparent triviality of subject matter, and loss of compositional structure. Used bolder pigments, thicker application, reliance on geometrical fields, and unnatural or arbitrary color choices.

Subgenres
- Cloisonnism: ca. 1885
- Synthetism: mid-1800s

Major Artists and Works
- Vincent van Gogh (1853–1890), *The Red Vineyard* (1888)
- Paul Gauguin (1848–1903), *The Painter of Sunflowers* (1888)
- Paul Cézanne (1839–1906), *The Card Players* (1892–1893)
- Georges Seurat (1859–1891), *A Sunday Afternoon on the Island of La Grande Jatte* (1884–1886)

Fauvism and Expressionism: 1900–1935

Origin: France
Description: Art focused on feelings. Developed pre–World War I. Was considered avant-garde, subjective and difficult to define. Intense colors, free-flowing brushwork, flat composition, favoring abstraction and simplification.

Subgenres
- Die Brücke: 1905–1913, Germany
- Flemish Expressionism: 1911–1940, Germany

Major Artists and Works
- Edvard Munch (1863–1944), *The Scream* (1893)
- Wassily Kandinsky (1866–1944), *Points* (1920)
- Henri Matisse (1869–1954), *La Danse* (1909)

American Realism: 1900–1970

Origin: United States

Description: Depicted contemporary social and personal lives of everyday people. As America went through huge social, economic, and industrial change, American Realists sought to define what was real, drawing on the techniques of the Realists, Impressionists, and Postimpressionists.

Major Artists and Works
- Henry Ossawa Tanner (1859–1937), *The Annunciation* (1898)
- Robert Henri (1865–1929), *Snow in New York* (1902)
- Edward Hopper (1882–1967), *New York Movie* (1939)

Cubism: 1907–1914

Origin: France

Description: Considered the most influential art movement of the twentieth century. Pre– and post–World War I art. Subjects are deconstructed, examined from more than one point of view, and then reassembled in an abstracted form. Very experimental, reordering forms to express life in a new era.

Subgenres
- Jack of Diamonds: 1909–1917, Russia
- Orphism: 1912, France
- Purism: 1918–1926, France

Major Artists and Works
- Pablo Picasso (1881–1973), *The Old Guitarist* (1903)
- Piet Mondrian (1872–1944), *Composition II in Red, Blue, and Yellow* (1930)
- Marc Chagall (1887–1985), *I and the Village* (1911)

Surrealism: 1920–1970

Origin: France

Description: Exploring the subconscious through art. Often incoherent juxtaposition of unrelated objects. Born from disillusionment, presented as an escape from reality.

Subgenres

- Lettrism: 1942
- Les Automatistes: 1946–1951, Quebec, Canada

Major Artists and Works

- Salvador Dalí (1904–1989), *The Persistence of Memory* (1931)
- René Magritte (1898–1967), *The Son of Man* (1946)
- Max Ernst (1891–1976), *The Temptation of St. Anthony* (1945)
- Frida Kahlo (1907–1954), *Self-Portrait with Thorn Necklace and Hummingbird* (1940)

Abstract Expressionism: 1940–1970

Origin: United States, post–World War II

Description: Art focused on ideas. Post–World War II. Expression without form, often directly tied to consumerism. Emotional intensity with anti-figurative aesthetic. Made New York City the center of the art world.

Subgenres

- Color Field Painting: mid-1940s
- Lyrical Abstraction: mid-1940s
- Abstract Imagists: mid-1940s

Major Artists and Works

- Jackson Pollock (1912–1956), *Autumn Rhythm (Number 30)* (1950)
- Mark Rothko (1903–1970), *No. 3/No. 13 (Magenta, Black, Green on Orange)* (1949)

Pop Art: 1945-1970

Origin: United Kingdom and United States

Description: Commentary on post–World War II culture, focused detachment from consumerism. Challenged traditional boundaries by using mechanical rendering techniques to reproduce images of popular culture and advertising in order to push back against pressures of cultural conformity.

Subgenres

- Color Field painting: 1960s
- Lyrical Abstraction: 1960s
- Abstract Imagists: 1960s

Major Artists and Works

- Eduardo Paolozzi (1924–2005), *I Was a Rich Man's Plaything* (1947)
- Roy Lichtenstein (1923–1997), *Drowning Girl* (1963)
- Andy Warhol (1928–1987), *Shot Marilyns* (1964)

SELECTED WORKS

Bailey, Anthony. *Vermeer: A View of Delft*. New York: Holt, 2001.

Bailey, Martin. *The Sunflowers Are Mine: The Story of Van Gogh's Masterpiece*. London: White Lion, 2019.

———. *Vermeer*. London: Phaidon, 1995.

Berkow, Ita. *Hopper: A Modern Master*. New York: New Line, 2006.

Berman, Avis. *Edward Hopper's New York*. San Francisco: Pomegranate, 2005.

Boser, Ulrich. *The Gardner Heist: The True Story of the World's Largest Unsolved Art Theft*. New York, HarperCollins, 2009.

Crenshaw, Paul. *Discovering the Great Masters: The Art Lover's Guide to Understanding Symbols in Paintings*. New York: Universe, 2009.

Etinde-Crompton, Charlotte, and Samuel Willard Crompton. *Henry Ossawa Tanner: Landscape Painter and Expatriate*. New York, Enslow, 2020.

Gayford, Martin. *The Yellow House: Van Gogh, Gauguin, and Nine Turbulent Weeks in Provence*. New York: Mariner, 2006.

Gowing, Lawrence. *Vermeer*. Berkeley: University of California Press, 1997.

Graham-Dixon, Andrew. *Caravaggio: A Life Sacred and Profane*. New York: Norton, 2011.

Hockney, David. *Secret Knowledge: Rediscovering the Lost Techniques of the Old Masters*. London: Thames and Hudson, 2009.

Lambert, Gilles. *Caravaggio*. Cologne: Taschen, 2019.

Levin, Gail. *Edward Hopper: An Intimate Biography*. New York: Knopf, 1995.

Marker, Sherry. *Edward Hopper.* East Bridgewater, MA: JG Press, 2005.

Marley, Anna O., ed. *Henry Ossawa Tanner: Modern Spirit.* Berkeley: University of California Press, 2012.

Mathews, Marcia M. *Henry Ossawa Tanner: American Artist.* Chicago: University of Chicago Press, 1969.

Morvan, Bérénice. *Impressionists.* Paris: Telleri, 2002.

Nash, J. M. *The Age of Rembrandt and Vermeer: Dutch Painting in the Seventeenth Century.* New York: Holt, Rinehart and Winston, 1972.

Néret, Gilles. *Michelangelo.* Cologne: Taschen, 2016.

Paolucci, Antonio, ed. *David: Five Hundred Years.* New York: Sterling, 2005.

Renner, Rolf Günter. *Hopper, 1882–1962: Transformation of the Real.* Cologne: Taschen, 2002.

Rewald, John. *Post-Impressionism: From van Gogh to Gauguin.* New York: Museum of Modern Art, 1975.

Rockness, Miriam Huffman. *A Passion for the Impossible: The Life of Lilias Trotter.* Grand Rapids: Discovery House, 2003.

———, ed. *A Blossom in the Desert: Reflections of Faith in the Art and Writings of Lilias Trotter.* Grand Rapids: Discovery House, 2007.

Scarry, Elaine. *On Beauty and Being Just.* Princeton, NJ: Princeton University Press, 2001.

Schneider, Norbert. *Vermeer: The Complete Paintings.* Cologne: Taschen, 2000.

Schütze, Sebastian. *Caravaggio: The Complete Works.* Cologne: Taschen, 2017.

Snyder, Laura J. *Eye of the Beholder: Johannes Vermeer, Antoni van Leeuwenhoek, and the Reinvention of Seeing.* New York: Norton, 2015.

St. John, Patricia Mary. *Until the Day Breaks: The Life and Work of Lilias Trotter, Pioneer Missionary to Muslim North Africa.* Bronley, Kent, UK: OM, 1990.

Steadman, Philip. *Vermeer's Camera: Uncovering the Truth Behind the Masterpieces*. Oxford: Oxford University Press, 2001.

Strand, Mark. *Hopper*, rev. ed. New York: Knopf, 2001.

Trotter, I. Lilias. *Parables of the Christ-Life*. New York: Start, 2013.

———. *Parables of the Cross*. Gloucester, UK: Yesterday's World, 2020.

Updike, John. *Still Looking: Essays on American Art*. New York: Knopf, 2005.

Wagstaff, Sheena, ed. *Edward Hopper*. London: Tate, 2004.

Wallis, Jeremy. *Impressionists*. Chicago: Heinemann, 2002.

Wellington, Hubert, ed. *The Journal of Eugène Delacroix*. Ithaca, NY: Cornell University Press, 1980.

Wheelock, Jr., Arthur K. *Vermeer*. London: Thames and Hudson, 1988.

Woods, Jr., Naurice Frank. *Henry Ossawa Tanner: Art, Race, Faith, and Legacy*. New York: Routledge, 2018.

NOTES

Foreword
1. Matthew 6:28.
2. "682: To Theo van Gogh. Arles, Tuesday, 18 September 1888," *Vincent van Gogh: The Letters*, www.vangoghletters.org/vg /letters/let682/letter.html.
3. Ephesians 2:10.
4. Ephesians 1:18.

Chapter 1: Beautifying Eden
1. Henri J. M. Nouwen, *The Return of the Prodigal Son: A Story of Homecoming* (New York: Crown, 2013), 35.
2. Though the most common view is that Vincent shot himself, recent scholarship questions whether van Gogh took his own life, suggesting it is possible he was shot in an accident that involved local teens taunting him with a gun. No one can say for sure, though most believe the wounds that caused his death were self-inflicted.
3. This petition, known as "the Arles Petition," can be read in full at "The Arles Petition: Petition, Report and Inquest, February–March 1889," www.vggallery.com/misc/archives/petition_e.htm.
4. Quoted in Martin Bailey, *The Sunflowers Are Mine: The Story of Van Gogh's Masterpiece* (London: White Lion, 2019), 12.
5. In L'Engle's book *Walking on Water: Reflections on Faith and Art* (New York: Convergent, 2016), she writes, "In a very real sense not one of us is qualified, but it seems that God continually chooses the most unqualified to do his work, to bear his glory" (54).

6. Psalms 27: 4, 13; 90:17; 119:68; Ecclesiastes 3:11; John 4:24; 14:6; 17:17; Galatians 5:22–23.

7. Peter Kreeft, "Lewis's Philosophy of Truth, Goodness and Beauty," in *C. S. Lewis as Philosopher: Truth, Goodness and Beauty*, ed. David Baggett, Gary R. Habermas, and Jerry L. Walls (Downers Grove, IL: IVP Academic, 2008), 23.

8. Genesis 1:31.

9. Genesis 2:16–17.

10. Genesis 3.

11. Genesis 1:27.

12. Genesis 2:19–20.

13. Maria Popova, "How Naming Confers Dignity Upon Life and Gives Meaning to Existence," BrainPickings, www.brain pickings.org/?s=how+naming.

14. Genesis 2:15.

15. Genesis 2:18.

16. J. R. R. Tolkien, *Tree and Leaf; Smith of Wootton Major; The Homecoming of Beorhtnoth, Beorhthelm's Son* (London: Unwin, 1975), 28.

17. C. S. Lewis, *Surprised by Joy: The Shape of My Early Life* (New York: Harcourt, 1955), 164.

18. Genesis 15:1–6.

19. Exodus 33:12–23.

20. Psalm 27:4.

21. Psalm 19:1.

22. Genesis 1:31.

23. Revelation 21:2.

24. See Psalm 149:4.

25. Matthew 28:18–20.

26. Elaine Scarry, *On Beauty and Being Just* (Princeton, NJ: Princeton University Press, 2013), 15.

27. Scarry, *On Beauty and Being Just*, 18.

28. Scarry, *On Beauty and Being Just*, 3.

29. Blaise Pascal, "The Art of Persuasion," in *Pensées and Other Writings*, ed. Anthony Levi (1995; repr., Oxford: Oxford University Press, 2008), 193.

30. Psalm 19:1.

31. Matthew 26:8–9.

32. Matthew 26:10.

33. Saint Augustine. *Confessions*, trans. R. S. Pine-Coffin (London: Penguin, 1961), 231.

34. Annie Dillard, *Pilgrim at Tinker Creek* (New York: HarperCollins, 1974), 8.

Chapter 2: Pursuing Perfection

1. Cited in Antonio Paolucci, ed. *David: Five Hundred Years* (New York: Sterling, 2005), 71.

2. I drew much of the detail I've included here about the origination and transportation of the stone from Sam Anderson's article "David's Ankles: How Imperfections Could Bring Down the World's Most Perfect Statue," *New York Times Magazine*, August 17, 2016, www.nytimes.com/2016/08/21/magazine/davids-ankles-how-imper fections-could-bring-down-the-worlds-most-perfect-statue.html.

3. Anderson, "David's Ankles."

4. Quoted in Charles de Tolnay, *Michelangelo: The Youth of Michelangelo* (Princeton, NJ: Princeton University Press, 1969), 11.

5. Gilles Néret, *Michelangelo* (Cologne: Taschen, 2016), 23.

6. Néret, *Michelangelo*, 23.

7. Néret, *Michelangelo*, 23.

8. Néret, *Michelangelo*, 23.

9. Néret, *Michelangelo*, 23.

10. Néret, *Michelangelo*, 23.

11. Cited in Robert Coughlan, *The World of Michelangelo, 1475–1564* (New York: Time-Life, 1971), 42.

12. Néret, *Michelangelo*, 7.

13. Néret, *Michelangelo*, 7.

14. Paolucci, *David: Five Hundred Years*, 33.

15. Néret, *Michelangelo*, 8.

16. 1 Samuel 16:12.

17. 1 Samuel 16:18 NIV.

18. 1 Samuel 17:42.

19. Genesis 12:11; 29:17; 39:6; 1 Samuel 9:2; and Esther 2:7, respectively.

20. 1 Samuel 13:14; Acts 13:22.

21. The story of David and Goliath is located in 1 Samuel 17. Many of the details in this portion are drawn from that text.

22. 1 Samuel 17:8–9, my paraphrase.

23. 1 Samuel 17:26, my paraphrase.

24. 1 Samuel 17:31–37, my paraphrase.

25. 1 Samuel 17:43–44, my paraphrase.

26. 1 Samuel 17:45–47, my paraphrase

27. Néret, *Michelangelo*, 8.

28. See Malcolm Gladwell, *David and Goliath: Underdogs, Misfits, and the Art of Battling Giants* (New York: Little, Brown, 2015).

29. Paolucci, *David: Five Hundred Years*, 74.

30. Quoted in Paolucci, *David: Five Hundred Years*, 74.

31. Quoted in "Michelangelo's David," www.accademia.org/explore -museum/artworks/michelangelos-david.

32. See Alan Cowell, "Michelangelo's David Is Damaged," *New York Times*, September 15, 1991, www.nytimes.com/1991/09 /15/world/michelangelo-s-david-is-damaged.html.

33. Anderson, "David's Ankles."

34. See Paolucci, *David: Five Hundred Years*, 28–29, 78–79; see also Elizabeth Wicks, "The Spring Cleaning of Michelangelo's David," Magenta Florence, March 1, 2016, www.magenta florence.com/10209-2.

35. 2 Corinthians 4:17.

36. Scarry, *On Beauty and Being Just*, 7.

Chapter 3: The Sacred and the Profane

1. Matthew 10:17–27.

2. John 4.

3. John 7:53–8:11.

4. Gilles Lambert, *Caravaggio: 1571–1610: A Genius Beyond His Time* (Cologne: Taschen, 2015), 15.

5. "Caravaggio: A Life Sacred and Profane," interview with Lois

Lindstrom on her program *The Bookman's Corner*, https://
bookmanscorner.com/programs.html.

6. Peter Robb, *M: The Caravaggio Enigma* (2000; repr., New York:
Bloomsbury, 2011), 35.

7. See Peter L. Berger, *A Rumor of Angels: Modern Society and the
Rediscovery of the Supernatural* (New York: Open Road Media,
2011), 15.

8. Cited in "Caravaggio - Artist Biography with Portfolio of
Paintings, Prints, Posters and Drawings," www.caravaggio.net.

9. Lambert, *Caravaggio: 1571–1610*, 7.

10. Sebastian Schütze, *Caravaggio: The Complete Works* (Cologne:
Taschen, 2017), 127.

11. Schütze, *Caravaggio*, 127.

12. See Lambert, *Caravaggio: 1571–1610*, 59.

13. Quoted in Lambert, *Caravaggio: 1571–1610*, 30.

14. Keith Christiansen, "Caravaggio (Michelangelo Merisi)
(1571–1616) and His Followers," The Met, October 2003, www
.metmuseum.org/toah/hd/crvg/hd_crvg.htm.

15. Genesis 22.

16. Quoted in Lambert, *Caravaggio: 1571–1610*, 11.

17. Nina Edwards, *Darkness: A Cultural History* (London: Reaktion,
2018), 91.

18. 1 Corinthians 13:12.

19. Matthew 9:9–13; quotes in the retelling of this story are my
paraphrases.

20. Hosea 6:6.

21. Acts 1:13–14.

22. John 20:27; Acts 9:4; Matthew 26:69–75.

23. Andrew Graham-Dixon, *Caravaggio: A Life Sacred and Profane*
(New York: Norton, 2011), 162.

24. Floris Claes van Dijk, a contemporary of Caravaggio in
Rome in 1601, quoted in John Gash, *Caravaggio* (London:
Bloomsbury, 1988), 13.

25. Quoted in Graham-Dixon, *Caravaggio: A Life Sacred and
Profane*, 293–94.

26. See Schütze, *Caravaggio: The Complete Works*, 239.

27. Lambert, *Caravaggio: 1571–1610*, 67.

28. As seen on the Nelson-Atkins Museum, Kansas City, Gallery label for Caravaggio's *Saint John the Baptist in the Wilderness*, 1604–1605.

29. John 19:5.

30. See Graham-Dixon, *Caravaggio: A Life Sacred and Profane*, 32.

31. Schütze, *Caravaggio: The Complete Works*, 239.

32. As seen on the Louvre, Paris, Gallery label for Caravaggio's *Death of the Virgin*, ca. 1605.

33. John 19:26–27.

34. Cited in "Caravaggio, Death of the Virgin," SmartHistory, www.youtube.com/watch?v=TkH-yjJ35vU.

35. 1 Peter 1:12.

36. See E. Sammut, "Caravaggio in Malta," *Scientia* 15, no. 2 (1949): 78–89.

37. See Lambert, *Caravaggio: 1571–1610s*, 78.

38. See Lambert, *Caravaggio: 1571–1610s*, 78.

39. See Schütze, *Caravaggio: The Complete Works*, 275.

40. Graham-Dixon, *Caravaggio: A Life Sacred and Profane*, 418.

41. Tom LeGro, "Conversation: Andrew Graham-Dixon, Author of 'Caravaggio: A Life Sacred and Profane,'" *PBS NewsHour*, December 2, 2011, www.pbs.org/newshour/arts/caravaggio.

42. Quoted in Lambert, *Caravaggio: 1571–1610: A Genius Beyond His Time*, 86.

43. See John Varriano, *Caravaggio: The Art of Realism* (University Park: Pennsylvania State University Press, 2010), 83.

44. See Schütze, *Caravaggio: The Complete Works*, 303.

45. Lambert, *Caravaggio: 1571–1610*, 89.

46. See Schütze, *Caravaggio: The Complete Works*, 303.

47. Art + Travel Europe, *Step Into the Lives of Five Famous Painters* (New York: Museyon, 2010), 135.

48. Giovanni Pietro Bellori, *Life of Caravaggio* [*Vite de' pittori, scultori ed architetti moderni*] (Rome 1672), http://arthistory resources.net/baroque-art-theory-2013/bellori-caravaggio

.html, as quoted in Walter Friedlaender, *Caravaggio Studies* (Princeton, NJ: Princeton University Press, 1955), 245–54.

49. Quoted in Lambert, *Caravaggio: 1571–1610*, 8.

50. Art + Travel Europe, *Step Into the Lives of Five Famous Painters*, 135.

51. Quoted in Lambert, *Caravaggio: 1571–1610*, 6.

52. John 18:37.

53. Matthew 19:16–22.

54. Ephesians 2:4.

55. Exodus 2:11–15.

56. Genesis 25:29–34.

57. 2 Samuel 11.

58. 1 Kings 11:1–13.

59. Jonah 1–4.

60. Matthew 21:28–32.

61. Matthew 9:9–13.

62. Matthew 4:18–22.

63. Acts 9:1–19.

Chapter 4: Rembrandt Is in the Wind

1. See Ulrich Boser, *The Gardner Heist: The True Story of the World's Largest Unsolved Art Theft* (New York: HarperCollins, 2009), 1–9.

2. Matthew 4:35–41.

3. Actually, August Rodin has told us what is on *The Thinker's* mind. *The Thinker* was created to be the capstone of a massive bronze sculpture called *The Gates of Hell*. *The Thinker* is Dante, and he is thinking about his epic poem *The Inferno*. Dante sits atop two massive doors—the gates of hell—and he is surrounded by tortured souls who are being taken into their eternal punishment. *The Thinker* is bent over with the burden of hell.

4. Luke 7:11–17; quotes in the retelling of this story are my paraphrases.

5. Luke 7:16–17.

6. Mark 4:38, my paraphrase.

7. Mark 1:29–2:12.

8. See Christopher Leslie Brown, Jan Kelch, and Pieter van Thiel, *Rembrandt, The Master and His Workshop: Paintings* (New Haven, CT: Yale University Press, 1991), 13.

9. See Boser, *Gardner Heist*, 48–52.

10. From a letter from Isabella to her art dealer and friend, Bernard Berenson, September 19, 1896 (see Rollin van N. Hadley, ed., *The Letters of Bernard Berenson and Isabella Stewart Gardner: 1887–1924* [Boston: Northeastern University Press, 1987], 66).

11. From Isabella Stewart Gardner's last will and testament, p. 3 (see "Will and Codicil of Isabella Stewart Gardner," www.law.harvard.edu/faculty/martin/art_law/gardner_will.pdf).

12. John Shiffman and Robert K. Wittman, *Priceless: How I Went Undercover to Rescue the World's Stolen Treasures* (New York: Broadway, 2011), 247.

13. From Isabella Stewart Gardner's last will and testament, pp. 8–9.

14. John Updike, *Endpoint and Other Poems* (New York: Knopf, 2009), 33.

15. Quoted in the documentary film *Stolen*, directed by Rebecca Dreyfus, Flourish Films, 2007.

16. Excerpted from the Isabella Steward Gardner Museum visitor guide (see "Dutch Room Guide," www.gardnermuseum.org/sites/default/files/uploads/files/Dutch%20Room%20Guide.pdf).

17. Alan Chong, ed., *Eye of the Beholder: Masterpieces from the Isabella Stewart Gardner Museum* (Boston: Isabella Stewart Gardner Museum, 2003), 145.

18. Quoted in Matt Lebovic, "Is the Hunt for Rembrandt's Stolen 'Galilee' Almost Over?", *The Times of Israel*, October 3, 2013, www.timesofisrael.com/is-the-hunt-for-rembrandts-stolen-galilee-almost-over.

19. See *What Happens to Stolen Art?* BBC News, August 23, 2004, http://news.bbc.co.uk/2/hi/entertainment/3590190.stm.

20. Cited in Robert M. Poole, "Ripped from the Walls (and the Headlines)," *Smithsonian Magazine*, July 2005, www.smith

sonianmag.com/arts-culture/ripped-from-the-walls-and-the
-headlines-74998018.

21. See Cornelius Poppe, "Seven Questions: A Reformed Stolen-
Art Dealer Tells All," *Foreign Policy*, February 20, 2008, https://
foreignpolicy.com/2008/02/20/seven-questions-a-reformed
-stolen-art-dealer-tells-all.

22. Quoted in Charles River Editors, *History's Greatest Artists:
The Life and Legacy of Rembrandt* (North Charleston, SC:
CreateSpace, 2017), 64.

23. Quoted in the documentary film, *Stolen*.

24. See Milton Esterow, "Inside the Gardner Case," *ARTnews*,
May 1, 2009, www.artnews.com/art-news/news/inside-the
-gardner-case-229.

25. Romans 8:26.

26. Matthew 6:19–24.

27. Revelation 21:3–4.

28. 2 Corinthians 4:8–10, 16–17.

29. 1 Peter 1:3.

30. Mark 4:39.

31. Revelation 21:1–5.

32. 1 Thessalonians 4:13.

Chapter 5: Borrowed Light

1. Isaiah 45:18.

2. Genesis 1:26.

3. Johannes and Catharina had fourteen children in total, three
of whom died young.

4. "Vermeer's Life and Art (part four): Last Five Years," Essential
Vermeer.com, www.essentialvermeer.com/vermeer's_life_04
.html.

5. Laura J. Snyder, *Eye of the Beholder: Johannes Vermeer, Antoni
van Leeuwenhoek, and the Reinvention of Seeing* (New York:
Norton, 2015), 273.

6. Snyder, *Eye of the Beholder*, 273.

7. See Norbert Schneider, *Vermeer, 1632–1675: Veiled Emotions* (Cologne: Taschen, 2000), 87.

8. Théophile Thoré-Bürger, "Van der Meer [Vermeer] de Delft," *Gazette des beaux-arts* 21 (October 1866).

9. See Malcolm Gladwell, *Blink: The Power of Thinking Without Thinking* (New York: Little, Brown, 2007).

10. See Gladwell, *Blink*, 8.

11. See Gladwell, *Blink*, 6

12. Martin Bailey, *Vermeer: Colour Library* (Berlin: Phaidon, 1995), 17.

13. See Arthur K. Wheelock Jr., *Vermeer* (London: Thames and Hudson, 1988), 37.

14. Lawrence Gowing, *Vermeer* (Berkeley: University of California Press, 1997), 137–38.

15. Snyder, *Eye of the Beholder*, 285.

16. Bailey, *Vermeer*, 17.

17. Quoted in Snyder, *Eye of the Beholder*, 295.

18. Anthony Bailey, *Vermeer: A View of Delft* (New York: Holt, 2001), 159.

19. See Bailey, *Vermeer: A View of Delft*, 165.

20. Bailey, *Vermeer: A View of Delft*, 157.

21. See Wheelock, *Vermeer*, 11–12.

22. Bailey, *Vermeer: A View of Delft*, 153.

23. See David Hockney, *Secret Knowledge: Rediscovering the Lost Techniques of the Old Masters* (London: Thames and Hudson, 2009); Philip Steadman, *Vermeer's Camera: Uncovering the Truth Behind the Masterpieces* (Oxford: Oxford University Press, 2001); and Snyder, *Eye of the Beholder*.

24. "Tim's Vermeer," Wikipedia, https://en.wikipedia.org/wiki/Tim%27s_Vermeer.

25. Wheelock, *Vermeer*, 34.

26. See Steadman, *Vermeer's Camera*, 36.

27. Wheelock, *Vermeer*, 45.

28. Quoted in Paul Richard, "No Ordinary Light," *Washington Post*, November 12, 1995, www.washingtonpost.com/archive

/lifestyle/style/1995/11/12/no-ordinary-light/e7d22010-8fa7
-477c-9a19-3e36f17f14f3.

29. "272: To Theo van Gogh. The Hague, Sunday, 15 October
    1882," Vincent van Gogh: The Letters, www.vangoghletters
    .org/vg/letters/let272/letter.html.

30. Bülent Atalay and Keith Wamsley, *Leonardo's Universe: The
    Renaissance World of Leonardo da Vinci* (Washington, D.C.:
    National Geographic, 2008), 96.

31. Snyder, *Eye of the Beholder*, 7.

32. Snyder, *Eye of the Beholder*, 4, 12.

33. Steadman, *Vermeer's Camera*, 161.

34. Steadman, *Vermeer's Camera*, 164–65.

35. Gowing, *Vermeer*, 25.

36. Steadman, *Vermeer's Camera*, 165.

37. Steadman, *Vermeer's Camera*, 165.

38. The phrasing of this line is modeled after C. S. Lewis's quote,
    "I believe in Christianity as I believe that the Sun has risen, not
    only because I see it, but because by it I see everything else"
    (1949; repr., *The Weight of Glory* [San Francisco: HarperSan
    Francisco: 2001], 140).

39. Old farmers used to define the duration of a workday as lasting
    from "can see to can't see."

Chapter 6: Creating in Community

1. Cited in "Frédéric Bazille: A Tragic Story," *WetCanvas*, June 20,
   2011.

2. Quoted in Hubert Wellington, ed. *The Journal of Eugène Delacroix:
   A Selection* (Ithaca, NY: Cornell University Press, 1980), xiv.

3. See Bérénice Morvan, *Impressionists* (Paris: Telleri, 2002), 68.

4. Quoted in Morvan, *Impressionists*, 10.

5. Quoted in Morvan, *Impressionists*, 46.

6. See "Frédéric Bazille: A Tragic Story."

7. See Morvan, *Impressionists*, 65.

8. Quoted in "Frédéric Bazille: Summary of Frédéric Bazille,"
   www.theartstory.org/artist-bazille-frederic.htm.

9. Malcolm Gladwell, *David and Goliath: Underdogs, Misfits, and the Art of Battling Giants* (New York: Little, Brown, 2013), 65.

10. Quoted in Morvan, *Impressionists*, 10.

11. Morvan, *Impressionists*, 10.

12. Morvan, *Impressionists*, 13.

13. Quoted in Morvan, *Impressionists*, 9.

14. Cited in John Rewald, *The History of Impressionism* (New York: Museum of Modern Art, 1955), 234.

15. Quoted in Jeremy Wallis, *Impressionists* (Chicago: Heinemann, 2002), 10.

16. Revelation 21:4–5.

17. 1 Peter 4:12.

18. John 15:13.

19. Philippians 4:8 NIV.

Chapter 7: The Striving Artist

1. "818: Octave Maus to Vincent van Gogh. Brussels, Friday, 15 November 1889," Vincent van Gogh: The Letters, www.van goghletters.org/vg/letters/let818/letter.html.

2. See Martin Bailey, *The Sunflowers Are Mine: The Story of Van Gogh's Masterpiece* (London: White Lion, 2019), 102–3.

3. "821: To Octave Maus. Saint-Rémy-de-Provence, Wednesday, 20 November 1889," Vincent van Gogh: The Letters, www .vangoghletters.org/vg/letters/let821/letter.html.

4. "693: To Eugène Boch. Arles, 2 October 1888," Vincent van Gogh: The Letters, www.vangoghletters.org/vg/letters/let693 /letter.html.

5. See Martin Gayford, *The Yellow House: Van Gogh, Gauguin, and Nine Turbulent Weeks in Provence* (New York: Mariner, 2008), 99, 119.

6. Josephine Cutts and James Smith, *Essential Van Gogh* (Bath, UK: Parragon, 2001), 136.

7. See Robert L. Herbert, *Neo-Impressionism* (New York: Solomon R. Guggenheim Museum, 1968).

8. "693: To Eugène Boch. Arles, 2 October 1888."

9. "717: To Theo van Gogh. Arles, on or about Saturday, 3 November 1888," Vincent van Gogh: The Letters, www.van goghletters.org/vg/letters/let717/letter.html.

10. "249: To Theo van Gogh. The Hague, on or about Friday, 21 July 1882," Vincent van Gogh: The Letters, www.vangogh letters.org/vg/letters/let249/letter.html.

11. "634: To Theo van Gogh. Arles, on or about Thursday, 28 June 1888," Vincent van Gogh: The Letters, www.vangoghletters .org/vg/letters/let634/letter.html.

12. Though Vincent would come to be known as a Postimpressionist painter, during his career he took his cues from the style of the Impressionists. On a technical level, the two schools are similar, with the primary difference being philosophical. The Postimpressionists thought Impressionism could be trivial, lacking in substance. But Postimpressionism spun off from Impressionism.

13. "712: To Theo van Gogh. Arles, on or about Thursday, 25 October 1888," Vincent van Gogh: The Letters, www .vangoghletters.org/vg/letters/let712/letter.html#translation.

14. Though the most common view is that Vincent shot himself, recent scholarship questions whether van Gogh took his own life, suggesting it is possible he was shot in an accident that involved local teens taunting him with a gun. No one can say for sure, though most believe the wounds that caused his death were self-inflicted.

15. See Khali Ibrahaim, "The Discovery of Van Gogh: From Shade to Light," Van Gogh Gallery, www.vggallery.com/visitors/017.htm.

16. See "815: To Theo van Gogh. Saint Rémy-de-Provence, on or about Friday, 25 October 1889," Vincent van Gogh: The Letters, www.vangoghletters.org/vg/letters/let815/letter.html.

17. Albert Aurier, "The Isolated Ones: Vincent van Gogh," *Mercure de France*, January 1890, www.vggallery.com/misc /archives/aurier.htm.

18. Octave Mirbeau, "Artists," *Echo de Paris*, 1 March 1891, www .vggallery.com/misc/archives/mirbeau.htm.

19. The Impressionists pushed against the Realists' commitment to depicting objects in their most natural state. The Post-impressionists pushed against the Impressionists' commitment to portraying light and color in their most natural state.

20. Quoted in Ian Dunlop, *Van Gogh* (Chicago: Follett, 1975), 199.

21. John Rewald, *Post-Impressionism: From Van Gogh to Gauguin* (New York: Museum of Modern Art, 1975), 374–75.

22. Quoted in Rewald, *Post-Impressionism*, 375.

23. See Bailey, *The Sunflowers Are Mine*, 105.

24. "855: To Anna van Gogh-Carbentus. Saint-Rémy-de-Provence, Wednesday, 19 February 1890," Vincent van Gogh: The Letters, www.vangoghletters.org/vg/letters/let855/letter.html.

25. The breakdown of Vincent's productivity that follows comes from an online list of all his works, arranged according to date. That list can be found at David Brooks, "The Vincent van Gogh Gallery," www.vggallery.com/index.html.

26. "117: To Theo van Gogh. Amsterdam, Wednesday, 30 May 1877," Vincent van Gogh: The Letters, www.vangoghletters.org /vg/letters/let117/letter.html.

27. "155: To Theo van Gogh. Cuesmes, between about Tuesday 22 and Thursday, 24 June 1880," Vincent van Gogh: The Letters, www.vangoghletters.org/vg/letters/let155/letter.html.

28. C. S. Lewis, *The Weight of Glory* (1949; repr., New York: HarperCollins, 2001), 40.

29. Ecclesiastes 2:20–21.

30. Ecclesiastes 1:14–15.

31. Romans 8:20.

32. Revelation 21:5.

33. C. S. Lewis, *The Weight of Glory, and Other Addresses* (New York: Macmillan, 1980), 15.

34. See Annie Dillard, *Pilgrim at Tinker Creek* (1974; repr., New York: HarperCollins, 1985), 8.

35. I'm borrowing an image here from the chapter called "Seeing" in Annie Dillard's Pulitzer Prize–winning book *Pilgrim at Tinker Creek*, in which she describes a recent cataract surgery patient

who sees an evergreen covered in dew in the morning sun for the first time and calls it "the tree with the lights in it" (*Pilgrim at Tinker Creek*, 33).

36. "717: To Theo van Gogh. Arles, on or about Saturday, 3 November 1888."
37. Ecclesiastes 1:8.

Chapter 8: Beyond Imagination

1. And often still does.
2. See Anna O. Marley, ed., *Henry Ossawa Tanner: Modern Spirit* (Berkeley: University of California Press, 2012), 35.
3. See Marley, *Henry Ossawa Tanner*, 20.
4. Quoted in Marley, *Henry Ossawa Tanner*, 19.
5. Marley, *Henry Ossawa Tanner*, 21.
6. Quoted in Naurice Frank Woods Jr., *Henry Ossawa Tanner: Art, Faith, Race, and Legacy* (New York: Routledge, 2017), 56.
7. Quoted in William R. Lester, "Henry O Tanner, Exile for Art's Sake," *Alexander's Magazine* 7, no. 2 (December 15, 1908): 69–73.
8. "Henry Ossawa Tanner, American, 1859–1937: Biography," National Gallery of Art, www.nga.gov/collection/artist-info .1919.html.
9. Quoted in Naurice Frank Woods Jr., "Henry Ossawa Tanner's Negotiation of Race and Art: Challenging 'The Unknown Tanner,'" *Journal of Black Studies* 42, no. 6 (September 2011): 891.
10. Woods, "Henry Ossawa Tanner's Negotiation of Race and Art," 895.
11. See Marley, *Henry Ossawa Tanner*, 23.
12. Quoted in Marley, *Henry Ossawa Tanner*, 23.
13. Marcus Bruce, "A New Testament: Henry Ossawa Tanner, Religious Discourse, and the 'Lessons' of Art," in *Henry Ossawa Tanner*, ed. Marley, 110.
14. Bruce, "A New Testament," 111.
15. Dewey F. Mosby, *Across Continents and Cultures: The Art and Life of Henry Ossawa Tanner* (Kansas City, MO: Nelson-Atkins Museum of Art, 1995), 38.

16. Alan C. Braddock, "Christian Cosmopolitan: Henry Ossawa Tanner and the Beginning of the End of Race," in Marley, *Henry Ossawa Tanner*, 136.

17. Henry Ossawa Tanner, "An Artist's Autobiography," *The Advance* (March 20, 1913), 14.

18. Marcus Bruce, "'I Invited the Christ Spirit to Manifest in Me': Tanner and Symbolism," in *Henry Ossawa Tanner*, ed. Marley, 119.

19. John 11.

20. Quoted in Marley, *Henry Ossawa Tanner*, 29.

21. Quoted in Marc Simpson, "*The Resurrection of Lazarus* from the *Quartier Latin* to the Musée du Luxembourg," in Marley, *Henry Ossawa Tanner*, 72.

22. Quoted in Marley, *Henry Ossawa Tanner*, 40.

23. This theme runs throughout the book of Jonah.

24. Zechariah 7:9–10.

25. Marcus Bruce, *Henry Ossawa Tanner: A Spiritual Biography* (New York: Crossroad, 2002), 33.

26. "Tanner Exhibits Paintings: Negro Artist Shows Pictures at Grand Central Art Galleries," *New York Times*, January 29, 1924, 9.

27. Quoted in Bruce, "A New Testament," 109.

28. See Simpson, "*The Resurrection of Lazarus*," 72.

29. Quoted in Simpson, "*The Resurrection of Lazarus*," 72.

30. Simpson, "*The Resurrection of Lazarus*," 72.

31. "The Paris Salons of 1897," *Art Journal* 59 (London, July 1897): 196.

32. Quoted in Simpson, "*The Resurrection of Lazarus*," 73.

33. Quoted in Simpson, "*The Resurrection of Lazarus*," 73.

34. Bruce, "A New Testament," 113.

35. Luke 1:28 NIV.

36. Daniel 8–9.

37. Leland Ryken, James C. Wilhoit, and Temper Longman III, eds., *Dictionary of Biblical Imagery* (Downers Grove, IL: InterVarsity, 2010), 32.

38. Luke 2:19.
39. Genesis 21:1–7.
40. Judges 13.
41. Luke 1:5–25.
42. Matthew 2:13–21.
43. Luke 2:35.
44. 2 Samuel 7:1–17.
45. Luke 1:34, my paraphrase.
46. Luke 1:36–37, my paraphrase.
47. Luke 1:38.
48. Isaiah 9:2.
49. Luke 2:8–21.
50. Matthew 2:1–18.
51. John 1:5.
52. "Henry Ossawa Tanner, *The Annunciation*, 1898, Philadelphia Museum of Art," Seeing Art History with James Romaine, www.youtube.com/watch?v=zs44P8zgfm0.
53. Luke 1:48–52.
54. Quoted in Marcia M. Mathews, *Henry Ossawa Tanner: American Artist* (Chicago: University of Chicago Press, 1969), 156–57.
55. Quoted in Sharon Kay Skeel, "A Black American in the Paris Salon," *American Heritage* 42, no. 1 (February/March 1991), www.americanheritage.com/black-american-paris-salon.

Chapter 9: What Remains Unsaid

1. Mark Strand, *Hopper*, rev. ed. (New York: Knopf, 2001), 48.
2. See Gail Levin, *Edward Hopper: An Intimate Biography* (Berkeley: University of California Press, 1998), 159–60.
3. Quoted in Levin, *Edward Hopper*, 88.
4. Quoted in Margaret Iversen et al., *Edward Hopper* (London: Tate, 2004), 53.
5. Quoted in Levin, *Edward Hopper*, 171.
6. Avis Berman, *Edward Hopper's New York* (Petaluma, CA: Pomegranate, 2005), 108.

7. See Levin, *Edward Hopper*, 12.
8. See Levin, *Edward Hopper*, 134, 222.
9. Quoted in Sherry Marker, *Edward Hopper* (East Bridgewater, MA: JG Press, 2005), 8.
10. Quoted in Marker, *Edward Hopper*, 17.
11. Quoted in Rolf Günter Renner, *Hopper, 1882–1962: Transformation of the Real* (Cologne: Taschen, 2002), 10.
12. Strand, *Hopper*, 31.
13. John Updike, *Still Looking: Essays on American Art* (New York: Knopf, 2005), 199.
14. Adrian Searle, "The Irreducible Business of Being," *The Guardian*, May 25, 2004, www.theguardian.com/culture/2004/may/25/1.
15. Updike, *Still Looking*, 199.
16. James Peacock, "Edward Hopper: The Artist Who Evoked Urban Loneliness and Disappointment with Beautiful Clarity," *The Conversation*, May 18, 2017, https://theconversation.com/edward-hopper-the-artist-who-evoked-urban-loneliness-and-disappointment-with-beautiful-clarity-77636.
17. Strand, *Hopper*, 30.
18. Updike, *Still Looking*, 195.
19. C. S. Lewis, *The Weight of Glory* (1949; repr., New York: HarperCollins, 2001), 46.
20. Robert Coles, "Art; On Edward Hopper, Loneliness and Children," *New York Times*, March 3, 1991, www.nytimes.com/1991/03/03/arts/art-on-edward-hopper-loneliness-and-children.html.
21. Coles, "Art; On Edward Hopper."
22. Coles, "Art; On Edward Hopper."
23. See Ita G. Berkow, *Edward Hopper: An American Master* (New York: New Line, 2006), 51.
24. See Berman, *Edward Hopper's New York*, 86.
25. Quoted in Renner, *Hopper, 1882–1962*, 11.
26. See Levin, *Edward Hopper*, 467.
27. Quoted in Avis Berman, "Hopper: The Supreme American

Realist of the 20th-Century," *Smithsonian Magazine*, July 2007, www.smithsonianmag.com/arts-culture/hopper-156346356.

28. Marker, *Edward Hopper*, 16.
29. Raquel Laneri, "The Woman Who Made Edward Hopper Famous Finally Seizes the Spotlight," *New York Post*, April 11, 2020, https://nypost.com/2020/04/11/woman-who-made -edward-hopper-famous-finally-seizes-the-spotlight.
30. Laneri, "The Woman Who Made Edward Hopper Famous."
31. Gaby Wood, "Man and Muse," *The Guardian*, April 25, 2004, www.theguardian.com/artanddesign/2004/apr/25/art1.
32. Gail Levin, "Writing about Forgotten Women Artists: The Rediscovery of Jo Nivison Hopper," in *Singular Women: Writing the Artist*, ed. Kristen Frederickson and Sarah E. Webb (Berkeley: University of California Press, 2003), 132, https://publishing .cdlib.org/ucpressebooks/view?docId=kt5b69q3pk&doc.view =content&chunk.id=ch10&toc.depth=100&brand=ucpress.
33. Quoted in Levin, *Edward Hopper*, 354.
34. Quoted in Levin, *Edward Hopper*, 463.
35. Berman, *Edward Hopper's New York*, 62.
36. Wood, "Man and Muse."
37. Strand, *Hopper*, 31.
38. Quoted in Sarah McColl, "Jo Hopper, Woman in the Sun," *Paris Review*, February 26, 2018, www.theparisreview.org/blog /2018/02/26/jo-hopper-woman-sun-woman-shadow.
39. Frederick Buechner, *Telling the Truth: The Gospel as Tragedy, Comedy, and Fairy Tale* (New York: HarperCollins, 1977), 3.
40. Matthew 23:37–38.
41. Wood, "Man and Muse."
42. Levin, *Edward Hopper*, 572–73.
43. Bernard Chambaz, *The Last Painting: Final Works of the Great Masters from Giotto to Twombly* (Woodbridge, UK: ACC Art Books, 2018), 12
44. Quoted in Levin, *Edward Hopper*, 577.
45. Quoted in Levin, *Edward Hopper*, 578.
46. Quoted in Levin, *Edward Hopper*, 579–80.

Chapter 10: Measuring a Life

1. Cited in Tom Mercer, "God's Grace in the Life of Lilias Trotter," sermon preached at Christ Covenant Church, Raleigh, North Carolina, August 24, 2018.

2. Patricia Mary St. John, *Until the Day Breaks: The Life and Work of Lilias Trotter, Pioneer Missionary to Muslim North Africa* (Bronley, Kent, UK: OM, 1990), 7–8.

3. Miriam Huffman Rockness, *A Passion for the Impossible: The Life of Lilias Trotter* (Grand Rapids: Discovery House, 2003), 42.

4. Rockness, *A Passion for the Impossible*, 50.

5. Cited in Tom Mercer, "God's Grace in the Life of Lilias Trotter."

6. Quoted in Rockness, *A Passion for the Impossible*, 61.

7. Cited in Tom Mercer, "God's Grace in the Life of Lilias Trotter."

8. The Ruskin School of Art remains part of the University of Oxford to this day.

9. Quoted in *Many Beautiful Things: The Life and Vision of Lilias Trotter* documentary film, written by Laura Waters Hinson, Oxvision Films and Image Bearer Pictures (October 17, 2015), https://amara.org/en/videos/np7it8gW9d1L/en/1071086.

10. Quoted in Katherine Halberstadt Anderson and Andie Roeder Moody, "'I Cannot Give Myself to Painting,'" *Behemoth* 32 (October 1, 2015), www.christianitytoday.com/behemoth/2015/issue-32/i-cannot-give-myself-to-painting.html; see also St. John, *Until the Day Breaks*, 14–15.

11. Quoted in St. John, *Until the Day Breaks*, 14–15.

12. Quoted in St. John, *Until the Day Breaks*, 15.

13. Quoted in Rockness, *A Passion for the Impossible*, 17.

14. Quoted in John D. Rosenberg, ed., *The Genius of John Ruskin: Selections from His Writings* (Charlottesville: University Press of Virginia, 1998), 91, italics in original.

15. See Rockness, *A Passion for the Impossible*, 74.

16. Quoted in *Many Beautiful Things* documentary film, https://amara.org/en/videos/np7it8gW9d1L/en/1071086.

17. Quoted in Rockness, *A Passion for the Impossible*, 92.

18. Quoted in Rockness, *A Passion for the Impossible*, 83.

19. Quoted in St. John, *Until the Day Breaks*, 17.

20. Iris Murdoch, *The Sovereignty of Good* (1970; repr., New York: Routledge, 2001), 36.

21. Quoted in St. John, *Until the Day Breaks*, 17–18.

22. Isabella Lilias Trotter, *Parables of the Cross* (Gloucester, UK: Yesterday's World, 2020), 13, italics in original.

23. See St. John, *Until the Day Breaks*, 20.

24. Quoted in Rockness, *A Passion for the Impossible*, 97.

25. See Rockness, *A Passion for the Impossible*, 122–23.

26. Quoted in Rockness, *A Passion for the Impossible*, 130.

27. It is with deepest respect that I borrow this line from Andrew Peterson's wonderful song "Is He Worthy?"

28. Ezekiel 36:26.

29. Isaiah 9:2; Matthew 4:16.

30. Quoted in Rockness, *A Passion for the Impossible*, 87.

31. Rockness, *A Passion for the Impossible*, 87.

32. Quoted in "The Lesson of the Dandelions," Miriam Rockness: Reflections on the Art and Writings of Lilias Trotter, March 15, 2013, https://ililiastrotter.wordpress.com/2013/03/15/the-lesson -of-the-dandelion.

33. Quoted in Rockness, *A Passion for the Impossible*, 324.

34. See St. John, *Until the Day Breaks*, 21.

35. Trotter, *Parables of the Cross*, 20.

36. Quoted in Rockness, *A Passion for the Impossible*, front matter.

37. Quoted in Rockness, *A Passion for the Impossible*, 203.

Epilogue: A World Short on Masters

1. Quoted in Hendrik Willem Van Loon, *R. V. R.: Being an Account of the Last Years and the Death of One Rembrandt Harmenszoon van Rijn* (New York: Literary Guild, 1930), 378.

2. Quoted in Tryon Edwards, ed., *A Dictionary of Thoughts: Being a Cyclopedia of Laconic Quotations from the Best Authors of the World, Both Ancient and Modern* (Detroit: Dickerson, 1908), 131.

3. Annie Dillard, *The Writing Life* (1989; repr., New York: Harper Collins, 2013), 58.

4. "534: To Theo van Gogh. Nuenen, on or about Saturday, 10 October 1885," Vincent van Gogh: The Letters, www.van goghletters.org/vg/letters/let534/letter.html, italics in original.

5. See C. S. Lewis, *The Voyage of the Dawn Treader* (1952; repr., New York: HarperCollins, 1994).